Flood Plain
Land Use Management

Other Titles in This Series

Energy and Water Management in Western Irrigated Agriculture, edited by Norman K. Whittlesey

Natural Radioactivity in Water Supplies, Jack K. Horner

Municipal Water Demand: Statistical and Management Issues, Clive Vaughan Jones, John J. Boland, James E. Crews, C. Frederick DeKay, and John R. Norris

Economic Benefits of Improved Water Quality: Public Perceptions of Option and Preservation Values, Douglas A. Greenley, Richard G. Walsh, and Robert Young

Water and Agriculture in the Western U.S., edited by Gary Weatherford, Lee Brown, Helen Ingram, and Dean Mann

Water and Western Energy: Impacts, Issues, and Choices, Steven C. Ballard, Michael D. Devine, and Associates

Also of Interest

Proceedings of the Second International Symposium on River Sedimentation: 11-16 October, 1983, Nanjing, China, edited by the Organizing Committee of the Symposium

Natural Resource Economics: Selected Papers of S. V. Ciriacy-Wantrup, edited by Richard C. Bishop and Stephen O. Anderson

Earth and the Human Future: Essays in Honor of Harrison Brown, edited by Fereidun Fesharaki, John P. Holdren, and Kirk R. Smith

Groundwater Pollution: Environmental and Legal Problems, edited by Curtis C. Travis and Elizabeth L. Etnier

*Environmental Planning and Management, John H. Baldwin

*Available in hardcover and paperback.

Studies in Water Policy and Management
Charles W. Howe, General Editor

Flood Plain Land Use Management:
A National Assessment

Raymond J. Burby and Steven P. French

with Beverly A. Cigler, Edward J. Kaiser,
David H. Moreau, and Bruce Stiftel

Flood plain land use management has been hailed as
the most likely approach for reducing flood hazards and
losses, but until now no systematic evidence has been
available to indicate what can be accomplished through
land use management programs or to indicate where this
approach is likely to prove most effective. This book
is the result of a major national assessment of flood
plain land use management, for which the authors examined
legislation and written guidelines developed in each of
the fifty states, interviewed administrators at all levels of government, and consulted leading hazards-manage-
ment scholars. Surveys of over 2,000 local governments,
583 regional agencies, and over 200 state officials, as
well as detailed on-site investigations have provided
data for this up-to-date, balanced, and comprehensive
report on land use management and its effectiveness.

Flood Plain
Land Use Management
A National Assessment

Raymond J. Burby and Steven P. French
with Beverly A. Cigler, Edward J. Kaiser,
David H. Moreau, and Bruce Stiftel

Studies in Water Policy and Management, No. 5

Westview Press / Boulder and London

Studies in Water Policy and Management

Copyright © 1985 by Westview Press, Inc.

Published in 1985 in the United States of America by Westview Press, Inc.; Frederick A. Praeger, Publisher; 5500 Central Avenue, Boulder, Colorado 80301

Library of Congress Cataloging in Publication Data
Burby, Raymond J., 1942-
    Flood plain land use management.
    Bibliography: p.
    1. Floodplain management--United States. 2. Land use--United States. I. French, Steven P. II. Cigler, Beverly A. III. Title.
TC423.B75 1985   363.3'4937'0973   85-10672
ISBN 0-8133-7070-1

Composition for this book was provided by the authors

Printed and bound in the United States of America

10 9 8 7 6 5 4 3 2 1

Contents

Tables

xiv

Figures

Foreword

This assessment of the effectiveness of flood plain land use management is the fifth volume in the Westview series "Studies in Water Policy and Management." The series is intended to make available information on a wide range of policy options for solving water-related problems to a broad public audience. The series emphasizes the economic, legal, political, and administrative dimensions of water resource systems.

The present volume concentrates on flood plain use management as a component of broader urban flood control programs that might also include structural measures, floodproofing of existing buildings, participation in the National Flood Insurance Program, preferential tax treatment, density transfers, and public information programs. Indeed, a major finding of the study is that flood plain land use management is most effective in communities that use a number of the flood control instruments just mentioned and in which the goal of flood control is integrated with other public objectives such as recreation, preservation of open space, and natural areas protection.

This volume, its findings and recommendations, will be of great value to public officials, consultants, and the interested lay public.

Charles W. Howe
General Editor

Charles W. Howe, editor of Westview's Studies in Water Policy and Management, is a professor of economics at the University of Colorado. He has served as director of the Water Resources Program, Resources for the Future, Inc., and on the Board of Editors of Land Economics and the American Geophysical Union Water Monograph series. Dr. Howe's previous books include Natural Resource Economics: Issues, Analysis, Policy and Managing Renewable Natural Resources in Developing Countries (Westview, 1982).

Acknowledgments

This book is a joint product of the two principal and four contributing authors. Raymond J. Burby assumed primary responsibility for chapters 1, 3, and 4 and contributed to chapters 5 and 8. Steven P. French assumed primary responsibility for chapters 6, 7, and 8. Beverly A. Cigler contributed to chapter 5 and helped with the 1983 community survey that is reported in chapters 3 and 6. Edward J. Kaiser assumed primary responsibility for chapter 2 and contributed to the case studies reported in chapter 7. David H. Moreau contributed to the policy evaluation model used in this research and helped with the case studies reported in chapter 7. Bruce Stiftel assumed primary responsibility for chapter 5.

We would like to acknowledge the assistance of Carolyn Jones, Barbara Rodgers, Asta Cooper, Lee Mullis, and Carroll Carrozza, who provided secretarial and administrative assistance. We owe a debt of gratitude to more that 2,500 local, regional, and state officials who responded to our requests for information about flood plain management. A final note of thanks is due Terry Sopher and William Anderson, the National Science Foundation program managers for the NSF grants that supported the research reported here.

The work on which this book is based was supported in part by funds provided by the National Science Foundation through grants DAR-7807603 and CEE-8209884. Of course, the opinions, findings, conclusions, and recommendations expressed herein are those of the authors and do not necessarily reflect the views of the National Science Foundation.

Raymond J. Burby
Steven P. French
Beverly A. Cigler
Edward J. Kaiser
David H. Moreau
Bruce Stiftel

1

Flood Plain Land Use Management: Evolution, Current Issues, and Research Approach

Flooding is a serious national problem. It affects every state, over half of the communities, and an estimated 7 percent of the land area of the United States.[1] (White 1975, 255) Over the past four decades, more than 4,000 persons have lost their lives in floods. Property losses from flooding are larger than from any other geophysical hazard. Rising flood losses and the potential for even greater flood catastrophes are largely attributable to rapid and continuing development of flood-hazard areas.

Flooding in and of itself is a natural phenomenon that helps create and sustain our biological life support system. The ecological systems found in flood plains, wetlands and estuaries contribute to the support of all forms of life. Fertile alluvial soils are associated with food production around the world. Flooding has historically replenished soils, recharged groundwater supplies, and aided in the migration of some fish species. (See New England River Basins Commission 1976.) Flooding becomes a problem when man competes with streams and rivers for the same space.

In numerous instances, urbanization of the flood plain has proceeded apace with the development of the remainder of the community. Among twenty communities studied by Sheaffer and Roland (1981b), an average of 18 percent of their flood plains (versus 29 percent of nonhazard areas) had been developed by 1975. In an earlier study of twenty-six cities across the nation, Schneider and Goddard (1974) found that on average 53 percent of their flood plains had been developed, but that some communities had as much as 84 percent of these hazardous areas in development. In a 1979 survey of 1,203 local jurisdictions conducted by the authors of this book, an average of 27 percent of their flood-hazard areas was in urban use (Burby and French 1981).

1

Extensive urbanization of the nation's flood plains has justified a sustained effort over the past four decades to keep floods away from people and damageable property through the construction of flood control structures. However, in spite of over $14 billion (over $7 billion in the last decade alone) in federal expenditures on dams and reservoirs, dikes, levees, floodwalls, channel alterations and other engineering solutions, the U.S. Water Resources Council (1979) noted that losses have continued to rise and may reach the staggering level of $5 billion per year by 1985.

In an effort to slow escalating flood losses and reduce mounting expenditures for structural protective works and flood disaster assistance, federal, state and local policy has been steadily shifting toward non-structural alternatives to protection works.[2] These nonstructural alternatives include improved warning systems, flood insurance, floodproofing, and land use management. According to White (1975, 89), the latter approach--flood plain land use management--may be "...the single adjustment most likely to lead to a decline in national flood losses."

The effectiveness of flood plain land use management, however, has been questioned on a number of grounds. James (1977) and others have suggested that it is simply not leading to a reduction in the continued encroachment on flood-hazard areas and is not likely to reduce flood losses appreciably because of difficulties in removing or modifying existing properties subject to flood damage. To this has been added concern that land use management has been too narrowly focused on mitigation of property damage and may be counterproductive if environmental values often concentrated in flood plains are ignored. (Whipple and Hufschmidt, et al. 1976) Finally, it has been noted that community adoption of land use management techniques is not likely to occur more quickly until their positive impact is amply demonstrated. (White, et al. 1976, 11-22) Because land use management is emerging as a central feature of the nation's approach to coping with floods, it is essential that questions surrounding its effectiveness be answered.

This book takes us a major step forward in resolving these questions by describing and assessing local flood plain land use management as it is being practiced in the United States. In addition to examining legislation and written guidelines, the authors have talked to administrators at all levels of government as well as to other scholars in this field. National surveys of over 2,000 local governments, 583

regional agencies, and officials in all 50 states provide the most broad-based set of data on flood plain
land use management yet assembled. In addition,
detailed on-site investigations were undertaken in
communities in three different states to probe the full
range of issues associated with flood plain management.
This multi-faceted inquiry has been designed to produce
an up-to-date, balanced and comprehensive report on
land use management and its effectiveness in attaining
societal objectives associated with flood hazard areas.

In the remainder of this chapter, the evolution of
land use management as an approach to flood problems is
briefly described, and a number of observers' perceptions of the need for more and better information
about effectiveness are summarized. With this background, the chapter concludes with a short discussion
of the issues that are addressed in the remainder of
the book and the methodologies that have been employed
in the study.

Basic responsibility for land use management programs rests with local government. Chapters 2 and 3
provide a careful definition of the concept,
"local flood plain land use management," and an overview of the status of land use management as it is
applied to flood-hazard areas in the United States
today. Two aspects of land use management programs are
examined in Chapter 2--one focusing on the components
of programs, such as goals and objectives, policies and
plans, and action instruments; the other on the sub-
stantive and operating characteristics of program
components. Based on two national surveys of flood-
prone local jurisdictions, Chapter 3 reviews the
current use of various land use management approaches
and examines local jurisdictions' commitment to solving
their own flood problems.

In our federal system, public functions tend to be
shared by all levels of government. As one observer
has noted, "In effect, everybody does everything."
(Mogulof 1974, 1) This national system of sharing is
as evident in flood plain management as in other
governmental matters. Because the federal government,
states and regions are heavily involved, before the
effectiveness of local management efforts can be
appraised, it is necessary first to understand how
programs originating with other levels of government
are affecting the use and management of flood plains.
In Chapter 4, three federal approaches to flood-
hazard mitigation--structural protection, flood-hazard
information, and the National Flood Insurance Program--
are explored in depth. The analysis focuses on the
distribution of program benefits among local juris-

4

dictions and how federal programs are affecting future flood plain encroachment and local flood plain management. The roles of state governments and regional agencies in flood plain management are discussed in Chapter 5. Based on surveys of state flood plain management personnel and regional agencies across the nation, the chapter looks at both the frequency with which various state and regional management approaches are used and also at local agencies' perceptions of the effectiveness of state and regional flood plain management efforts.

Chapters 6 and 7 analyze the effectiveness of local flood plain land use management using two different approaches. In Chapter 6, the experiences of over two thousand local jurisdictions are compared in an effort to isolate key factors associated with more successful local management programs. Particular attention is given to the interplay between characteristics of the community and flood hazard on the one hand and characteristics of the management program on the other. Based on this analysis, suggestions are developed for fitting flood plain management programs to particular local circumstances. In Chapter 7, the analysis goes one step deeper into the evaluation of local program effectiveness by examining the full range of economic, fiscal, social, and environmental impacts that may flow from local flood plain land use management activities. While focusing on impacts that were uncovered during detailed field investigations in three communities, the chapter discusses a number of lessons that have implications for the practice of flood plain land use management in other communities.

The book concludes in Chapter 8 with an exploration of how policies at each level of government might be improved to produce more satisfactory results at the local level. At the present time, federal policy is in a state of flux. A major redirection in the National Flood Insurance Program has been under way since 1980. The shift toward a greater local role in flood plain management that was promised by the Water Resources Development Act of 1974, the U.S. Water Resources Council's "Unified National Program for Flood Plain Management," and President Carter's Executive Order 11988 on Flood Plain Management has slowly been unfolding. In Chapter 8, suggestions are offered for focusing federal and state efforts on those local program elements and those types of communities where local efforts can be most effective in mitigating flood losses and achieving other objectives for flood hazard areas. Finally, we conclude by offering suggestions for future research on local flood hazard mitigation.

EVOLUTION OF FLOOD PLAIN LAND USE MANAGEMENT

Flood plain land use management is concerned with the wise use of flood plains as "...an integral part of a community and of a total river, shore, or coastal system." (U.S. Water Resources Council, 1976, 11-1) It is one of three basic strategies that may be used alone or in combination to cope with flood problems. The more traditional approach is to modify flooding; that is, to keep flood waters away from people and property, usually through various types of engineering flood control structures. A second approach is designed to modify the impact of flooding on people and property through a variety of means, such as insurance, flood emergency procedures, and post flood disaster relief. Increasingly, however, attention is shifting toward the third strategy for coping with flood hazards--reducing the susceptibility to flood damage by keeping people and property away from flood-prone areas (the land use management approach).

Federal Policies in Transition

Federal involvement with flood control measures began in 1917 following a series of floods on the Mississippi River. During the next thirty years, a series of Congressional acts authorized the Corps of Engineers to reduce property damage from flooding through the construction of protective works; established the Tennessee Valley Authority, in part, to control flooding of the Tennessee River and its tributaries; expanded the Bureau of Reclamation's authority to build reservoirs for flood control purposes; and authorized the Department of Agriculture to construct flood control projects and upstream watershed projects. With these acts the federal government assumed almost total responsibility for flood protection in the United States, and embarked on a program of flood plain management that focused almost exclusively on structural solutions. The Flood Control Act of 1936 established the principle of cost sharing with local interests, but cost-sharing requirements were drastically reduced in subsequent flood control acts passed in 1937 and 1938. As a result, "...local communities, believing themselves to be adequately protected from floods through federal intervention, took little interest in the use of land within their own floodplains." (Platt 1979, 8)

In the absence of local intervention to protect flood plains from urban encroachment, federal construction of various protective works made possible continued and even more intensive use of flood-hazard areas. (White, 1958) Beginning with White's (1945) seminal study in the early 1940s, however, a number of experts in a variety of fields began to suggest that all flood problems could not be economically solved by water control structures and that preventive measures were also necessary.[3] By 1953, this point had been recognized by the Tennessee Valley Authority, which started providing local communities with flood-hazard information that could be used in local planning and land use management to discourage urbanization in hazardous flood-prone areas. With passage of the Flood Control Act of 1960, the TVA approach was expanded to the nation as a whole. In Section 206 of the act, Congress recognized the need to support greater state and local participation in flood plain management and authorized the Corps of Engineers to prepare flood plain information studies requested by state and local governments.

During the fifteen years preceeding 1965, federal interest in nonstructural approaches to flood problems steadily grew, but little response was forthcoming at the local level. In the mid-1950s, Hoyt and Langbein (1955, 95) observed, "Flood zoning, like almost all that is virtuous, has great verbal support, but almost nothing has been done about it." By the end of that decade, Murphy (1958) surveyed national experience with local flood plain management and found only about fifty communities with a local program. He concluded, "...the extensive field investigation of past and present uses made of channel-encroachment laws, flood plain zoning provisions, subdivision regulations, building codes, and other methods of flood plain regulation indicate that as now applied they do not halt continued increase in flood losses" (Murphy 1958, 161). Community interest in flood plain land use management varied from state to state, but it is noteworthy that a decade later (at the end of the 1960s) a review of local activity in North Carolina found, "None of the cities represented...has been successful in the adoption of flood plain zoning ordinances (so that)...flood plain encroachment continues" (Water Resources Research Institute of the University of North Carolina 1969, 56).

The nation's response to the flood hazard problem tends to be episodic. National interest in devising solutions to flooding rises sharply after a disaster and then wanes until the next catastrophe occurs. During the first half of the 1960s a series of hurricanes and coastal storms (Donna in 1960, the "northeaster" of March 1962, Hilda in 1964, and Betsy in 1965) was the apparent impetus for a complete reevaluation of federal flood control policy and

subsequent efforts to bring about effective local
participation in flood hazard mitigation. In 1965 two
studies were commissioned to review national policy.
One, a Task Force on Federal Flood Control Policy
formed by the U.S. Bureau of the Budget and chaired by
Gilbert White, was charged with reviewing national
flood control policy and recommending appropriate
changes. A second study, directed by Marion Clawson,
was undertaken by the U.S. Department of Housing and
Urban Development to explore the feasibility of a
national flood insurance program. Both studies contributed to a major redirection in federal policy.

The 1966 report of the Task Force on Federal Flood
Control Policy strongly recommended taking steps to
ensure that local planning and land use management
decisions give "proper and consistent" recognition to
flood hazards. To strengthen the local role in flood
plain management, among its sixteen recommendations
the Task Force urged (1) improvements in basic knowledge about floods and flood hazards through expansion
and refinement of flood plain mapping and other
measures; (2) coordination and planning of federal and
state activities affecting flood plains through federal
grants-in-aid and greater state involvement in managing
flood hazard areas; (3) improvement in technical
services to flood plain managers; and (4) changes in
policy for flood control project survey and cost
sharing to provide for greater state and local contributions. In transmitting the Task Force report to
Congress, President Johnson emphasized that the success
of a "unified national program for managing flood
losses" rested on state and local governments and on
property owners in flood-hazard areas.

To provide the federal leadership necessary to
stimulate state and local efforts, in 1966 President
Johnson issued Executive Order 11296 directing federal
agencies to help prevent uneconomic flood plain
development. Subsequently, a number of federal
agencies strengthened their nonstructural flood plain
management programs. The Corps of Engineers expanded
its program to include technical services and guidance
to local governments in the preparation of flood plain
regulations, public information on floodproofing, and
assistance in comprehensive flood damage prevention.
The U.S. Water Resources Council began working toward a
uniform technique for determining flood frequency, and
the U.S. Geological Survey began preparing hydrological
atlases.

Both the Task Force report and the report of the
Department of Housing and Urban Development study (U.S.
Senate Committee on Banking and Currency 1966) recom-

mended inaugurating a federal flood insurance program
as a means of (1) meeting insurance needs in flood-
prone areas;[4] (2) shifting the costs of flood plain
occupancy from the federal government (structural protection and disaster assistance costs) to the private
beneficiaries of flood plain locations; and
(3) encouraging the development of local regulations to
reduce future losses from flooding. To encourage
participation by the owners of existing flood plain
structures, who could be faced with extremely high
insurance costs, the HUD study recommended that their
insurance rates be subsidized, but that full actuarial
rates be applied to future structures built in the
flood plain to reflect the risk of flood damage
inherent in their locations. To prevent the availability of flood insurance from producing a boom in
flood plain development, the HUD study also recommended
requiring adoption and enforcement of local flood plain
regulations before subsidized flood insurance could be
sold in a community. These recommendations were enacted
into law on August 1, 1968, with passage of the
National Flood Insurance Act. The trend in federal
policy toward expanded local involvement and reduced
flood plain encroachment is clearly evident in this
legislation, which was designed, in part, to
"...(1) encourage state and local governments to make
appropriate land use adjustments to constrict the
development of land which is exposed to flood damage...
[and] (2) guide the development of proposed future
construction, where practicable, away from locations
which are threatened by flood hazards ..." (P.L. 90-
448, Sec. 1302 [e].

As first enacted, flood insurance could not be
sold in a community until detailed studies had
established actuarily sound rates and had mapped the
special flood hazard zone (designated by the Secretary
of HUD as the 100-year flood plain) where new construction would be regulated to be certain that it was
reasonably free of flooding. Because of the length of
time needed to complete the required studies, by the
end of 1969 only four communities had qualified for the
National Flood Insurance Program (Anderson 1974, 582).

In the aftermath of Hurricane Camille in August
1969, which caused extensive damage to a number of
communities where flood insurance was not yet available, Congress amended the program in December of that
year to create an "emergency phase" that would allow
communities to participate pending completion of their
flood hazard boundary maps and flood insurance rate
maps. Under the emergency phase, subsidized insurance
was made available to existing and new structures
located in participating communities. To be eligible

for the sale of insurance, communities had only to
apply for the program and agree to adopt minimum land
use management measures to control the development of
their flood-hazard areas. Nevertheless, community
participation, which was voluntary, was far from
overwhelming.

When some of the worst flooding in the nation's
history occurred in June 1972 (Hurricane Agnes, with
estimated damages in excess of $2 billion, and the
Rapid City, South Dakota, flood, with damages of $100
million), it was found that fewer than one-fifth of the
communities with identified flood hazard areas had
chosen to participate in the National Flood Insurance
Program (NFIP) by adopting the required regulations.
To correct this weakness in the program, the Flood
Disaster Protection Act of 1973 made community
participation in the NFIP virtually compulsory. The
act required states and local communities, as a
condition of future federal financial assistance for
property acquisition or construction, to participate in
the flood insurance program and to adopt flood plain
ordinances with effective enforcement provisions (consistent with federal standards) to reduce or avoid
future flood losses. The act also established severe
sanctions for the owners of flood-prone property if
their local government chose not to join the program.
Besides not being able to purchase flood insurance,
they would not be eligible for federal disaster
assistance for any flood-related damages; they would
not be eligible for loans (such as home mortgages) from
any federally supervised, regulated, or ensured
agencies or institutions; [5] and they would no longer be
eligible for direct federal grants and loans, such as
assistance from the U.S. Small Business Administration.
Those sanctions were enough to spur a massive increase
in community participation in the flood insurance
program--from fewer than 3,000 communities in 1973 to
more than 16,500 a decade later.

The trend in federal policy away from structural
flood control measures and toward nonstructural
measures was strengthened further by the Water
Resources Development Act of 1974, Disaster Relief Act
of 1974, and Executive Order 11988 (1977) on Flood
Plain Management.[6] Section 73 of the Water Resources
Development Act states that in planning or designing
any federal project involving flood protection, consideration shall be given to nonstructural alternatives
to prevent or reduce flood damages. The Disaster
Relief Act of 1974 requires that as a condition for
disaster loan or grant assistance, communities evaluate
natural hazards where the funds are to be applied and
take steps to mitigate the hazards through various

means, including safe land use and construction practices (Section 406).

Executive Order 11988 was issued by President Carter on May 24, 1977, in order to "...avoid to the extent possible the long-and short-term adverse impacts associated with the occupancy and modification of floodplains and to avoid direct and indirect support of floodplain development wherever there is a practicable alternative" (see U.S. Water Resources Council 1978). This new executive order was issued in response to federal agencies' failure to fully implement President Johnson's Executive Order 11296 of August 1966. According to the General Accounting Office, as of 1975 federal agencies were continuing to support new construction in or near the 100-year flood plain and were not providing enough assistance to local government in delineating flood hazard areas (see Comptroller General of the United States 1975). To rejuvenate agencies' concern with flood hazards, E.O. 11988 required them to avoid the 100-year base flood plain in their facility location decisions; to implement the Water Resources Council's (1976) Unified National Program for Flood Plain Management; and to include adequate provision for the evaluation and consideration of flood hazards in the regulations and operating procedures used in license, permit, loan, and grant-in-aid programs that they administer.

Mounting State Interest in Flood Plain Land Use Management

In spite of some difficulties in implementation, the Flood Disaster Protection Act of 1973, the Water Resources Development Act of 1974, the Disaster Relief Act of 1974, and Executive Order 11988 issued in 1977 provide a strong federal mandate for effective flood plain land use management. In turn, the states have become increasingly involved in this field. For example, between 1962 and 1978 the number of states with flood plain regulations or equivalent programs more than doubled, increasing from fewer than one-fifth to over one-half of the states. (U.S. Water Resources Council 1979, VII-13). The Federal Emergency Management Agencies' State Assistance Program, begun in 1980, further stimulated state activity to manage flood hazards, so that by 1983 every state had in place at lease a minimal program designed to mitigate flood hazards.

State approaches to flood plain management include stream channel encroachment regulations, state permit systems for construction in designated flood plain

areas, state requirements for local flood plain land
use regulations (with provision for state regulation if
localities fail to act), requirements that local regulations be consistent with state standards, and
assistance to localities with existing or potential
flood problems. In some instances, states require
that localities qualify for participation in the
National Flood Insurance Program through local or, if
necessary, state adoption of the required minimum
building and land use regulations. Besides these
direct state flood plain land use management programs,
most states have enabling legislation that allows local
governments to regulate flood plains (see U.S. Water
Resources Council 1971, 112-118). In fact, including
state model ordinances, critical areas legislation, and
enabling legislation, Sheaffer and his associates
(1976) found "...that the majority (92 percent) of the
states have become involved in the problem of flood
hazard area land use control."

Local Government and the Issue of Effectiveness

The federal government and states have provided
incentives and a framework for flood plain land use
management, but the primary responsibility for program
implementation lies with local government. In response
to the requirements of the National Flood Insurance
Program, thousands of communities across the nation
have initiated land use and building regulations for
flood-hazard areas. The experience gained in those
communities, in turn, makes it possible for the first
time to examine issues related to program
effectiveness.

To date, considerable attention has been devoted
to identifying approaches local governments can use to
manage the use and development of flood hazard areas.
In addition, model ordinances have been prepared (U.S.
Water Resources Council 1971/1972) and several
excellent guidebooks are available for local use (see
Kusler and Lee 1972; Kusler 1976; and Owen and Wall
1981). On the other hand, little attention has yet
been given to determining (1) how well federal and
state mandates for flood plain land use management are
working; or (2) how effective local flood plain
management programs are in achieving various land use
objectives. As a result, it is difficult to determine
(1) whether or in which circumstances land use management is an appropriate supplement or alternative to
conventional structural flood damage prevention
approaches; (2) the social, economic, and environmental
consequences of land use management in comparison with
alternative flood hazard adjustments; (3) the
consequences of pursuing alternative land use manage-

ment approaches and policy mixes; and (4) the circumstances in which one land use management policy or mix
of policies is preferable to another. Studies
conducted for the Department of Housing and Urban
Development by Sheaffer and Roland (1981) show wide
variation in potential flood losses with different
degrees of flood plain regulation. Thus, the development of information about the effectiveness of land use
management as a flood hazard adjustment is of crucial
importance to federal, state, and local policy makers.

INFORMATION NEEDS

Concern for the effectiveness of land use management has been widespread among close observers of
national flood hazard management policies. The basic
issue is "How well does it work?" For example, the
success of the Unified National Program for Flood Plain
Management depends on a cooperative federal, state, and
local governmental effort. Yet, a number of observers
have questioned whether such an effort will be forthcoming from any level of government. The U.S. General
Accounting Office (1975) criticized federal agencies'
efforts to comply with President Johnson's executive
order dealing with flood plain management, and the U.S.
Water Resources Council (1980) was dismayed at the
slowness of agencies' response to President Carter's
Executive Order 11988. Although the National Flood
Insurance Program requires communities to adopt flood
plain land use and building regulations as a condition
for eligibility, the U.S. General Accounting Office in
two reviews of the program (1976, 1977), found that
communities were not adequately enforcing the regulations. Even if local governments do enact and enforce
the required regulations, research by Sheaffer and
Roland (1981) indicates that the absolute level of
flood losses in the United States will continue to
rise. In addition, since the actions of one community
may exacerbate or ameliorate flood hazards experienced
by neighboring communities, local efforts may be mean-
ingless unless they are accompanied by strong
intergovernmental planning and cooperation (see Platt
and McMullen 1979; Platt 1982).

The question of program effectiveness gives rise
to two additional questions: in which types of communities do particular land use management approaches
work best, and, more generally, what factors are
associated with more successful programs? James (1977,
26-27), for example, has written,

Instead of establishing uniform nationwide flood
plain management practices, we need to seek out

locations where nonstructural approaches can prove effective and can be implemented. We need to learn how to vary program design to fit local needs. We need to learn how to implement more effectively in measured local contexts...The economic implications of flood plain management for the $250 billion worth of development currently located on 100-year flood plains are surely sufficient to justify the needed research...

In a similar vein, Whipple, Hufschmidt and their associates (1976, 15) noted,

Few if any land-water plans and management programs are adequately monitored to obtain information on how well they have been meeting their intended purposes and what unintended side effects have been generated. Without systematic collection of specific information on measures of performance and evaluation of programs as they are implemented, it is not possible to modify existing programs im to formulate new ones with much assurance that the programs will achieve the intended objectives and not generate serious side effects.

They then go on to call for comparative studies of current urban land-water management programs to identify key variables that relate to success or failure.

The "Principles and Standards for Planning Water and Related Land Resources" adopted in 1973 by the U.S. Water Resources Council require careful consideration of the economic, social, and environmental effects of proposed water resources projects. A similarly broad-based evaluation is not typical prior to the application of land use management approaches. Nevertheless, some observers have indicated that flood damage prevention is too narrow a basis for flood plain management and have stressed the need for information about the effects of land use management programs on other community objectives. Whipple, Hufschmidt, and their associates (1976, 30), for example, have suggested that the National Flood Insurance Program's emphasis on delineation and protection of the minimum floodway[7] may encourage development and filling of the floodway fringe,"...thereby destroying potentially important elements of the natural resource base, limiting flood storage, and creating a scenario for catastrophic damage and loss of life should floods in excess of the design frequency occur." (Also see Baker and McPhee 1974, 108 and White 1975, 89.) In short, it

is clearly not enough to consider flood plain management soley in terms of flood loss abatement. The
successes and failures of local managment programs in
meeting other objectives for flood hazard areas also
must be addressed if a full assessment of the performance and potential of the land use management
approach to flood problems is to be achieved.

A final area of concern relates not to the effects
of management programs but to the sources of community
flood problems. It has become increasingly apparent
that land use changes outside a local jurisdiction can
affect that jurisdiction's flood problem. When land is
developed, for example, runoff into streams and rivers
can increase from two to six times as absorbent
vegetation is replaced by impervious cover (National
Science Foundation, 1980). According to Allee and
Walter (1977, 11), "Until we face the issue of upland
management, we won't be able to control downstream
flooding." What is more, upstream develoment may make
obsolete maps and other studies that provide the
technical base for downstream flood plain management
(Kusler, 1982). Also, by filling on one side of a
stream a local jurisdiction can remove flood storage
capacity and "shove" flood-waters onto adjacent jurisdictions. This potential for adverse impacts extending
across jurisdictional boundaries has led to a call for
improved intergovernmental coordination of flood plain
management at the local level (Baker and McPhee
1975,110; Platt et al. 1980; Platt 1982).

In summary, local flood plain land use management
has been widely hailed as an alternative or supplement
to structural flood control measures and has drawn
increasingly strong support in the policies of the
federal and many state governments. As the preceding
discussion illustrates, however, a number of aspects of
the effectiveness of land use management have been
questioned. Until the performance of land use management in actual practice is assessed, its use in flood
damage abatement programs must depend more on the
personal preferences of policymakers than on the results of rational decision processes. In addition,
until more is known about how the effectiveness of land
use management varies with local circumstances and is
affected by federal and state programs, it will be
difficult to devise better approaches at any level of
government.

RESEARCH AIMS AND PROCEDURES

The research reported here was undertaken to
answer many of the questions that have been raised

about flood plain land use management and to provide baseline information and analyses needed to improve current policies and programs. As a first step in this direction, research was begun to provide a better capability for evaluating the effectiveness of flood plain land use management programs. The results of that effort are reported in two volumes: A Conceptual Framework for Evaluating the Effectiveness of Flood Plain Land Use Management (Burby, French, and Kaiser 1979) and Managing Flood Hazard Areas: A Field Evaluation of Local Experience (French, Miller, Burby, and Moreau 1980). In the present book, we draw on the data assembled for the initial methodological research and the results of subsequent national surveys of state, regional, and local agencies to assess the state of the art and the performance of land use management programs being applied to flood hazard areas. Although the focus of this research is on the performance of local programs, the roles of federal and state programs in local policy formulation and policy effectiveness are also explored.

Assessing the Current State of the Art

A literature that describes various approaches to flood plain land use management has been slowly evolving, but it tends to lag behind the current state of the art in actual practice. Therefore, it is necessary to ascertain from people working on the local scene, as well as from those in regional and state agencies, what programs and measures are being used now. This was done through mail and telephone surveys of flood hazard management officials working in local and state government.

Local agency surveys were conducted during the springs of 1979 and 1983. The 1979 survey was sent to 1,415 jurisdictions across the United States. A sampling frame was constructed based on the 16,500 cities, counties, towns, townships, and boroughs participating in the National Flood Insurance Program.[8] Participation in the NFIP ensured that the communities to be selected for study were subject to flooding. To ensure that jurisdictions had some need for flood plain land use management and were capable of establishing a management program, two additional criteria were applied to the master list of NFIP jurisdictions.[9] Jurisdictions with fewer than 5,000 population in 1970 were excluded, since many of them lacked the resources to mount more than a minimal management effort (see Hutton and Mileti 1979). Jurisdictions that did not issue a permit for construction in a flood hazard area in 1977 also were eliminated, in order to exclude

communities with no development pressure on their flood
plains and thus less need for flood plain land use
management. Those two exclusions reduced the sample
frame from 16,500 to 3,410 jurisdictions.

Within this sampling frame, the communities'
status in the National Flood Insurance Program (regular
or emergency) was used to form two sampling strata. All
communities in the regular phase of the NFIP and a 20
percent random sample of those in the emergency phase
were selected. Note that this is not an entirely
representative sample because communities in the
regular program are over-represented. However, because
all the communities in the National Flood Insurance
Program will eventually enter the regular phase and
because, at the time of this survey in 1979 communities
were converting to the regular phase at a rapid rate,
we believed this sampling strategy was preferable to
drawing a random sample that would have been dominated
by communities in the emergency phase of the NFIP.

A second survey of local governments was undertaken in the spring of 1983, primarily to evaluate the
effects of state governments' flood plain management
programs at the local level. The 1983 survey served
another purpose as well, however, since it provided a
basis for testing the continued validity of findings
that emerged from the 1979 data. Although one must be
cautious in interpreting results based on samples, our
confidence in research findings is enhanced
considerably when they are confirmed on the basis of
data from another sample at a different time.

Because of our interest in evaluating state
governments' flood hazard management programs, the 1983
survey of local governments was directed to a sample of
1,219 communities drawn to represent communities in
each of the fifty states. Twenty-five jurisdictions
per state were sampled from communities participating
in the regular and emergency phases of the National
Flood Insurance Program. Jurisdictions were selected
randomly; the probability of inclusion in the sample
was directly proportional to the size (acres) of each
community's flood hazard area.

The 1979 and 1983 local government surveys were
conducted using mail survey techniques developed by
Dillman (1978). The initial survey instrument was
sent to all of the communities sampled with a cover
letter and description of the project. One week after
the initial mailing a post card reminder was sent to
all communities. Three weeks after the initial mailing, a replacement questionnaire and cover letter were
sent to communities that had not responded. Seven

weeks after the initial mailing, another questionnaire
and cover letter were sent by certified mail to communities that still had not responded. To maximize the
reliability of the data returned by communities, each
letter and questionnaire was sent to the person listed
in the files of the Federal Insurance Administration as
the local flood plain coordinator. If that information
was unavailable, the letter was personally addressed
to the planning director (if one existed) or to the
chief executive officer of the jurisdiction. In each
case, the addressee was asked to refer the questionnaire to the person in the jurisdiction who was most
knowledgeable about local flood problems and the local
flood hazard management program. Responses were received from 1,203 (85 percent) of the 1,415 communities
surveyed in 1979 and from 956 (78 percent) of the 1,219
communities surveyed in 1983.

    Characteristics of the communities in the 1979 and
1983 samples are summarized in Table 1. The communities tend to be relatively small; those in the 1983
sample (which was not limited to communities of more
than 5,000 people) were significantly less populous
than the communities sampled in 1979. Flood hazard
characteristics of the communities in each sample,
however, tend to be similar. Just over half of each
group indicated that flash flooding of creeks, streams,
and drainageways was their principal flood hazard.
Urbanization of flood hazard areas varied widely among
the communities studied: relatively few communities in
either sample reported heavy development (more than 60
percent of the flood plain in urban use). Flood plains
of the 1983 sample communities tended to be less
developed than those of the communities sampled in
1979, but similar proportions of both groups of
communities--about 20 percent--rated flooding as a
serious community problem. Among both sets of communities, about the same proportions--approximately 40
percent--reported that hazard-free sites for new
development were either limited or not available at all
within the community boundaries.

    There is a high degree of correlation among several
key flood plain characteristics. As might be expected,
communities that have developed their flood hazard
areas intensively tend to be those with limited
alternative sites for development. The perceived
seriousness of the flood problem is directly associated with the extent of flood plain development and
the existence of intensive land uses (apartments, commercial, and industrial uses) in the hazard area.
Those are also the communities, however, in which a
higher proportion of new construction is occurring in
flood zones.

TABLE 1-1
Characteristics of communities studied

Community Characteristic	1979 Sample N = 1,415	1983 Sample N = 956
Population (median)	17,592	3,221
Principal type of flood hazard (percent)		
Flash floods	51	57
Riverine floods	33	31
Coastal floods	16	12
Seriousness of property loss from floods (percent)		
Very serious	21	17
A problem, not serious	57	51
Not a problem	22	33
Extent of flood plain development (percent)		
Heavy (60 percent or more developed)	18	12
Moderate (30-59 percent developed)	27	20
Slight (10-29 percent developed)	30	26
Undeveloped (under 10 percent developed)	26	42
Land uses in flood hazard area (percent with use)		
Single family	86	75
Multiple family	41	27
Commercial	47	33
Industrial	46	28
Development sites outside of flood plain (percent)		
Readily available	57	55
Limited	39	38
Not available	4	6
National Flood Insurance Program status (percent)		
Regular phase	65	56
Emergency phase	35	44
Percent of building in last year in flood plain (mean)	7.5	5.3
Years in flood insurance program (mean)	6.0	8.0

The ways in which communities can address their flood-related problems are discussed in Chapter 2, which provides a conceptual overview of flood plain land use management. In Chapter 3, the actual use of various management approaches among the sample communities is described. Particular attention is given in Chapter 3, to explaining community adoption of different land use management approaches in terms of community goals for the use of flood plains, flood hazard characteristics and socioeconomic characteristics of the community. Attention also is given to the stringency of the management approach adopted and to the efforts communities have made in program implementation.

Although regional agencies, in most cases, do not administer regulatory programs, they can play an important role in technical assistance, flood hazard information, flood plain planning, and coordination of local land use management activities. To date little study has been made of regional agencies' roles in the nation's Unified National Program for Flood Plain Management, and little is known of their activities in that field. To improve our understanding of the potential for regional approaches to flood hazard mitigation, a survey instrument was prepared and sent, using procedures described above, to each of the 648 member agencies of the National Association of Regional Councils. Responses were received from 583 agencies (90 percent). The data obtained from this survey, which was conducted in the spring of 1979, are analyzed in Chapter 5, which also includes an evaluation of state efforts in flood plain land use management.

Information about state flood hazard management programs was obtained through two surveys conducted in the fall of 1982 and spring of 1983. The initial step, undertaken in the fall of 1982, was to conduct a telephone survey of state officials in order to build comprehensive lists of state flood hazard management personnel and programs. In each of the fifty states calls were made first to the state water resources director, the state coordinator for the NFIP, the state disaster preparedness director, and the director of the state's water resources research center or institute. Additional calls were placed to people identified in the first round so that program information was obtained from personnel who were directly involved rather than secondhand.

In the spring of 1983 state officials were asked to complete a ten-page questionnaire dealing in depth with organization and management issues.

Questionnaires were sent to six officials in
each state, including the state water resources
director, the NFIP Coordinator, the disaster assistance
director, and three other lead officials whose
positions varied from one state to the next, depending
on how flood hazard management responsibilities were
distributed among state agencies. The response rate
was 78 percent after a postcard reminder and two
follow-up mailings.

In combination, the two local government surveys,
regional agency survey, and the state agency telephone
and mail surveys provide for the first time a
comprehensive picture of the nation's efforts to control
flood losses through the management of flood hazard
areas. The question still remains, however, whether
those efforts have been effective.

Evaluating Effectiveness

An effective program is generally considered to be
one that produces desired results. The concept of
effectiveness can be broken into three components:
determining effects; determining the causes of the
effects; and valuing the effects in terms of goals and
objectives. Thus the definition of effectiveness in a
particular evaluation depends on the set of goals and
objectives chosen to value effects. In the case of
flood plain land use management, evaluating effectiveness in terms of a set of goals is complicated because
the objectives of public programs often are not stated
clearly enough for this purpose. According to the
Office of Technology Assessment (1978, 80, 88), for
example,

> First, there are no national goals which are
> straight forward, clear, and action-oriented with
> regard to flood hazard management. Second, the
> more detailed programs involving flood hazard
> areas are disintegrated and at cross-purposes.
> The absence of specific national objectives in
> flood plain management is in conflict with the
> need for means of evaluating progress.

In addition, because programs affecting land use
management involve not only different federal
bureaucracies but also different levels of government,
a mix of goals--some complimentary and some
conflicting--is likely to be applied to the flood
plains of any given locale.

These difficulties were resolved in two ways.
First, a set of nationally relevant criteria for

evaluating the effectiveness of flood plain land use management were extracted from the literature on flood problems in the United States. These national criteria ("goals") serve as benchmarks against which we have judged the effectiveness of programs in local jurisdictions. With this approach, effectiveness is evaluated in general terms and not in terms of the goals and objectives of any particular governmental unit--federal, state, or local. Second, because the goals and objectives of particular governmental units are likely to vary from one jurisdiction to another, in this research we have viewed local program goals as components of flood plain land use management that can contribute to or detract from a program's effectiveness as judged by national criteria.

Nationally, land use management has been advanced as one way to reduce damages and resulting economic losses from flooding. Beginning with the Flood Control Act of 1917, minimizing damages caused by floods has been a goal of every flood-related statute enacted by Congress. Current federal policy, at least as exemplified by the various flood insurance acts and Executive Order 11988, seems designed to encourage state and local governments to constrict the development of land that is exposed to flood hazard and to minimize damages caused by flood events. Because of this overriding national concern with flood damages, the major evaluative criterion used in this research is the extent to which land use management programs have protected property from flood damage.

In examining the reduction in flood damage potential, several key distinctions must be made. Currently, the National Flood Insurance Program focuses on the reduction of loss from the 100-year flood through the use of elevation and floodproofing techniques, rather than discouragement of development in the flood plain. By focusing on site design rather than location, potential losses from floods that recur at intervals shorter than every one hundred years may be reduced from what they would have been without the land use management techniques, but potential losses from rarer flood events may be increased, particularly if site design measures, such as elevation of structures and floodproofing, result in greater feelings of safety among hazard zone occupants and greater development of hazard areas than would have otherwise occurred. This is an important distinction, inasmuch as previous research indicates that floods greater than the 100-year event caused more than 60 percent of flood damage experienced in the United States (see Sheaffer, Roland et al. 1976, 49, and Baker 1976, 8). Accordingly, one important indicator of effectiveness is the extent to which flood plain land use management has reduced the risk of catastrophic and other flood losses <u>by preventing new urban development from locating in the flood plain</u>. Although policies being pursued by the National Flood Insurance Program are not designed to eliminate development of flood hazard areas, that outcome is suggested by Executive Order 11988 on Floodplain Management, which requires federal agencies to avoid direct and indirect support of flood plain development.

Besides the distinction between the protection of development and location of development, a distinction must also be made between new development and existing development. Most flood plain land use management measures are designed to prevent increases in damage potential by affecting the design (and location) of <u>new</u> development. With the exception of relocation measures and measures regulating the improvement of existing structures, they are not designed to reduce potential damage to <u>existing</u> development. As a result, recent studies indicate that land use management programs such as those promulgated by the National Flood Insurance Program will not lead to an overall reduction in national flood losses from their present levels, although they will reduce the increment in future losses associated with new urban development (Sheaffer and Roland 1981). Accordingly, it seems appropriate to examine the effectiveness of flood plain land use management in protecting <u>existing</u> and <u>new</u> flood plain development separately.

A number of community values--economic, social, and environmental--may be affected by the way land is used in flood hazard areas. Therefore, in evaluating effectiveness we must consider more than physical occupancy of the flood plain. This is particularly important because individual and community resistance to programs is often based on apprehension about the "secondary" effects of land use management. Adverse economic effects that are often attributed to flood plain land use management include reduction in property values, reduction in community economic growth and development, reduction in the tax base, and increased construction costs. Adverse social effects can include increased community conflict over regulation and inequitable costs to low- and moderate-income households (see Frieden 1979). Adverse environmental effects can include the loss of natural habitats if the management program encourages flood plain encroachment, as suggested above. On the other hand, positive secondary effects also might result from flood plain management efforts. The preservation of natural areas and open space, for example, can result from public land acquisition or the discouragement of development in flood hazard areas. Each of the secondary effects discussed here must be considered in a comprehensive program evaluation.

Two approaches were used to gather information with which to gauge the effectiveness of flood plain land use management: (1) the surveys of local jurisdictions described above and (2) case study analyses based on actual field measurements within three communities, which are described below. The use of survey research methods to evaluate land use management programs is based on the assumption that knowledgeable community informants can provide reliable information about the location of new development taking place in their community and that they can also make reasonable assessments of the effectiveness of their community's land use management programs. Specific effectiveness measures used and the results obtained from analyses of the survey data are presented in Chapter 6.

The case study approach to the evaluation of effectiveness involved the formulation of a detailed methodology for field-level measurements and evaluation in particular communities. Development of the methodology included the specification of program impacts relevant to flood plain land use management and procedures for measuring them in communities. Results obtained when the methodology was applied in three communities are described in Chapter 7. Although the three communities--Raleigh, North Carolina, Jackson, Mississippi, and Littleton, Colorado--do not represent the full range of flood plain land use management programs that can be found throughout the country, the in-depth explorations of their experiences provide a useful supplement to the survey data on effectiveness.

Fitting Land Use Management Program to Local Conditions

In formulating appropriate mixes of land use management policies, it is important to consider how policies interact with local conditions to produce particular outcomes. For example, traditional land use management measures, such as flood plain zoning and floodway encroachment regulations, may not be very effective when a community's flood plains have high locational advantages or when there is a scarcity of developable land outside of flood-hazard areas. In those instances, land use management might more appropriately stress public acquisition rather than regulation (or levees might be more appropriate). A

number of other state and local conditions may also
influence how well various land use measures actually
work. These include factors that cannot be manipulated
by policymakers, at least in the short run (such as
hydrologic and physiographic characteristics of the
flood plain and community socioeconomic status), as
well as factors that can be changed by public policy
(such as prevailing state policies or the priority the
community attaches to the solution of flood problems).

As noted earlier in this chapter, a number of
observers have stressed the importance of finding out
in which communities particular management approaches
seem to be working best. In an effort to provide that
information, data were collected on a number of
contextual factors that previous research and the
experience of the investigators suggested would be
associated with program effectiveness. The collection
and analysis of these data were guided by the
conceptual model illustrated below.

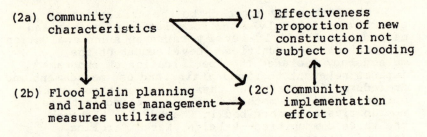

Figure 1-1
Simplified conceptual model

The diagram depicts the relationships among the
four elements of the model: (1) effectiveness of the
program; (2a) the characteristics of the community in
which planning and land use management efforts are
undertaken; (2b) the planning and land use management
measures themselves; and (2c) characteristics of the
community's implementation effort. We also recognize
that the choice of measures and the vigor with which
they are implemented are themselves likely to depend in
part on community factors, so that community characteristics may influence effectiveness directly and
indirectly through their influence on the
adoption/implementation of land use management
measures. This simple conceptual model is elaborated in
Chapter 6, which also reports the results of
statistical tests conducted to test the various
relationships suggested by the model.

SUMMARY

   In an effort to reduce national flood losses,
federal and state policies have increasingly stressed
the need for community land use management of flood
plains as an alternative and/or supplement to
structural flood control measures. The effectiveness
of flood plain land use management techniques, where
adopted, however, has been questioned on a number of
grounds, so that the nation may be pursuing flood plain
policies that are less than optimal. Before better
policies can be devised, the practice and impacts of
flood plain land use management must be better understood. This book takes a step in that direction by
describing and evaluating flood plain land use management as it is currently practiced in the United States.

   In this chapter, the evolution of flood plain
management approaches has been traced, with particular
attention to the rise of nonstructural approaches such
as land use management. Various observers' perceptions
of the problem of program effectiveness have been reviewed, along with their observations regarding
information needs for further policy and program
development. Finally, the approach of this research in
providing the needed information has been described.
With this background, in the next chapter we examine
the conceptual foundations for local flood plain land
use management.

NOTES

   1. In urban areas, the proportion of land subject
to flooding is even higher . Schneider and Goddard
(1974), for example, found in a study of twenth-six
cities that 16 percent of the urbanized areas were
located in flood plains. Similarly, Sheaffer and
Roland (1981) found in a study of twenty cities that an
average of 19.7 percent of their area was located in a
flood-hazard zone. In a 1979 survey by the present
authors, which included 1,204 jurisdictions with
counties as well as cities, the median jurisdiction had
9 percent of its land area located in the 100-year
flood plain.
   2. The role of each level of government is
discussed in the U.S. Water Resources Council's (1979)
report A Unified National Program for Flood Plain
Management.
   3. Some of the disciplines represented in the
growing recognition that nonstructural measures had a
place in national flood hazard mitigation policy
included engineering (Goddard 1958); planning (Gray

1961); economics (Krutilla 1967); and law (Dunham 1959), as well as White and his colleagues' work in the Department of Geography at the University of Chicago.

4. Because of the problem of _adverse selection_-- the only persons interested in purchasing insurance are those who face a very high probability of experiencing flood losses--the insurance industry has historically not promoted the sale of flood insurance. See Kunreuther, _et al._, 1978, 24-26.

5. The 1977 amendments to the Flood Disaster Protection Act weakened the legislation somewhat by allowing federally regulated banks and savings and loan institutions to lend to uninsured purchasers in flood hazard areas of nonparticipating communities. Lenders, however, are required to notify buyers or lessees that the property in question is located in a flood hazard area and that they will not be eligible for disaster relief.

6. A number of other federal programs with a less direct effect on flood plain land use management, such as the National Environmental Policy Act, Section 404 of P.L. 92-500 (dredge and fill permits), and the Coastal Zone Management Act, are discussed in Chapter Four.

7. The minimum floodway is that portion of the flood plain required to discharge the 100-year flood without raising the water surface elevation (i.e., causing flood waters to back up) more than one foot above the base flood level at any point. See Institute of Rational Design, 1977.

8. For ease of discourse the terms "jurisdiction" and "community" are used interchangeably in this book in referring to the governmental units studied.

9. Data for choosing this sample were provided by the Federal Insurance Administration in the U.S. Department of Housing and Urban Development (now called the Office of Federal Insurance and Hazard Mitigation of the Federal Emergency Management Agency).

2
The Community Flood Plain
Land Use Management Program

A community's flood plain land use management program consists of those measures local governments use to influence the development of flood hazard areas and the site design and construction practices there. It includes goals, objectives, policies, and plans as well as regulations, incentives and disincentives, public information programs, property acquisitions, capital improvements, and other actions. It incorporates the ways those measures are administered in practice and the ways they are stated in ordinances and other documents. This chapter describes the land use management program and its parts. It lays the foundation for subsequent analyses of local adoption and administration of management measures and for judging their effectiveness.

The flood plain land use management program may be conceived as one part of a more comprehensive flood-hazard management system. The broader system has several other parts: (1) flood control measures, often called structural or engineering measures; (2) emergency preventive measures; and (3) loss alleviation measures. Flood control measures include dams and reservoirs, levees, channel improvements, and other engineering works that are aimed at modifying flooding behavior. By contrast, land use management is aimed at modifying human behavior; at man's use of the flood plain rather than the flood's use of it; at keeping people out of the flood's way rather than keeping the flood out of the people's way. Emergency preventive measures, such as flood warning systems, temporary floodproofing, and temporary evacuation of flood-hazard areas, also attempt to modify human behavior, but not land-using behavior, and not permanently. Loss alleviation measures are designed to lessen the effects of flood losses on individuals and organizations. They include insurance, disaster relief, and tax write-offs. They are applied during and after a flood event, rather

than before and are ameliorative rather than
preventive. Both emergency preventive and loss
alleviation measures have a valid role in a flood-
hazard management system because no reasonable
combination of structural and land use measures, and
certainly no optimal one, would avoid all flooding or
all flood damage permanently.

In any ideal sense, the flood plain land use
management system should not be conceived or analyzed
independently of the other three components of comprehensive flood-hazard management. Most urban flood-
hazard management programs for flood-prone areas should
include all four parts. Flood control is as valid as
behavior modification. Furthermore, the design of land
use management measures should consider the effect of
flood control structures on the nature and geographic
pattern of the remaining risk of flood damage.
Temporary preventive measures taken at the time of the
flood event to modify the loss burden are as necessary
as the more permanent measures of flood control and
land use management. Given this context of an overall
flood-hazard management system, the present research
focuses on one part of that system--the flood plain
land use management component. The other components of
an ideal flood-hazard management system--structural
measures, emergency preventive measures, and loss
alleviation measures--are treated as exogenous factors
that can influence both the nature of the land use
management program and its impacts or effects.

The term "flood plain land use management program"
implies that the program is conscious, intentional,
designed, and controlled. Those are the aspects of
flood plain land use management that are emphasized in
this research, as well as in the literature. Nevertheless, a de facto flood plain land use management
program also exists. It includes other local
governmental goals, policies, plans, and actions that
significantly influence land use decisions, site
design, and construction practices in the flood plain
for better or for worse, even though these measures are
not designed for that purpose. For example, an open
space acquisition program takes some flood plain land
out of the marketplace and thereby contributes to flood
hazard management. On the other hand, an extension of
public water and sewer lines into the flood plain may
encourage urban development there and aggravate the
flood hazard. Thus de facto flood plain land use
management measures must be considered if we are to
suggest how policies could be modified to achieve more
effective management programs.

In this study we are concerned primarily with

local programs. Federal and state goals, policies and plans, and hazard management programs are included only to the extent that they are adopted as part of a local government's land use management system. For example, the adoption of a state model ordinance by a locality would be included, but the National Flood Insurance Program would not, except as represented by whatever land use regulations a local government adopts and enforces in order to participate in the program. This is not to imply that we are not interested in the effects of federal and state policies on the course of action pursued by localities. In Chapter 4 we give particular attention to the extent to which federal programs have shaped local flood plain land use management efforts. We also recognize that past federal and state flood-hazard mitigation projects, such as the provision of structural protection measures, can counteract or reinforce local land use management measures. The role of federal and state policies in local program effectiveness is explored in Chapter 6.

Local governments examined in this study are general-purpose local governments eligible for membership in the National Flood Insurance Program. Land use management efforts of special-purpose local governments, such as drainage and flood control districts, are included only to the extent that they are integrated by a general-purpose local government into its land use management program. Otherwise they are considered part of the inter-governmental component of the contextual milieu that reinforces or confounds the effectiveness of local programs.

In the remainder of this chapter, the flood plain land use management program is defined more explicitly. First, flood plain land use management is conceptualized as an array of specific measures of different types, grouped into categories. Not all of these possible measures or categories of measures are necessarily included in every program, but the list helps define the building blocks of such a program. Most of the literature on flood plain management takes this "component listing" approach. (See, for example, Sheaffer, Roland, et al. 1976 and Wall 1969.)

The second part discusses the key dimensions of a program. These dimensions define the characteristics of flood plain land use management that determine the degree and direction of influence that the adopted measures and the management program as a whole will have upon the use and development of the flood plain. Ultimately, they determine the flood plain land use management program's effectiveness. This second approach is more representative of political

scientists' and policy analysts' methods of studying
governmental programs and is not often found applied to
flood plain programs. Sabatier and Mazmanian (1979) are
representative of this perspective in the literature on
regulatory policy, of which flood plain land use
management programs may be considered an example.[1]   In
the literature that focuses explicitly on flood plain
land use management, only Hutton and Mileti (1979) have
explored questions related to policy implementation in
any depth.

COMPONENTS OF THE FLOOD PLAIN LAND USE MANAGEMENT
PROGRAM

Although planners have conceptualized urban
land use management programs in a number of ways (see,
for example, Reps 1964 and Chapin 1963), one of the
earliest schemes directly related to flood hazard
management was formulated within the Tennessee Valley
Authority.[2]   In the initial TVA approach, the comprehensive flood damage prevention program consisted of
corrective measures and preventive measures. The land
use management program was called "flood plain regulations," under preventive measures. It consisted of
zoning ordinances, subdivision regulations, building
codes, health regulations, and others. Development
policies, open space, urban redevelopment, and floodproofing, all of which we consider to be examples of
land use management, were scattered among other head-
ings in this initial TVA scheme. The TVA approach was
refined over time so that land use management measures
received more explicit consideration. In a later,
refined conceptual scheme (Wall 1969), two types
of land use measures were identified. One, land use
controls, included zoning, encroachment statutes, subdivision regulations, building codes, and developmental
policies. The second, termed adjustments, included
relocation, open space acquisition, urban renewal, and
watershed treatment.

Sheaffer, David and Richmond proposed another
typology in 1970:

Modify the flood
    Flood protection (affecting the stream flow)
    Watershed treatment (affecting runoff)
    Weather modification (affecting precipitation)
Modify the damage susceptibility
    Land use changes
    Floodproofing
    Planned unit development
Modify the loss burden
    Flood insurance
    Tax write-off

> Disaster relief grants and loans
> Emergency measures (e.g., flood warning,
>   temporary floodproofing)

The flood plain land use management program covers the
second of these three components--modifying damage
susceptibility. The typology was used fruitfully in
several tables that related flood plain management
alternatives to their compatibility with local goals,
federal programs, applicability to various land uses,
private versus public cost-bearing and beneficiaries,
and cause of flooding.

More recently Sheaffer has distinguished between
safe land use practices (land acquisition, development
policies, and regulatory activities such as zoning,
subdivision regulations, and special flood hazard regulations) and safe construction practices (floodproofing, building codes, and construction practices in
the watershed) in modifying damage susceptibility
(Sheaffer, Roland, et al 1976, 3). This typology
clarifies the distinction between approaches designed
to change the location of development and technological
(engineering and construction) approaches that reduce
the damage susceptibility of development that is still
at risk.

Our flood plain land use management program model
is based on a synthesis of these and other ideas in the
flood plain management literature, together with ideas
stemming from the land use planning and management and
the policy analysis literatures. In addition, our
conceptual approach reflects our ultimate interest in
gauging the effectiveness of land use management
programs and identifying factors influencing variation
in effectiveness. It is different from, but not inconsistent with, most other conceptualizations of flood-
hazard management.

Our conceptual model consists of three main
categories of land use management measures: (1) goals
and objectives; (2) policies and plans; and (3) action
or implementation instruments. Goals and objectives
are included as integral parts of the program rather
than as exogenous factors because they will vary among
local governments and because they help determine at
least an initial measure of the appropriateness of
policies, plans, and actions. In addition, as noted by
Sabatier and Mazmanian (1978), "Statutory objectives
which are precise and clearly ranked in importance
serve as an indispensible aid in program evaluation, as
unambiguous directives to implementing officials, and
as a resource available to supporters of those

objectives both within and external to the implementing agencies."

Policies and plans are included for their contributions as (1) bridges from goals to the formulation of action instruments in the planning process; and (2) general guides to the administration of action instruments and in their periodic revision. In addition, policies and plans shed further light on the real (perhaps tacit) goals and objectives of the governmental body; help ascertain consistency between goals and action/implementation instruments; indicate integration of various action instruments; and indicate general strategies.

Action instruments are the components of the management system that intervene most directly in decisions regarding flood plain land use, development, and redevelopment. The conceptualizations in the flood plain land use management literature tend to discuss action strategies and instruments separately both from goals and objectives and from policies and plans. (See, for example, Sheaffer, Davis, and Richmond 1970.) In the next three sections the major components of flood plain land use management programs--goals and objectives, policies and plans, and action instruments--are described in greater detail.

GOALS AND OBJECTIVES

Goals and objectives that may be incorporated in a flood plain land use management program include those that have been explicitly adopted and those that serve as implicit guides to decision making, even though they have not been formally adopted and have no legal standing. Some of both types of goals may come from federal, state, and regional governments, such as the sections of model ordinances that summarize the purpose of regulation.[3] Goals derived from other governments are considered to be goals of the local flood plain land use management program if they have been consciously adopted as the community's own; otherwise they are viewed as another category of exogenous factors, against which effectiveness may or may not be measured. We hypothesize that federal and state goals will be achieved more effectively if local governments consciously adopt them as their own, and will be achieved less effectively to the degree that local governments substitute or add other goals. Goals may be identified from a number of sources, including resolutions, legislation, policy statements, plans, and other governmental documents. In addition, goals may be discovered through interviews with or questionnaires returned by community decision makers and officials responsible for implementing the land use management program.[4]

Categories of goals can be formulated, based on the flood plain management and policy analysis literature. Various goals that have been associated with flood plain land use management include

    Economic
        Economic efficiency
        Fiscal efficiency
        Economic development
        Equity

    Social
        Equity
        Health-safety-security
        Continuity of social organization

    Environmental
        Environmental quality
        Natural resource conservation
        Amenity-aesthetics

Economic Goals

The economic goals are straightforward. Economic efficiency suggests the objective of minimizing the total flood-hazard costs in the private and public realm. These include the costs of running the program, costs incurred by those affected by the land use management program plus the remaining expected private and public flood damage costs. Fiscal efficiency refers to the balancing of public costs incurred in operating the program, floodproofing public investments, and lost property tax revenues from flood plain land whose value is depressed by the land use controls versus the savings realized in disaster relief costs and damages avoided to public capital improvements. One could classify fiscal efficiency as merely a special category of economic efficiency. It is a particularly salient goal for most local governments, however, and for that reason it is desirable to think of a separate category for fiscal efficiency objectives.

Economic development goals emphasize use of the flood plain resource and conceivably the resources created by flood control measures (e.g., the recreation potential of a reservoir) for improving the locality's economy. Equity suggests a fair distribution of the costs and benefits flowing from occupation of the flood

plain and the costs (and even benefits) flowing from
the flood-hazard management program. The term "fair"
may imply a redistribution of benefits/costs to favor
those least well off. Alternatively, it might imply
having those who benefit from flood plain occupancy
assume the full costs of that occupancy, rather than
shifting them to neighbors and society at large. The
equity goal may fit equally well under the social
heading.

Social Goals

Under the category social goals, equity goals
include those discussed above. They may also
incorporate the legal/constitutinal sense of equity--
equal protection, due process, and avoidance of the
taking of private property for public purposes without
compensation. Provision of a wider range of choices
for people also may be viewed as a variation of the
equity goal. Finally, equity may include giving special
consideratin to the effects of flood management
measures on the "have nots" of society. Health,
safety, and security, both real and perceived, are
basic social and human values that may be affected by
floods and the solutions to floods. Continuity of
social organization may be interpreted as the avoidance
of community or neighborhood disruption by flood
catastrophe or the flood hazard management solution
(e.g., relocation, urban renewal, building a dam and
reservoir).

Environmental Goals

Environmental goals also are generally accepted as
purposes of flood plain land use management. Environmental quality refers to maintenance of standards for
water and air quality. Resource conservation speaks to
wise preservation and long-term use of environmental
processes and the supply of natural materials and
places. Finally, the amenities or aesthetics goal
addresses the promotion of culturally valued characteristics of the flood plain landscape, such as views,
open space, unique features, and the preservation of
places associated with culturally important events or
people.

Other Expressions of Goals

Goals are sometimes expressed in ways that are
more specific to flood hazards and flood plain management than the goals just discussed. While they are less
abstract, they are also less general. Some of these

goals are:

1. Protection of adjacent, upstream, and downstream private and public landowners and residents from direct and substantial increases in flood damages. (This speaks to the principle of avoiding the imposition of externality costs by one landowner upon others, a notion related to equity.)

2. Avoidance of the costs to society of alleviating the flood losses of private and public property owners or of building expensive public works to control floods to protect such property (related to the goals of fiscal efficiency and equity).

3. Prevention of victimization and fraud. (This goal should not be interpreted as one of keeping people from harming themselves in spite of themselves. In our society, according to the Constitution, people are free to make unwise choices, provided that information about possible adverse consequences of such choices has not been withheld from them. Thus, if a person wishes to locate in the flood-hazard area and bear the risks, he may be allowed to do so without violation of this goal, as long as forewarning is provided.)

4. Equitable distribution of flood hazard costs (i.e., having the person who benefits from flood plain occupancy also pay the costs associated with that occupancy, such as by requiring insurance coverage at full actuarial rates or by creating a special assessment district, with boundaries coterminous with the flood plain, to raise funds for flood relief from those landowners who are obtaining the benefits of flood plain use).

There are other goals that are often found in statements of legislative intent, but that thoughtful observers tend to discount. These goals include keeping the flood plain free of urban uses (which should be discounted, since such uses might be economically justified in some circumstances); minimizing flood losses (this might be unreasonable if the costs of doing so are not also considered); promoting the general welfare (too vague); and promoting wise land use patterns (also too vague).

Flood plain land use management goals and

objectives are hypothesized to have a significant, if indirect, effect on decisions regarding flood plain use and development and on the ultimate effectiveness of the management program. They are also hypothesized to help explain the composition and stringency of the other two components of the program--policies and plans, and action instruments.

POLICIES AND PROGRAMMATIC PLANS

Policies are expressions of governmental intention. They constitute a set of principles to guide whole classes of subsequent decisions by governmental decision makers and sometimes nongovernmental decision makers as well. Their purpose is to maintain consistency in a long-term stream of incremental decisions to achieve constant progress toward a goal. Policies also may include goal statements if they have that purpose. Examples of policies include comprehensive plans and most land use plans (which normally propose general policy even though they are called plans), as well as adopted policy statements or resolutions. Programmatic plans, on the other hand, propose specific programs of action. Examples include capital improvement programs, water resource plans, and community facilities plans.

For purposes of this research, plans provide an interpretation of goals (which are often included within such plans), and more significantly they are an indication of the degree of analysis and coordination underlying action instruments. It is hypothesized that land use management programs are more effective when they have a more solid analytical foundation and have been coordinated through planning.

ACTION INSTRUMENTS

Flood plain land use management programs may involve the use of seven categories of action instruments. Within each type, program managers may employ one or more measures. The categories include: (1) police power regulations; (2) capital improvements; (3) land acquisition; (4) relocation of development; (5) incentives and disincentives; (6) information and advice; and (7) measures applied outside of the flood plain but in the watershed.

Police Power Regulations

Police power regulations are measures prohibiting

or requiring various actions, usually from the private sector, in developing, building, and rebuilding in flood-hazard areas. A number of different police power regulations that have been applied to flood plain land use management are briefly described below.

Flood plain zoning, as described by Kusler and Lee (1972), "...involves the division of a governmental unit into districts and the regulation, within these districts, of the use of structures and land; the height and bulk of structures; and the size of lots and density of use." Regulations usually differ from district to district so that special standards can be established for land in flood-hazard areas. Flood plain zoning is generally characterized as "single-district" or "two-district" depending on how it handles the floodway within the floodplain. Single-district approaches are suitable for situations where a flood-hazard area can be distinguished, but where data are not adequate to distinguish the floodway (portion of the flood plain consisting of the stream channel and overbank area needed to convey a selected flood discharge within designated heights) from the remainder of the flood plain (usually called the floodway fringe). Where the floodway and floodway fringe can be differentiated, two-district zoning may be used, specifying different regulations for the floodway and floodway fringe districts.

Subdivision regulations apply to the division of parcels into lots, usually for purposes of sale and subsequent building. The regulations require the developer or subdivider to prepare a map (plat) of the subdivision, which must be approved by the local jurisdiction. Subdivision ordinances contain various standards for lot layouts, street patterns and widths, minimum widths and depths of lots, stormwater drainage, water and sewer lines, and the like. For purposes of flood plain land use management, the regulations may require that lots be free of flooding or that they contain a sufficiently large, buildable portion free of flooding; that adequate drainage facilities be provided; that encroachment of structures into floodway areas be prohibited; and that roads and utilities be elevated above some minimum flood-protection height.

Floodproofing involves the requirement of emergency, contingency, or permanent measures that are designed to render buildings, contents, and grounds less vulnerable to flood damage. Elevation requirements involve raising the structure above the flood level, either by filling low-lying areas with compacted

soil or by elevating the foundation through the use of
posts, piles, piers, walls, or pedestals. For detailed
explanations of floodproofing and elevation measures,
see Sheaffer, et al. (1967); Office of the Chief of
Engineers, U.S. Army (1972b); and Federal Insurance
Administration (1976). Floodproofing and elevation
requirements are often contained in building codes,
which specify standards that must be met when
structures are built or rebuilt. As noted by Kusler
and Lee (1972, 9), standards may be used to
"(1) prevent flotation of buildings by requiring proper
anchorage, (2) establish minimum construction
elevation consistent with flooding potential, (3) restrict use of materials which deteriorate when exposed
to water, and (4) require structural design consistent
with water pressures and flood velocities."

Sanitary codes and septic tank regulations govern
the use of on-site water supply and waste disposal
systems and may control dumping in hazard areas. They
often prohibit the use of on-site sewage disposal
systems in flood-hazard areas.

Transfer of development rights regulations assign
development rights to parcels based on land capability
and other studies. These rights are separable from the
land and may be transferred to other parcels. In flood
plain land use management, if a parcel's zoning allows
development that would be unwise because of the flood
hazard, transfer of development rights regulations may
permit the parcel owner to sell his development rights
to the owner of another parcel in a receiving area
deemed by the community to be more suitable for
development in return for reducing allowable density
within the flood plain.

Capital Improvements

In contrast with regulatory measures, which
directly control development and building within the
flood-hazard area, capital improvements may be
manipulated to shape development through various
secondary effects. For example, the presence of certain public facilities, such as highways, water and
sewer lines, schools, and parks, may induce land use
changes. (See Urban Systems Research and Engineering,
Inc. 1976.) When these and other facilities are
located in or near flood-hazard areas, they may
encourage unwise urban encroachment on the flood plain.
Conversely, locating major public facilities away from
hazardous areas may have the opposite effect.
Developers and builders may be induced to locate on the

flood-free sites where public facilities will be provided, particularly if flood-hazard areas will not be
served with public infrastructure. Besides policies
regarding the location of facilities, the effects of
public facilities may be mitigated by changing the
scale of facilities, their design, and conditions
related to their use, such as the number of tap-ons
allowed for a new sewer line (The Research Group, Inc.
1978).

In contrast with the indirect effects of public
facilities, capital improvement policies also may deal
with various direct effects. For example, capital
improvement policies may call for avoidance of flood
hazard areas not because of a concern for induced
private-sector development, but simply to avoid the
threat of flood damage to public property. In
addition, capital improvement policies often are aimed
at mitigating direct environmental damage from facility
development.

Land Acquisition

One of the seemingly most effective means of protecting flood-hazard areas and reducing flood damages
to public and private property is the acquisition of
flood plain land for park, open space; and other public
uses with low flood-damage potential. Since fee-simple
acquisition is expensive and often requires the provision of funds from other levels of government, a
number of supplementary means of acquiring flood plain
property are useful. In a number of states, for
example, mandatory dedication provisions can be applied
as part of the subdivision regulation process.
Mandatory dedication regulations require that
developers give to the public (or reserve for public
acquisition) land that meets certain standards. These
standards can be designed to include land with various
development limitations, such as steep slopes and flood
hazards. Also, easements or partial rights for
development (purchase of development rights) can be
acquired to limit intensive development in flood-hazard
areas. Although these rights may be costly to acquire
in urban areas where development is imminent,
acquisition of partial rights in land may be used with
greater effect in rural areas to protect sensitive
environments. The Massachusetts Wetlands Act, for
example, is said to rely heavily on such easements to
limit coastal development and damage from coastal
flooding (The Institute of Rational Design, Inc. 1977,
66).
A number of other techniques for reducing acquisition costs may be applied depending upon local
circumstances (Kusler 1979). They include selective

acquisition of a limited number of sites, such as those
sites most likely to lead to a reduction in flood
damages; active solicitation of private land donations;
"official mapping" of wetlands and flood plains to
prevent development that would add to future
acquisition costs; legislative taking, where land
prices are frozen pending acquisition for a public
facility or park; bargain sales, where landowners may
be induced to sell flood-hazard property to public
agencies at below-market rates if the difference
between the sales and market prices can be classed as a
charitable deduction for tax purposes; purchase and
resale, where land is purchased and resold for private
development with covenants that restrict its future
use; and purchase and leaseback, where property is
purchased and is leased for various uses in an effort
to reduce the fiscal impact of the acquisition program.
In sum, a number of land acquisition techniques are
available to reduce somewhat the costs of using the
acquisition approach to flood plain land use
management.

Relocation

Relocation, which involves moving structures and
occupants from the flood plain to hazard-free
locations, is much more expensive and difficult to
accomplish than the acquisition of vacant land. Nevertheless, a number of communities have found that
relocation is the most cost-effective solution to their
flood problems. After the Rapid City, South Dakota,
flood in June 1972, for example, a non-structural
recovery program was mounted that involved the
acquisition of 1,400 parcels in the Rapid Creek floodway. Other recent major relocation efforts include
acquisition and relocation of 246 flood-prone dwellings
by Baltimore County, Maryland; relocation of a portion
of the central business district of Soldier's Grove,
Wisconsin, out of the Kickapoo River floodway;
relocation of 350 dwellings from an area experiencing
subsidence and tidal flooding in Baytown, Texas; relocation of 80 families from the Kingery West subdivision
in the Salt Creek watershed of DuPage County, Illinois;
purchase of 116 properties in Lilydale, Minnesota; and
relocation of the entire community of Clinchport,
Virginia, by the Tennessee Valley Authority (Kusler
1979; Platt 1979). While those are among the best-
known cases, they are not unique. A recent survey by
Ables, Schwartz and Associates/Ralph M. Field
Associates, Inc. (1979) of community experience with
land acquisition for flood-hazard mitigation found that
of 92 successful acquisition projects, 42 involved the
acquisition and subsequent demolition or relocation of

structures.

Incentives and Disincentives

Incentives and disincentives are another set of tools that may be used to achieve public land use objectives in flood-hazard areas. Preferential taxation is widely used to discourage the premature conversion of open, agricultural land to urban uses. Typically, land is assessed for tax purposes at its value in nonurban uses with a provision that deferred taxes must be paid if development occurs within a specified period. A more direct form of incentive is the payment of subsidies to households to floodproof their property or to relocate from the hazard area. Another form of incentive is built into the National Flood Insurance Program, which provides subsidized insurance to existing occupants of flood-hazard areas in order to encourage them to purchase insurance. On the other hand, the requirement that new development using federally ensured loans purchase flood insurance at actuarial rates provides a disincentive for flood plain development, since the flood plain occupant is forced to pay for the costs of potential flood losses. Moreover, to the extent that requirements to floodproof or elevate new construction raise building and development costs, they are a disincentive to locating in the flood plain.

In contrast with their indirect effect, incentives may be used directly to influence builders and developers to take certain actions. Density transfer or clustering provisions of zoning ordinances, for example, may be used to allow landowners to shift development rights from flood-prone portions of their property and build at higher-than-normal densities on that portion of the parcel outside of the hazard zone. Density transfer and clustering provisions are often incorporated into zoning regulations through a planned unit development ordinance.

Information and Advice

The provision of information about the flood hazard is one of the oldest nonstructural techniques for discouraging the development of flood-hazard areas. A number of approaches to informing the public have been devised. They include educational programs, publication and dissemination of flood-hazard area maps, and posting of warning signs. In addition, communities may require that builders, developers, real estate agents, and others involved in the real estate industry disclose the flood hazard before property is sold. Moreover, subdivision regulations often require that the flood-hazard area boundary be delineated on plats, so that prospective lot purchasers know of the hazard and later can avoid inadvertently locating damageable property in areas subject to flooding.

Watershed Measures Applied Outside of the Flood Plain

A final class of flood plain land use management measures is applied to property located outside of the flood plain. Such measures include regulations limiting the proportion of a site that may be paved, requiring on-site detention of stormwater, encouraging stormwater drainage into pervious soils, and other measures to slow runoff rates. Those provisions are usually incorporated into a community's subdivision regulations and apply to the entire planning jurisdiction.

Summary

The preceding listing and discussion of action instruments makes clear that if communities wish to solve their flood plain problems, a variety of methods and measures can be employed for that purpose. We hypothesize that if a greater number and wider range of action instruments are used, the flood plain land use management program will be more effective in terms of the community's flood plain land use management goals and objectives. There is little empirical evidence, however, about the relative effectiveness of the various individual instruments or combinations of instruments.

KEY DIMENSIONS OF THE FLOOD PLAIN LAND USE MANAGEMENT PROGRAM

The "components approach" to defining the flood plain land use management program discussed above outlines the silhouette of a system and identifies its parts. It is primarily descriptive and cannot fully explain variation in the effectiveness of flood plain land use management. The "key dimensions" perspective discussed here evolved from this study's interest in explaining variation in program effectiveness. The key dimensions perspective sets forth a number of hypotheses about significant aspects of the flood plain land use management program that determine (1) the program's effects on private-sector decisions regarding

flood plain development and use; (2) the flow of consequences (benefits and adverse impacts) from those
decisions; and (3) the flow of benefits and costs that
emanate directly from the flood plain land use management program itself, rather than through effects on
private-sector decisions. The concepts developed here
rely heavily on the work of Sabatier (1977), Mazmanian
and Sabatier (1978, 1979), and, indirectly, on other
political science policy analysis literature, such as
Van Meter and Van Horn (1975).

There are two major dimensions of a flood plain
land use management program, each of which is composed
of a series of variables. The two major dimensions are
the legislative content of the program (the program on
paper); and the operational dimension of the program
(the program as implemented).

The Legislative Dimension

The dimension of legislative content consists of
two subdimensions--the types and scope of measures
included in the flood plain land use management program
and the program's legislative stringency. These may be
briefly summarized as follows:

1. Types and Scope of Measures Included

    a. Existence/nonexistence of specific land
        use management measures and the total
        number of measures being used.

    b. Pattern of measures, such as relative
        emphasis on police power versus emphasis
        on policies and plans or on
        capital improvements.

    c. Systematic nature of the legislative con-
        tent, including the degree of coordination
        among measures and the positive and
        negative interaction of measures (positive
        interaction being conscious or fortuitous
        integration and mutual support; negative
        interaction being conflicting or offset-
        ting influences).

2. Legislative Stringency

    a. The effort needed to implement the
        measures.

    b. Existence and clarity of goals and
        objectives specified in ordinances and

other legislation.[5]

    c.   The difficulty of obtaining variances and exceptions.[6]

    d.   The probability of detection for those violating regulations.

    e.   The type and severity of sanctions for violators who are detected. (Rosenbaum 1978)

    f.   Concentration or fragmentation of authority to implement the program, including the number of possible veto points.[7]

In examining legislative stringency, our main interest is whether a land use management program has teeth. A stringent program should provide evidence of a community's commitment to manage its flood-hazard areas.

The Operational Dimension

After examining legislative lative content, only the "paper" program has been considered. The operational dimension of flood plain land use management focuses on how the paper program is implemented in practice. The operational dimension has three important subdimensions: (1) structural commitment or resources; (2) administrative commitment; and (3) procedural character. These may be briefly summarized as follows:

1. Structural Commitment

    a.   Size of the implementation staff, relative to the implementation workload (Sabatier and Mazmanian 1979).

    b.   Qualifications of the staff, including leadership, prior experience with land use management, particularly flood plain land use management, and stature in the local government (Van Meter and Van Horn, 1975).

2. Administrative Commitment

    a.   Attitudes of administrators toward flood plain land use management and commitment

to the implementation of the program
(Dunshire 1978).

b. Assertiveness of implementation staff in
administering the flood plain land use
management program, as indicated by
adherence to program objectives and
standards in negotiations with permit
applicants, the extent of searching for
violations, inspection of permit
recipients for compliance with permit
conditions, prosecution of violators,
aggressiveness of land acquisition, and
other related measures.

c. Commitment of quasi-judicial appeals
boards and the legislative body toward the
flood plain land use management program,
as indicated by the number and nature of
variances and exceptions granted.[8]

3. Procedural Character

a. Organizational arrangement, including
location of the implementation unit in
relation to the locus of decision-making
authority, degree of centralization of
decision making related to flood plain
land use management, degree of autonomy of
decision makers.

b. Work processes, including degree of
standardization, level of technical knowledge required, number of separate
operations involved, complexity of
processes.

c. Character of interaction with other
organizations involved with flood plain
land use management, including degree of
interdependence, frequency of contacts,
shared values, and related variables.

Each of the factors and variables outlined above
is expected to influence the effectiveness of local
flood plain land use management. Precise hypotheses to
give meaning to these relationships are discussed along
with the empirical results of this study in the
succeeding chapters.

SUMMARY

This chapter has presented a conceptual framework for identifying and measuring local flood plain land use management programs. Local flood plain management is viewed as part of a larger flood hazard management system that includes structural flood control measures, measures to alleviate losses, and emergency preventative measures, as well as land use management. Because of the focus of this research on land use management approaches, other components of an ideal flood hazard management system are treated as exogenous factors that can influence both the nature and the effects of the land use management program. Flood plain land use management is conceptualized in two ways: first, as an array of specific measures of different types grouped into categories; and second, in terms of key dimensions that cut across measures and in large part determine the degree of influence that individual management measures have on the character of flood plain development and use.

Three categories of land use management measures are defined: (1) goals and objectives; (2) policies and plans; and (3) action or implementation instruments. Action instruments intervene most directly in decisions regarding flood plain development and use. The seven categories of action instruments discussed in this chapter are police power regulations, public investments, acquisition of property rights, relocation of development, incentives and disincentives, information and advice, and measures applied outside of the flood plain. The greater the number and wider the range of action instruments employed by a jurisdiction, the more effective its land use management program should be.

Two major dimensions cut across the specific measures of a jurisdiction's land use management program: the strength and pattern of the legislative content of the program (the program on paper); and the strength and pattern of the program's operational content (the program in action). Legislative content comprehends both the type and scope of measures used as part of the local program and the notion of legislative stringency--the teeth given to program measures, in terms of goals and objectives sought, range and type of targeted groups and decisions, geographic coverage, and concentration of implementation authority. The operational dimension has three important subdimensions: (1) structural commitment; (2) administrative commitment; and (3) procedural character. The strength of these legislative and operational dimensions and subdimensions, as well as the combination of specific measures incorporated in a flood plain land use manage-

ment program, may change over time. Similarly, some
effects of the program may be immediate, while others
may not appear for some time.

In the following chapter, our examination of local
flood plain land use management moves from the
conceptual considerations discussed here to an
examination of flood plain management as it is actually
practiced across the nation. In addition, attention is
given to factors associated with the adoption of
broader, more stringent measures and to the commitment
of local jurisdictions to flood plain management as
indicated by the funding of program implementation.
The legislative and operational dimensions of flood
plain management are further explored in Chapter Seven,
which summarizes the results of an in-depth exploration
of flood plain land use management in three
communities.

NOTES

1. The literature on policy implementation, most
of it dealing with the implementation of federal
policies, has been growing rapidly over the past ten
years. Besides Sabatier and Mazmanian, conceptual
models have been developed by, among others, Williams
(1975); Van Meter and Van Horn (1975); Bardach (1977);
and Hutton and Mileti (1978, 1979). Key empirical
studies of implementation include Pressman and
Wildavsky (1973) and Rodgers and Bullock (1976).
2. The Tennessee Valley Authority approach to
flood hazard management has been described in numerous
places. In particular, see Wall 1969.
3. For example, many communities have adopted the
Department of Housing and Urban Development's model
ordinance developed for the National Flood Insurance
Program. The suggested model ordinance includes the
following statement of purpose:

It is the purpose of this ordinance to promote the
public health, safety, and general welfare, and to
minimize public and private losses due to flood
conditions in specific areas by provisions
designed: (1) to protect human life and health;
(2) to minimize expenditure of public money for
costly flood control projects; (3) to minimize the
need for rescue and relief efforts associated with
flooding and generally undertaken at the expense
of the general public; (4) to minimize prolonged
business interruptions; (5) to minimize damage to
public facilities and utilities such as water and
gas mains, electric, telephone and sewer lines,
streets and bridges located in areas of special

flood hazard; (6) to help maintain a stable tax
base by providing for the safe use and development
of areas of special flood hazard so as to minimize
future flood blight areas; (7) to ensure that
potential buyers are notified that property is in
an area of special flood hazard; and (8) to ensure
that those who occupy the areas of special flood
hazard assume responsibility for their actions.

4. A methodology for identifying community goals
is presented in Sheaffer, David, and Richmond 1970,
98-101.
5. See Sabatier and Mazmanian 1978 and Van Meter
and Van Horn 1975.
6. Even though much land-use decision making
occurs in negotiations between implementation officials
and target groups, and thus never reaches the point at
which variances are requested, provisions regarding
appeals from administrators' decisions are another
factor that can have a strong influence on the
effectiveness of flood plain land use management. For
example, according to Levin, Rose, and Slavet (1974,
18, 67), "...within municipalities, there has been a
consistent pattern of critical land use decision making
made piecemeal through variances, zoning amendments,
special use permits, and exceptions. Justified mainly
on the basis of individual owner hardships, these cases
have had cumulative effects in achieving fundamental
alterations in the nature of entire neighborhoods.
bodies, planning and zoning principles are constantly
eroded for the benefit of individual property owners."
In an early study of zoning exceptions and variances,
Delafons (1962, 84-87) found that in Philadelphia
during the period 1935-1955, one thousand zoning amendments, 35,000 variances, and 3,500 exceptions were
granted, so that by the end of the period, 5 percent of
the property in the city was not in compliance with
provisions of the zoning ordinance. Also see Salamon
and Wamsley (1975) for another discussion of zoning
amendment, variance, and special use permit practices.
7. See Pressman and Wildavsky (1973, Chapter 5)
for a discussion of how the number of decision points
can delay program implementation and, potentially,
render a program ineffective.
8. The number of variances granted can be mis-
leading, since in some cases the granting of variances
and special use permits may serve a valid function as a
safety valve that is "...in large part a response to
the existing inadequate system." (Salamon and Wamsley
1975, 147)

3
The State of Practice: Community Adoption of Flood Plain Land Use Management Measures in the United States

Since inauguration of the National Flood Insurance Program in 1968, the number of places engaging in flood plain land use management has increased from a handful of local jurisdictions to some 16,500 communities. Now that more than a decade of experience has accumulated in communities all across the nation, it is possible to take a close look at how local governments are actually undertaking the task of flood plain management. This chapter provides a broad overview of the state of practice in the United States. It covers local perceptions of flood plain problems; current use of various management system components (goals, plans and policies, and action instruments) that have been adopted to address flood plain problems; and the human and financial resources that communities are devoting to this effort. Some communities have adopted more stringent flood plain land use management programs, while others have not moved beyond a token effort to comply with the minimum requirements of the National Flood Insurance Program. This chapter explains why that has occurred and suggests how federal and state policies can stimulate greater local attention to flood hazard mitigation.

A CLOSER LOOK AT THE PROBLEM

Flood losses are clearly a critical national problem. But, are floods also a serious local problem? No, according to most local officials. Nevertheless, some jurisdictions do perceive flooding as a serious problem and, as shown later in this chapter, are taking steps to mitigate the hazard. Recent data assembled by Wright, Rossi, Wright, and Weber-Burdin (1979) at the University of Masachusetts-Amherst and by Friesema (1979) and his colleagues at Northwestern University indicate that communities suffer few if any long-term adverse effects from floods, hurricanes or other

natural disasters. The University of Massachusetts
study found that the average county affected by a flood
disaster during the entire decade of the 1960s
experienced only one fatality, four dwellings
destroyed, and twenty-one dwellings with major damage.
In comparison with the average of more than 32,000
dwellings in a typical flood-stricken county, the
damages experienced, although serious for the people
who suffered them, are not generally a major loss from
a county- or community-wide perspective. That finding
led the University of Massachusetts researchers (1979,
33) to conclude, "...Policies designed to deal with the
national disaster problem and which appear to be
rational and effective from that viewpoint may be seen
as burdensome, irrational, inefficient, and perhaps
even counterproductive from the viewpoint of the
communities to which they are applied."

Most people discount the probability of loss from
infrequently occurring events such as floods.[1] Burton
(1972, 184) observed, "Despite the recurrence of
floods, earthquakes, droughts, tornadoes, and similar
phenomena, human populations have not only occupied
hazard zones in large numbers but have almost
invariably moved back into such areas after a disaster
has occurred, sometimes in greater numbers than before
the disaster." It is not surprising, therefore, that
previous research has uncovered little concern with
natural hazards as a community problem. Based on a
survey of 2,000 political and community leaders in 20
states and 100 communities, Rossi, Wright, and Weber-
Burden (1982) reported, "The major thrust of the findings here is quite straightforward: for the most part,
political decision makers in the states and local communities do not see environmental hazards as a very
serious problem, least of all in comparison to the many
other problems that these governmental units are
expected to be doing something about."

Among the broader samples of 1,203 local jurisdictions included in our 1979 survey and 956
jurisdictions surveyed in 1983, flooding was not viewed
as a critical or even a very serious issue (see Table
1-1 in Chapter 1). More than 50 percent of the
responding local officials in both surveys, however,
were aware that property loss from flooding was a
problem in their communities. They just did not
consider it to be a very important one.

Officials queried in the 1979 survey were also
asked about other problems occurring in their communities' flood-hazard areas. Erosion and
sedimentation was the only problem besides property
loss from floods that was cited by a majority of those

jurisdictions. One-third were concerned about damage to public facilities from flooding and flood-related disruption of economic activity. Encroachment on natural areas also was considered to be a problem in about a third of the communities. Few communities-- less than 10 percent --cited social issues, such as concentrations of poor housing or poverty in flood hazard areas, as a community problem.[2]

Just as most flood plain problems are not widely perceived, their solution is usually not given highest priority among the whole gamut of problems facing a community. Concern for flooding ranked twelfth (just behind pornographic literature) among eighteen community problems respondents were asked to evaluate in the University of Massachusetts study of local leaders (Rossi, Wright, and Weber-Burdin 1982). Among the local governments we surveyed in 1979 and 1983, fewer than 10 percent indicated that highest priority had been assigned to solving flood plain problems.

Previous research has shown that past personal experience with flooding is a consistent predictor of the accuracy of individuals' perceptions of flood hazards (Roder 1961; Kates 1971), belief in hazard warnings (see Mileti, Drabeck, and Haas 1975), and adoption of hazard adjustments, such as the purchase of flood insurance (Kunreuther et al. 1978; Miller 1977). The University of Massachusetts researchers found that the only strong and consistent predictor of how com- munity leaders rated the seriousness of flood problems was the previous experience of the community (not the individual) with flooding (Rossi, Wright, and Weber- Burden 1982). Thus, there is strong reason to believe that although flooding is not a very high priority issue in the average community in the United States, it may be taken more seriously in communities where severe floods have occurred.

Data from our 1979 and 1983 surveys confirm this expectation. The proportion of communities that gave high priority to solving flood plain problems was much larger than average among jurisdictions with severe flood plain problems. In the 1979 survey, for example, 79 percent of local governments experiencing serious riverine flooding and 77 percent of those experienceing serious coastal flooding gave high priority to solving their flood problems, compared with only 32 percent and 39 percent, respectively, of the riverine and coastal communities where flooding had not yet become a serious problem.

To summarize briefly, it has been shown that while flooding is a serious national problem, it is not

perceived as a very important concern in most communities in the United States. Potential property
losses from floods are the most widely recognized
problem of flood-hazard areas. In addition, a number
of communities are also aware of environmental problems
within the bounds of their flood plains. In general,
communities do not attach very high priority to solving
flood plain problems. Where problems are most serious,
however, communities do seem to be concerned and are
placing a high priority on governmental action to
resolve them. The key policy question emerging from
that finding is this: If communities do not become
concerned about flooding until _after_ they have allowed
a flood problem to arise by permitting urban development to encroach on flood hazard areas, is it then too
late to take effective action to mitigate the hazard
through land use adjustments. This issue is addressed
in Chapter Eight.

COMMUNITY GOALS FOR FLOOD PLAIN LAND USE

Specifying goals is one of the first steps in
formulating a land use management program to cope with
flood plain problems. In the previous chapter, a
number of potential goals for flood-hazard areas were
identified. Here we look at the proportion of
communities that have actually adopted goals for their
flood plains and at the specific goals they are
pursuing.

Participation in the National Flood Insurance
Program requires that communities take official
cognizance of their flood problems and pledge to
minimize the exposure of future development to
flooding. It is not particularly surprising, therefore, that a very high proportion of the communities--
more than 80 percent of those surveyed in 1979 and
1983--have officially adopted one or more goals for
flood plain land use. Communities reported an average
of four goals for their flood-hazard areas in 1979, but
as shown in Table 2, only two specific goals--reducing
property loss from flooding and protecting the
population--were being used by most to guide their
flood plain land use management programs. The two
goals mentioned least often were encouraging economic
development and distributing flood plain management
costs equitably. Environmental goals, such as reducing
erosion and sedimentation and preserving natural areas,
had been adopted by a modest proportion (30 percent to
40 percent) of the communities. The 1983 survey asked
about goals in a different manner, but as shown in
Table 3-1, produced similar findings.

TABLE 3-1
Percent of communities adopting various goals

Goals	Percent Reporting Adoption	
	1979 Survey	1983 Survey
Reduce property loss	66%	60%[a]
Protect safety of population	63	(b)
Reduce flood damage to public property	44	33
Reduce erosion and sedimentation	40	(b)
Preserve natural areas	39	38
Minimize fiscal impacts of floods	39	(b)
Preserve open space and recreation areas	38	(b)
Maintain good water quality	30	(b)
Encourage economic development	21	8[c]
Distribute management costs equitably	10	(b)

[a]In the 1983 survey, local governments were asked about two aspects of this goal: losses to future development and losses to existing structures located in flood hazard areas. Sixty percent, as noted in the table, reported adopting a goal to reduce losses to future development. Fewer, only 43 percent, had adopted a goal to reduce flood losses to present structures.
[b]Data not obtained in 1983 survey.
[c]In the 1983 survey, local governments were asked about two aspects of this goal: increase commercial and industrial potential of hazard area and increase residential development potential of hazard area. Eight percent, shown in the table, had adopted the former goal, and 7 percent the latter.

The flood plain goals adopted by communities across the nation provide a reading on the potential effectiveness of a number of federal programs that are designed, in part, to affect the use of flood-hazard areas. These data show the National Flood Insurance Program is having a clearly discernible effect at the local level. The property loss mitigation objectives of the NFIP are evident in the goal most frequently adopted by local governments--reducing property loss from flooding. There also are sharp differences in the proportions of emergency and regular-phase communities that have adopted goals related to property loss: much higher proportions of communities in the NFIP's regular phase have adopted property loss reduction goals, but there are no differences between regular and emergency-phase communities in their attention to environmental goals.

In fact, federal environmental objectives for flood hazard areas do not seem to have filtered down to the local level to any great degree. The water quality objectives of the Federal Water Pollution Control Act Amendments of 1972, for example, have not had much impact on community flood plain management goals. Only 30 percent of the communities surveyed in 1979 were pursuing maintenance of good water quality as an objective for flood plain land use, and only a slightly higher proportion, 40 percent, had adopted an official goal of reducing erosion and sedimentation. Preservation of critical natural areas is encouraged by the Coastal Zone Management Act of 1972 and in the programs of the U.S. Fish and Wildlife Service, but had not been adopted as a goal for local flood plain land use by a majority of the coastal communities we studied (176 of the communities surveyed in 1979 and 50 of those surveyed in 1983 listed coastal flooding from storms, hurricanes, and/or tsunamis as their principal flood hazard). Finally, and most strikingly, while federal policy is moving strongly toward sharing flood plain management costs among federal, state, and local agencies and between the public and private sectors, equitable distribution of costs is apparently of little interest to local governments. Only 10 percent of the communities surveyed in 1979 had adopted "fair distribution of management costs" as a goal for their flood plain land use management efforts. If federal equity and environmental objectives for flood plains are to be promoted at the local level, it seems likely that much more effort must be devoted to convincing local governments of their wisdom and to securing local adoption of related goals.

COMPREHENSIVE PLANNING AND FLOOD PLAIN LAND USE
MANAGEMENT

Until now, most attention in flood plain land use
management has been given to the regulation of flood-
hazard areas. Management regulations may be much more
effective, however, if they are conducted within the
framework provided by a comprehensive land use plan.
In the previous chapter we noted that a comprehensive
plan can be a useful tool in coordinating various
action instruments, such as regulations, to achieve a
community's goals for its flood plains. White (1975,
91) has underscored the need for such coordination. He
observed that without close coordination among management measures, regulations can prove to be counterproductive if they lead to the prolonged existence of
buildings beyond their economic life. In addition,
flood plain land use management may not be fully
effective unless it integrates the entire range of
objectives communities may have for their flood plains
(Whipple, Hufschmidt, et al 1976, 31) and unless it
also considers the simultaneous need for the management
of upland areas that can contribute to downstream
flooding (Allee and Walter 1977, 11). Comprehensive
planning provides a means of achieving this necessary
integration so that multiple means can be coordinated
successfully to serve the multiple objectives
communities may have for their flood-hazard areas.

Sixty percent of the communities surveyed in 1979
and 55 percent of those questioned in 1983 employed
comprehensive land use planning in the management of
their flood plains. There was little difference in the
proportions of NFIP emergency phase and regular phase
communities using comprehensive planning. That is not
particularly surprising, since the National Flood
Insurance Program has encouraged, but not required,
communities to plan for the future use of flood-hazard
areas. Comprehensive planning is most likely to be
used in communities that are seeking to accomplish more
than hazard mitigation in managing their flood plains.
In fact, the goal most closely associated with the use
of comprehensive planning is fair distribution of flood
plain management costs. That reflects the traditional
role of planning as a means of minimizing spillover
costs from urban growth and development. In addition,
communities are more likely than average to use comprehensive planning when they want to achieve various
environmental goals for their flood plains, including
preserving open space and recreational areas, preserving natural areas, and maintaining water quality.

USE OF ACTION INSTRUMENTS IN COMMUNITY FLOOD PLAIN
MANAGEMENT

Communities can employ a number of methods to
achieve their objectives for flood-hazard areas. These
methods, termed "action instruments" in this study,
include police power regulations, such as zoning and
floodproofing rquirements; capital improvements designed to attract new development to locate outside of
flood-hazard areas; public land acquisition in the
flood plain to preclude private development; relocation
of development; tax and other incentives to maintain
low-density uses in the flood plain; and the provision
of public information about the flood hazard.[3]
Communities' use of each of these types of action
instruments is summarized in Table 3-2.

Police Power Regulations

Regulations are the most commonly used methods for
influencing the location and character of development
in flood-hazard areas. As shown in Table 3-2, three
types of regulations--elevation requirements, subdivision regulations, and zoning--had been adopted by
most of the communities contacted in our 1979 and our
1983 surveys. In addition, a majority of the communities contacted in 1979, which tended to be more
populous (see Table 1-1) had adopted floodproofing
requirements and special floodway regulations. Each of
the other types of regulations communities were asked
about--septic tank permits, sedimentation and erosion
control, wetlands protection measures, critical areas
designation and regulations, and sand dune
regulations--had been adopted by fewer than half the
communities surveyed in 1979 and 1983.

Communities participating in the emergency and
regular phases of the National Flood Insurance Program
differed in the proportion that had adopted various
regulations: NFIP regular-phase communities were significantly more likely to have adopted specific
elevation requirements, flood-proofing requirements and
floodway laws. These differences are attributable to
NFIP program regulations and to the associated quality
of the flood-hazard maps the NFIP provides to
communities. Participation in the regular phase of the
NFIP is based on the availability of a Flood Insurance
Rate Map (FIRM), which is compiled from extensive field
surveys and computations of flood magnitudes and water
levels. The map includes precise definitions of the
flood-hazard area and minimum safe first-floor elevations of structures in the hazard zone, and it
designates the channel or floodway required to
discharge the 100-year flood (or the coastal high

TABLE 3-2
Action instruments used by communities to manage flood
hazard areas

Action Instruments	Percent Using 1979 Survey[a]	Percent Using 1983 Survey
Police Power Regulations		
Elevation requirements	77%	60%
Subdivision regulations	75	51
Zoning	75	58
Floodproofing requirements	59	41
Special floodway regulations	52	44
Septic tank permits	42	35
Sedimentation and erosion control regulations	29	22
Wetlands protection regulations	25	13
Critical areas designation	18	(b)
Density exchange/cluster development regulations	6	6
Sand dune regulations	6	3
Capital Improvement Policies		
Location of public facilities outside of flood hazard areas	22	8
Land Acquisition		
Land acquisition for open space, parks and other public uses	34	17
Relocation of existing hazard area development	3	2
Incentives		
Preferential taxation	9	3
Information and Advice		
Public information about hazard	37	32

[a]Communities with 5,000 or more population only.
[b]Data not obtained in 1983 survey.

58

hazard area subject to hurricane waves or tsunamis).
With the FIRM in hand, communities have
a sound basis for and are required by the NFIP to (1)
require new residential construction to be elevated
above the 100-year flood level; (2) require new nonresidential construction to be elevated above the 100-
year flood level or to be floodproofed; and (3) desig-
nate a regulatory floodway or coastal high hazard area
within which no development may occur. In coastal
areas new development must be located landward of the
reach of the mean high tide. NFIP emergency phase
communities, which do not have as precise information
upon which to base their flood plain regulations, are
not required by the NFIP to regulate floodway
encroachment.

Besides differences between communities participating in the emergency and regular phases of the
National Flood Insurance Program, differences in regulations adopted by riverine and coastal communities
also were discovered. Coastal communities in both the
emergency and regular phases of the National Flood
Insurance Program, for example, were more likely than
riverine communities to require that new construction
be elevated above the base (100-year) flood level.
Coastal communities were also somewhat more likely to
have adopted regulations to protect wetlands and other
types of critical areas, and, of course, to have
adopted regulations to protect sand dunes.

Capital improvements policies, land acquisition,
incentives/disincentives, and public information

Local governments were much less likely to be
using various nonregulatory approaches to managing
their flood hazard areas than they were to have enacted
regulations. One commonly suggested nonregulatory
approach is to locate public facilities outside of
flood hazard areas, not only to protect those
facilities from flood damage, but also to avoid inadvertently increasing the attractiveness of flood plains
for urban development. This approach is advocated by
current federal flood plain management policies. As
noted in Chapter 1, Executive Order 11988 directs
federal agencies to "avoid to the extent possible the
long and short term adverse impacts associated with the
occupancy and modification of floodplains and to avoid
the direct and indirect support of floodplain development, whenever there is a practicable alternative."
Table 3-2 shows, however, that few local agencies have
enacted counterpart policies. Only about one in five
of the local governments contacted in 1979 and fewer
than one in ten of those surveyed in 1983 were con-

sciously locating public facilities outside of all
flood-hazard areas in order to reduce future flood
losses. Little difference in the use of this policy
was evident between coastal and riverine communities or
between communities in the emergency and regular phases
of the National Flood Insurance Program. Rather than
avoiding flood hazard locations, the data summarized in
Table 3-3 indicate that in the past communities located
a variety of facilities in areas where they are
threatened by flooding. Whereas parks and open space
serve to protect the natural values of flood-hazard
areas, the location of roads, utility lines, offices,
and other public facilities in the flood plain should
have an opposite effect, stimulating and supporting
urban encroachment.

Besides avoiding flood plain locations in siting
public facilities, federal policies have begun to move
slowly toward land acquisition and relocation as ways
to reduce national flood losses. (See Kusler 1979;
Ralph M. Field Associates 1981.) In that case, however, rather than lagging behind federal initiatives,
local agencies clearly are leading the way for national
policy makers. Acquisition and relocation authorities
are contained in Section 1362 of the Flood Insurance
Act of 1968 and Section 73 of the Water Resources
Development Act of 1974. Section 1362, as amended in
1977, authorizes the federal government to acquire
selected properties insured under the National Flood
Insurance Program and substantially or repeatedly
damaged by flooding. This provision of the act has not
been implemented, but based on unpublished studies that
indicate selective acquisiton would be cost
effective (Abeles, Schwartz, et al 1979), in 1979 the
Federal Emergency Management Agency began requesting
funds to move forward with Section 1362. Section 73 of
the Water Resources Development Act of 1974 requires
federal agencies to consider the acquisition of flood
plain lands for recreation, fish, and wildlife, and
other public purposes as a matter of course in the
survey planning, and design of flood control projects.
That provision also has not been implemented,[4] but the
same act (P.L. 93-251) authorized the Corps of
Engineers to undertake specific nonstructural
acquisition programs in the Charles River Basin of
Massachusetts, and also in Littleton, Colorado (see
Chapter 7), and Prairie du Chien, Wisconsin. Several
other cases of federally sponsored acquisition
and relocation have been reported (Ralph M. Field
Associates 1981), but in general the federal government
has been reluctant to use acquisition as an approach to
flood plain land use management. Local governments,
however, have not been reluctant to use acquisition as
an approach to flood plain land use management or

hesitant in acquiring flood plain property. As shown
in Table 3-3, some 90 percent of the communities surveyed in 1979 and 78 percent of those surveyed in 1983
have some portion of their flood plains in public
ownership. The most common uses of this publicly owned
land are parks and recreation, undeveloped open space,
and roads. A number of these communities were using
land acquisiton as a conscious element of their flood
plain land use management programs. In a very few
cases, communities reported that they also had begun to
relocate existing flood plain development. (For recent
examples of relocation, see David and Mayer 1984 and
Perry and Mushkatel 1984.)

Incentives and disincentives are another approach
communities can use to discourage the development of
flood hazard areas. Two types of incentives were explored in this study--preferential taxation to maintain
agricultural or open space uses of the flood plain, and
density exchanges that allow developers to build at
higher densities than normally allowed in non-hazard
areas in return for maintaining lower-than-required
densities in the flood plain. Neither approach, as
Table 3-2 illustrates, is widely used at this time.

About a third of the communities surveyed in 1979
and 1983 were using public information to discourage
flood plain development. Since misinformation about
the flood hazard is often a large factor undermining
the effectiveness of community flood plain management
efforts (see Chapter Seven), flood plain management
programs might be more successful if more communities
inform citizens of the nature of the flood hazard.
Apparently communities either have become discouraged
about the undertain effectiveness of public information
(see Roder 1961; Kates 1962; and James, Laurent, and
Hill 1971), or, more likely, lack the manpower and
financial resources to undertake a continuing public
informatin program. Communities in the regular phase
of the National Flood Insurance Program were much more
likely than emergency phase communities to be using
public information as a management tool, which suggests
that maps and other assistance provided as part of the
regular phase of the NFIP are helping communities to
increase the breadth of local management efforts.

THE SCOPE AND FOCUS OF LOCAL FLOOD PLAIN MANAGEMENT

Two measures provide indicators of local governments' commitment to land use planning and management
of flood hazard areas: program scope and program
focus. Program scope measures the range of planning
and action instruments employed by a community. We

TABLE 3-3
Public ownership of flood hazard areas

Indicator	Percent of Communities 1979 Survey	1983 Survey
Communities with any of flood hazard area in public ownership	90%	78%
Uses of Publicly Owned Flood Plain Property:		
Parks and recreation	69	51
Undeveloped open space	54	(a)
Roads and bridges	56	58
Sewage and/or water Treatment plants	38	32
Public utility lines and Right-of-ways	38	47
Public works yards	17	13
Offices	11	(a)

[a]Data not obtained in 1983 survey

hypothesize that the more methods a community uses to achieve its flood plain objectives, the more likely those efforts are to be effective. Program focus measures the use of action instruments that are succeedingly more direct in their ability to mitigate flood losses and to achieve other flood plain objectives. We hypothesize that communities that employ more direct measures, such as land acquisition and relocation, will be more likely to have effective programs. The contributions of program scope and focus to the accomplishments of flood plain land use management programs are evaluated in Chapter Six. In the present chapter we develop an explanation for the wide variation that exists in the scope and focus of local communities' flood plain management efforts.

Variation in program scope and focus is illustrated in Tables 3-4 and 3-5. Although the average community surveyed in 1979 had adopted six action instruments, a sizable proportion of those communities had much more robust programs consisting of nine or more action instruments, while some communities were barely complying with the minimum requirements of the National Flood Insurance Program. Similar variation is apparent in the focus of the program adopted. Less than a

TABLE 3-4
Scope of flood plain land use management programs

Program Scope	Percent of Communities	
	1979 Survey	1983 Survey
Number of action instruments used by community[a]		
0-2	10%	26%
3-5	33	28
6-8	33	25
9 or more	24	21

[a]This measure of program scope consists of the number of measures listed in Table 3-2 that had been adopted by a community.

TABLE 3-5
Focus of flood plain land use management programs

Program Focus[a]	Percent of Communities	
	1979 Survey	1983 Survey
0- None of the following goals or action instruments used	22	17
1- Any goal and use of zoning and/or subdivision regulations	20	12
2- Goal to reduce losses and use of elevation and/or floodway regulations	37	53
3- Goal to preserve natural values/protect open space and use of land acquisition	18	16
4- Goal to reduce property losses and use of relocation of development	3	2

[a]This measure of program focus is a Guttman scale (coefficient of reproducibility =.95; coefficient of scalability =.80) formed by combining community flood plain goals and action instruments adopted.

quarter of the communities surveyed in 1979 had programs that comprehended subdivision or zoning regulations, elevation requirements or floodway regulations,
and land acquisition or relocation (see program focus
categories 3 and 4, Table 3-5). Thirty-seven percent
had gone as far as enacting elevation or floodway
regulations (category 2), while one-fifth had adopted
programs that were limited to the use of traditional
subdivision or zoning regulations (category 1), and a
fifth had not adopted zoning, subdivions, elevation, or
floodway regulations, but were relying on their
building codes to reduce future flood losses (category
0). Communities surveyed in 1983, which, on average,
were smaller than those surveyed in 1979, were using
fewer action instruments in their flood plain land use
management programs, but the measures they were
employing tended to be as focused, or more so than
those used by communities in the 1979 survey. See
Tables 3-4 and 3-5.

In both 1979 and 1983, communities participating in
the regular phase of the National Flood Insurance Program tended to have adopted broader flood plain land
use management programs than communities in the
emergency phase.[5] While differences between riverine
and coastal communities that were participating in the
NFIP regular phase were minimal, some differences are
apparent among emergency-phase communities. Reflecting
the heightened perception of flood hazards in coastal
areas (Burton, Kates, and Snead 1969; Mitchell 1974),
coastal communities participating in the NFIP emergency
phase were more likely to have broader programs than
riverine communities in the emergency phase.

Other factors contributing to variation in program
scope and focus also were explored. Based on the work
of Hutton and Mileti (1979), community adoption of
flood plain land use management measures was viewed as
a function of four sets of factors: (1) objective
characteristics of the flood plain that contribute to
flood risk; (2) community officials' perception of
flood risk; (3) community concern for solving flood
plain problems; and (4) objective characteristics of a
community that affect its ability to respond to problems in an effective manner. Each of these factors is
discussed in turn.

Characteristics of the flood plain that contribute
to the risk of flooding and flood damage in a community
were examined first. Studies of community participation in the National Flood Insurance Program have
reported that the first communities to enter the program had more recent and more severe flooding than
communities that delayed their participation in the

NFIP (Preston, Moore, and Cornick 1976; Moore and Cantrell 1976). This finding parallels other research results that indicate public policy responds to observable needs. As school-age children in a community increase, for example, more schools are provided; as the number of buildings increase, more fire protection is provided, and so on (Burby 1968). In a similar vein, communities that have more severe flood problems should adopt broader flood plain land use management programs.

The threat of damage from coastal flooding seems to be taken more seriously by communities than damage from riverine flooding. As a result, coastal areas are more likely to use more direct hazard management measures than riverine communities (see Table 3-6). Among riverine communities, the threat of damage from flash flooding, with its attendant greater possibility for loss of life, should stimulate the adoption of flood plain land use management measures, but that has not yet occurred. On the other hand, community use of flood hazard areas, and the associated greater risk of property loss from flooding, does appear to be related to community flood plain land use management efforts.

In general, riverine communities are most interested in land use management when they are experiencing an intermediate level of risk. Communities with the broadest, most stringent programs had more than 5 percent but less than 50 percent of the community located within the flood-hazard area and from 10 percent to 60 percent of the flood plain developed in urban uses. Apparently, communities with less intensive flood plain development do not view the flood problem as serious enough to warrant a major management effort, whereas those with more heavily developed flood plains look to other solutions for their problems, such as flood control structures. In addition, since no association was found between the number of buildings located in riverine flood hazard areas and program scope and focus, it could be that after development reaches a certain point, the flood plain is viewed more as a land resource suitable for development and less as a hazard area (see also Sheaffer, Davis and Richmond 1970, 9).

Although the land use management efforts of riverine communities tailed off when development of the flood-hazard area reached high levels, that did not occur in coastal communities. The broadest, most direct land use management programs in coastal communities are found in communities with the highest proportion of the community in the flood-hazard zone,

TABLE 3-6
Factors associated with the scope and focus of
local programs

	Correlation Coefficients (simple r's)[a]			
	Program Scope		Program Focus	
Factors	1979 Survey	1983 Survey	1979 Survey	1983 Survey
Flood Plain Characteristics				
Percent of community land area in flood plain	.08	ns	ns	ns
Number of buildings	ns	ns	.12	ns
Land uses				
Multiple family residential	.17	.19	.17	.11
Commercial (stores, offices)	.18	.21	.18	.17
Industrial	.09	.21	.11	.15
Flooding				
Type: coastal	ns	.13	.14	ns
Serious flood during past ten years	(b)	.12	(b)	.10
Frequency of damage due to inadequate storm drainage	(b)	.19	(b)	.15
Flooding exacerbated by actions of neighboring jurisdictions	ns	ns	ns	.07
Community Perception of Risk				
Severity of risk of flood damage	.20	.18	.22	.19
Community Concern with Hazard				
Priority assigned to solution of flood problems	.21	.40	.23	.37
Enrollment in regular phase of NFIP	.20	.30	.17	.23
Use of structural flood control works	.14	.25	.45	.24

(continued)

TABLE 3-6 (cont.)

Factors	Program Scope 1979 Survey	Program Scope 1983 Survey	Program Focus 1979 Survey	Program Focus 1983 Survey
	Correlation Coefficients (simple r's)[a]			

Community
  Characteristics

Factors	Program Scope 1979 Survey	Program Scope 1983 Survey	Program Focus 1979 Survey	Program Focus 1983 Survey
Urbanization				
Population	.16	.16	.10	.09
Population growth rate 1970-75	ns	(c)	ns	(c)
Building permits issued in previous year	.27	.30	.28	.19
Metropolitan location	.19	(c)	.21	(c)
Affluence				
Median family income	.16	(c)	.10	(c)
Median housing value	.21	(c)	.11	(c)
Government/Policy				
Type of Jurisdiction: City	.08	(c)	.11	(c)
Extent of land use management experience before joining NFIP	.33	na	.08	(c)
Direct state regulation of flood hazard	.11	.22	ns	.15
Availability of non-hazard sites for new development	ns	.22	.14	.23

ns = not staticially significant at .05 level.
[a] Values for correlation coefficients shown are statistically significant at the .05 level.
[b] Data not obtained in 1979 survey.
[c] Data not obtained in 1983 survey.

with the greatest intensity of development in the
hazard zone, and with the greatest absolute amount of
hazard zone development. One reason for coastal communities' continued interest in land use management as
a hazard mitigation adjustment, even when they have
experienced high levels of hazard-area development, is
that structural solutions are not as viable an alternative as they are for riverine communities. While
riverine communities can turn to channel improvements,
dams, levees, flood walls, and similar measures to
mitigate the hazard, structural measures such as sea
walls have not proven to be particularly effective over
the long term in preventing losses from hurricanes and
major coastal storms.

Besides examining the proportion of the community
at risk and the extent of flood plain development, we
also looked at the relationship between types of flood
plain land uses and the adoption of land use management measures. We expected that communities that had
flood plain land uses with greater loss potential, such
as multi-family residential, commercial, and industrial
uses, would be more likely to have adopted broader,
more direct management programs. In general, that
expectation was supported by the data assembled in 1979
and 1983 (see Table 3-6).

Actual flood plain characteristics and flood problems are related to the adoption of flood plain land
use management programs, but community perceptions of
this risk and concern for resolving flooding problems
are even better predictors of program scope and focus.
As the perceived risk of loss increases, for example,
the potential payoff from pursuing a management program
also increases, so that communities are more likely to
have adopted broader, more direct management programs
(see Hutton and Mileti 1979). In addition, we found
that the more concerned communities are with their
flood plain problems--as indicated by enrollment in the
regular phase of the NFIP and assignment of high
priority to solving flood plain problems--the more
likely they are to have adopted broader and more direct
management measures.

Finally, program scope and focus varied system-
atically with a number of community characteristics.
Counties were less likely than cities or minor civil
divisions to be pursuing aggressive management programs, in part because they were less likely to have
advanced to the regular phase of the National Flood
Insurance Program. Larger communities, which have more
fiscal resources and governmental personnel to pursue
land use management, had broader, more direct programs.
Previous land use management experience also was a

critical factor. More than half of the communities
surveyed in 1979 that had extensive experience with
land use management prior to joining the National Flood
Insurance Program reported using nine or more land use
management measures. By way of contrast, only 5 percent of the communities with no land use management
experience prior to joining the NFIP, and only 17
percent of those with minimal experience, reported
using nine or more methods. Thus, communities with the
resources to support a land use management program and
that have used management measures in the past seem to
have the least difficulty in mounting a vigorous
effort. Similar findings have been reported by Moore
and Cantrell (1976), Luloff and Wilkinson (1979), and
Hutton and Mileti (1979) based on studies of factors
contributing to early community participation in the
National Flood Insurance Program.

Programs also tended to be broader in scope and
more direct in affluent, middle-class communities than
in poorer communities. One explanation is that land
use planning and management measures tend to be favored
by the middle class, which is more likely to have
"public-regarding" rather than "private-regarding"
values than working and lower classes (Banfield and
Wilson 1963). Another is that land use management can
be more easily supported by more affluent communities
with greater resources (Hutton and Mileti 1979).

Urbanization is another factor that seems to have
a pervasive influence on the strength of community
flood plain land use management programs. Hutton and
Mileti (1979) note that increasing urbanization is
associated with greater resources and capacity to implement public policies. Thus, we expect larger
communities to be more likely than smaller communities
to have adopted a whole array of policies, including
land use management measures, to deal with problems
they are facing. To others urbanization indicates
"structural differentiation" in the population (see,
for example, Moore and Cantrell 1976 and Luloff and
Wilkinson 1979). As urbanization increases, more
individuals and groups in a community are likely to
become concerned with particular problems and to have
the expertise to stimulate community action to resolve
them. Accordingly, communities that are more urban
should be more likely to have adopted policies to deal
with particular problems, including flood problems,
than less urban communities are. These expectations
are supported by the analyses summarized in Table 3-6.
Communities with larger populations, those growing at a
faster rate, and those located in metropolitan areas
are more likely than others to have adopted broader and
more direct flood plain land use management programs.

Finally, the availability of development sites located outside the flood plain also affects a community's interest in pursuing a virorous land use management program. Communities are more likely to use more land use management measures, and also measures that are more direct, when sites for community growth and development outside the flood plain are widely available. When alternative sites for development are limited, community enthusiasm for flood plain land use management diminishes substantially.

Multiple regression analysis was used to develop a concise explanation of factors influencing the scope and focus of the land use management programs pursued by communities. The results are summarized in Table 3-7. The variables discussed above explain about one-quarter of the variance in both program scope and program focus. Variables from each of the four categories of influence factors—hazard-area characteristics, perceived hazard-area problems, community concern for the problems, and community characteristics—made statistically significant contributions to the final regression models.

The regression models provide a means of isolating a set of key factors influencing the scope and degree of focus of community flood plain land use management programs. Based on standardized beta coeffecients in the final regression equations, the top five factors contributing to the scope of a community's program in 1979 were:

1. Extent of previous land use management experience
2. Median housing value
3. Priority given to the solution of flood plain problems
4. Enrollment in the Regular Phase of the NFIP
5. Population

In essence, the model shows that communities employ a wider range of land use management measures when they have had previous experience in using land use management to deal with other community problems, assign some priority to solving flood plain problems, and have the resources (property value/population) to mount a vigorous program. In addition, requirements of the Regular Phase of the National Flood Insurance Program and availability of additional technical information about the flood hazard enables communities to do more in flood hazard management. Although a different set of variables was tested with the 1983 data (information on land use management experience and housing values was not obtained), the results of the regression analysis were similar, as shown in Table 3-7.

To the extent that the key factors may be shaped by federal and state policies, they indicate how local governments could be induced to broaden their land use management efforts. For example, intergovernmental grants-in-aid, such as various planning assistance programs and the Community Development Block Grant program, could be used to augment community resources available for flood plain land use management. Further, even with the present minimal land use management requirements of the NFIP, communities should accumulate land use management experience that over time will enable them to adopt broader local programs. The positive influence of the NFIP could be increased if the more sophisticated hazard zone mapping associated with conversion from the emergency to regular phase of the program were applied to more communities. Finally, NFIP and state governments' technical assistance programs could be targeted at smaller communities, which currently are less likely to pursue broader hazard management programs.

The multiple regression models summarized in Table 3-7 also indicate key factors associated with the **focus** of communities' flood plain land use management programs. In this case, the five key factors in 1979 were:

1. Priority assigned to solution of flood problems
2. Median housing value
3. Enrollment in regular phase of the NFIP
4. Availability of hazard-free sites for new development
5. Severity of risk of flood damage

Since more direct programs have been defined as those that go beyond elevation requirements to include land acquisition and relocation, it is logical that these approaches would be used only where the risk of flood damage is most severe and high priority has been assigned to reducing the risk of loss. Enrollment in the regular phase of the NFIP, as noted above, provides communities with the technical data needed to pursue more sophisticated land use management programs. Because land acquisition and relocation are more

TABLE 3-7
Key factors associated with the scope and focus
of flood plain land use management programs

	Standardized Regression Coefficients[a]	
Key Variables	Program Scope	Program Focus
1979 DATA		

Flood Plain
  Characteristics

Commercial land uses in hazard area	.06	.08

Community Perception
  of Risk

Severity of risk of flood damage	.08	.09

Community Concern
  with Hazard

Priority assigned to solution of flood problems	.16	.16
Enrollment in regular phase of NFIP	.11	.14
Use of structural flood control works	(b)	.08

Community Characteristics

Population	.09	(b)
Median housing value	.16	.16
Availability of hazard-free sites for new development	(b)	.11
Land use management experience	.28	(b)
R^2 for equation	.25	.15

(continued)

72

TABLE 3-7 (cont.)

Key Variables	Standardized Regression Coefficients[a]	
	Program Scope	Program Focus

1983 DATA

Flood Plain Characteristics

Coastal community	.08	(b)
Industrial land use in hazard area	.09	.19

Community Perception of Risk

Severity of risk of flood damage	(b)	.07

Community Concern with Hazard

Priority assigned to solution of flood problems	.27	.27
Enrollment in regular phase of NFIP	.19	.15
Use of structural flood control works	.15	.16

Community Characteristics

Building permits issued in previous year	.15	.07
Availability of hazard-free sites for new development	.18	.20
Direct state regulation of flood plain	.14	.08
R^2 for equation	.37	.25

[a]Standardized beta weights shown are statistically significant at .05 level or less.
[b]Variables not statistically significant at .05 level.

expensive than other techniques, it is not surprising that median housing value--an indicator of community wealth--is highly associated with program focus. The importance of the availability of hazard-free sites for new development suggests that communities will pursue more direct land use management programs if the program does not threaten continued growth and development of the community. Again, regression analyses run with the 1983 data produced results similar to those obtained with the 1979 data.

The findings imply that if communities gain a better understanding of the problems of their flood-hazard areas--possibly through a comprehensive planning program, as suggested earlier--they can be expected to mount more vigorous efforts to solve those problems. In addition, however, the data indicate that if more communities are to pursue more focused flood plain management programs, financial assistance from states and the federal government may be required.

GOVERNMENTAL RESOURCES DEVOTED TO FLOOD PLAIN LAND USE MANAGEMENT

Most communities indicated that very little funding or staff time was devoted to flood plain land use management (see Table 3-8). Overall, 47 percent of the communities surveyed in 1979 had spent less than $1,000 on flood plain land use management during the past fiscal year. (That information was not gathered from the 1983 respondents.) Almost half of the 1979 sample (49 percent) and fully three-quarters of the communities surveyed in 1983 (which had much lower populations, on average) allocated less than one person-hour per week to flood plain land use management. There was little difference between riverine and coastal communities in the fiscal and staff resources devoted to land use management. There was a difference, however, between communities in the emergency and regular phases of the National Flood Insurance Program. As would be expected by their broader programs, communities in the regular phase of the NFIP were spending a significantly greater amount of funds and staff time on their programs. Even among regular-phase communities, however, flood plain land use management was not particularly expensive. Only 26 percent of the regular-phase communities surveyed in 1979 spent more than $5,000 per year on their flood plain programs, and only about 14 percent were devoting as much as one person-day per week to flood plain management.

The low level of resources communities devote to managing their flood-hazard areas is in keeping with

TABLE 3-8
Implementation of local programs

Indicator	Percent of Communities 1979 Survey	Percent of Communities 1983 Survey
Weekly Staff Time		
Less than 1 person hour	49	75
1-7 person hours	36	20
8-39 person hours	9	3
40 or more person hours	5	2
Annual Funding		
Less than $1,000	49	(a)
$1,000-$4,999	25	(a)
$5,000-$9,999	9	(a)
$10,000-$24,999	8	(a)
$25,000 or more	9	(a)
Qualified Personnel		
Lack of qualified personnel an obstacle to successful implementation	21	21
Not an obstacle	79	79

[a]Data not obtained in 1983 survey

the low probability of suffering serious, long-term
losses and accordingly modest priority given to flood
plain problems. Without the incentive for managing
their flood plains provided by the National Flood
Insurance Program, experience prior to 1968 indicates
that most communities would probably not bother to
adopt and continue implementing flood plain land use
management measures. With the NFIP incentive, most
communities have adjusted their ongoing land use
management programs to include special provisions for
flood-hazard areas. As shown here, this adjustment has
not been particularly burdensome for most communities.
Whether it has been particularly effective is examined
in Chapter 6.

SUMMARY

This chapter has examined the practice of flood
plain land use management in the United States. We

have seen that although flooding is a serious national problem, in most places it is not perceived as a serious problem at the local level. As a result, in comparison with other problems facing communities, solving problems that occur in flood-hazard areas is often not given high priority. Nevertheless, some communities do have serious local flooding problems and consider solving those problems to be a matter of high local concern. Those communities tend to have a large proportion of their land area located within the flood-hazard zone and to have a large number of structures and high proportion of the community population at risk.

The first step in developing a flood plain land use management program is specifying goals for the flood plain. Most of the communities studied had taken that step. Two goals, reducing property loss from flooding and protecting the population, have been widely adopted. Environmental goals for flood hazard areas, however, have not been adopted by a majority of the communities surveyed, and even fewer communities are pursuing goals related to the fair distribution of flood plain management costs. The goals communities are following in flood plain land use management show that the National Flood Insurance Program has had a major effect on community concerns, but that other national objectives for flood plains have had less impact at the community level.

Communities can move directly from the specification of goals to the adoption of various regulations and other action instruments, but their efforts may be more effective if they are guided by a comprehensive plan. About 60 percent of the communities studied, in fact, were using comprehensive planning in their flood plain management programs. The use of comprehensive planning was associated with the pursuit of equity and environmental goals for the flood plain, suggesting that if planning is required as a condition for participation in the National Flood Insurance Program, it may promote a more balanced approach to flood plain land use than has occurred in the past.

Regulations are now the most commonly used method of achieving community flood plain goals. Three types of regulations--subdivision ordinances, zoning, and elevation requirements--have been adopted by a majority of riverine and coastal communities and by a majority of communities participating in the regular and emergency phases of the National Flood Insurance Program. The NFIP has had a strong effect on the types of management measures being used. Participants in the NFIP regular phase were much more likely than emergency-phase communities to be using elevation, floodproofing, and floodway regulations in their land use management programs. On the other hand, little difference between regular- and emergency-phase communities is evident for the use of less-commonly employed measures, including locating public facilities outside hazard areas, land acquisition and relocation, preferential taxation, and density exchanges to maintain low density use of the flood plain.

The adoption of broader, more directly focused flood plain land use management programs was associated with four sets of factors: hazard-area characteristics, perceived hazard-area problems, community concern for the problems, and community characteristics not related to the flood hazard. In general, communities tend to use a wider array of land use management measures when they have had extensive previous experience in using land use management to deal with community problems, when they assign some priority to solving flood plain problems, and when they have more resources to mount a vigorous management program.

Although many communities have adopted goals for flood plains, formulated comprehensive plans that consider flood plain problems, and enacted regulations to address those problems, few devote significant funds or staff resources to program implementation. For the most part it appears that flood plain management measures and responsibilities have been grafted onto other programs, so that communities have been able to respond to the federal mandate for local flood plain management at minimal cost. The federal role in local flood plain management is explored in greater depth in the next chapter. The effectiveness of local programs--whether they are actually reducing flood losses to existing and new development and leading to the accomplishment of other objectives for flood plains--is evaluated in Chapter 6.

NOTES

   1. Previous research on the accuracy of hazard perception is summarized in Mileti, Drabek, and Haas 1975, 23-25. Also see Kunreuther et al. 1978.
   2. A number of studies of flood-hazard area occupants in the United States have found that most households are reluctant to relocate. Three factors have been offered as an explanation for this finding. First, comparative advantage appears to be a major consideration. Some households move into flood hazard

areas knowing of the flood risk because they view the advantages of a flood plain location as outweighing the disadvantages. Others who were ignorant of the hazard when moving nevertheless would remain for the same reason (James, Laurent, and Hill 1971; Roder 1961). A second factor is evidently lack of concern on the part of flood plain occupants. For example, a study of Davenport, Iowa, concluded, "The people living within the area by their own admission were not afraid of being flooded, they were merely afraid of what would happen when they tried to sell their property. As a result...the attempt to have the regulation program adopted by the city council failed." (Johnson 1969, 110) The third factor producing resistance to relocation is social rigidity and the stake of economic influentials in the continued use of the flood plain. (See Singer and Walzer 1975; Roder 1961; and Rossi, Wright, and Weber-Burdin 1982.)

3. The use of a seventh method, watershed treatment, was not examined in the sample of local communities.

4. The St. Paul District (1979) of the Corps of Engineers has reported a number of factors that have contributed to the Corps' reluctance to implement nonstructural measures. As reported by Platt (1979), they include (1) lack of experience with nonstructural proposals in a number of Corps districts; (2) lack of personnel capable of using social science techniques needed for some nonstructural measures; (3) lack of local acceptance in comparison with structural projects; and (4) unfavorable benefit/cost ratios.

5. As noted previously, communities in the regular phase of the National Flood Insurance Program have been provided more detailed maps and other technical information on which to base their flood plain land use management programs. Thus, they are technically more capable of adopting a broader, more stringent program than are emergency-phase communities. In addition, the Office of Federal Insurance and Hazard Mitigation has attempted to convert communities with more serious flood hazards to the regular phase of the NFIP before communities with less severe problems (see National Institute for Advanced Studies 1978) so that the more serious problem faced by regular phase communities could also contribute to the adoption of broader, more stringent programs.

4
The Intergovernmental Web: Federal Programs and Local Flood Plain Land Use Management

In our federal system, public functions tend to be shared by all levels of government. Land use management is often thought of as a purely local function, but the system of sharing is as evident here as with other governmental matters (U.S. Water Resources Council 1979). Because the federal government, states, and regions are involved in managing flood plains, before we can assess the effectiveness of local land use management programs, we first need to understand how the actions of other layers of government are affecting local flood problems and their solutions.

During the past ten years, there has been a remarkable expansion in interest in intergovernmental relations and policy analysis, but most of this work has focused on the local implementation of programs originating with the federal government and the states (e.g., Van Horn and Van Meter 1976; Bingham 1976; Hutton and Mileti 1979; Mazmanian and Sabatier 1980, 1981, 1982). As a result, there is still no coherent conceptual framework for examining how intergovernmental factors support or confound policies originating at the local level. It is useful to think of both vertical and horizontal aspects of intergovernmental influence. Vertical aspects refer to the effects of federal, state, and regional policies and programs on local program effectiveness. Horizontal aspects refer to the effects of other local governments' policies and actions. The focus in this and the next chapter is on the vertical dimension, but horizontal effects (which are considered in Chapter Six) are also critical (Platt and Kusler 1978).

In considering the vertical elements of the intergovernmental web, we believe there are three main avenues through which federal, state, and regional policies and programs can affect the outcomes of local land use management. One avenue is indirect and

operates through local land use management programs.
Federal and state policies provide inducements and
assistance for local flood plain land use management
and set standards for local programs. In the preceding
chapter we showed how the National Flood Insurance
Program has affected the goals communities have adopted
for their flood plains and the types of regulations
they are able to employ in program management. In
fact, it is unlikely that without the NFIP many communities would even consider local land use management
as a flood-hazard adjustment.

A second avenue of intergovernmental influence is
through public actions that change the nature of the
flood hazard. One of the primary justifications of
structural flood control measures has been the
opportunity for increased development and use of the
"protected" flood plains. Various public investments
also may have serious unintended or secondary effects.
Damages caused by a disastrous flood in Jackson,
Mississippi, during Easter 1979 (see Chapter Seven and
Platt 1982), for example, were increased by backwaters
from public bridges and highways that impeded the flow
of the Pearl River. Private development located within
the Pearl River flood plain, in part because of public
investments in levees, highways, bridges, and other
facilities, increased accessibility and provided some
(but inadequate) safety from flooding (Platt 1980, 11,
28; Platt 1982). Because of the potential for adverse
effects from public investments in flood-hazard areas,
as noted in Chapter 1, Executive Order 11988 requires
that if at all possible, federal agencies avoid direct
and indirect support of flood plain development, and
the Barrier Islands Act of 1982 eliminated federal
support of development on designated, undeveloped
barrier islands. A third avenue of intergovernmental
influence is through federal and state programs that
directly affect flood plain occupants, either by regulating their use of the flood plain or by helping to
mitigate the effects of flooding. These policies and
programs may either support or undermine the objectives
of local flood plain land use management. Direct
federal regulation of hazard areas through the administration of dredge-and-fill regulations authorized by
the Rivers and Harbors Act of 1899 and Section 404 of
the Federal Water Pollution Control Act Amendments of
1972 (P.L. 92-500), for example, may discourage hazard-
area development. On the other hand, federal insurance
designed to mitigate personal hardships caused by
flooding may, in some circumstances, encourage development in areas subject to flood risk (Miller 1975;
Miller 1977a; Miller 1977b; Kusler 1982).

The ways in which federal policies can affect local

flood plain management provide a framework that will be used in exploring key federal programs that have evolved to deal with the national flood problem. For each program, this chapter examines its distribution or use among communities across the nation and then indicates how it has affected continued flood plain development and community flood plain land use management. The key federal flood-hazard mitigation policies studied include the provision of various types of structural protection, the National Flood Insurance Program, and provision of flood plain information and other technical assistance.

FLOOD CONTROL PROGRAMS AND STRUCTURAL PROTECTION

Land use management measures may be effective in limiting the exposure of new development to flood damage, but in most cases they are not designed to cope with problems associated with the flooding of existing development. In the usual course of events, communities allow flood plain development to occur, experience a flood and the resulting damage to flood plain property, and then seek to mitigate future losses by constructing various engineering works to control the flood waters. These engineering works or structures may include dams and reservoirs; dikes, levees, floodwalls, and seawalls; channel alterations; high flow diversions and spillways; and land treatment measures.[1] In many cases, federal programs have been promulgated to design and construct various protective works and to defray, in large part, the required capital costs. By 1980, federal expenditures on structural flood control measures through those programs approached $14 billion (Platt 1980).

Use of Structural Measures in Flood-Prone Communities

Structural flood control measures were providing some degree of protection in more than 70 percent of the 1,203 communities surveyed in 1979 and 67 percent of the 956 communities surveyed in 1983. A third of the communities surveyed in each year had adopted more than one type of measure. Channel improvements were used most often (see Table 4-1), but more than one of every six communities surveyed in both 1979 and 1983 had employed small watershed projects, dikes and/or levees, and dams and reservoirs to provide some protection from flooding.

The proportion of communities that had adopted various structural protection measures varied somewhat depending upon the nature of the local flood hazard.

TABLE 4-1
Use of structural solutions to community flood problems

Types of Structural Method	Percent Using Method 1979 Survey	1983 Survey
Channel improvements	45	36
Small watershed projects	24	17
Dikes and/or levees	23	20
Dams and reservoirs	22	18
Seawalls, groins, jetties	10	4
Subsurface (piped) storm drainage systems	(a)	27
Diversions and bypasses	(a)	10

[a]Data not obtained in 1979 survey.

In riverine areas, for example, almost 85 percent of the communities had adopted some form of structural protection. Riverine communities were more and more likely to have adopted structural protection measures as the number of residential and/or nonresidential structures located in the flood-hazard area increased. In coastal regions, the use of structural measures was positively associated with the number of large storms a community had experienced during the previous fifteen years and also with the proportion of the community subject to flood damage and the number of residential and nonresidential buildings located in the flood-hazard area. In general, in both riverine and coastal areas communities were increasingly likely to have employed structural flood control measures as the potential for damage to existing development increased.

Structural Protection Issues

Four issues related to the effects of structural protection on local land use management have received national attention. The most serious of them is the high potential for environmental damage that accompanies most structural flood control measures. This issue has received extensive treatment in environmental literature over the past decade and therefore will not be explored further here. Three other issues have received less attention and were examined in this study:

1. The potential for structural measures to give communities a false sense of security from

flood losses, which may result in less-than-optimal local actions to mitigate the hazard.

2. The potential for structural measures to induce further encroachment on and use of the flood plain, which may increase the potential for losses if less than complete structural protection is provided and/or if a catastrophic event exceeds the design levels of the structural works.

3. The potential for structural measures to be treated as an alternative rather than as a complement to nonstructural mitigation measures, which also may result in less-than-optimal local actions to mitigate the hazard.

Each of these issues was analyzed using date collected from the 1979 survey of flood-prone jurisdictions.

Contrary to popular belief, the provision of structural protection does not seem to lead local officials to a false sense of security based on a feeling that local flood problems have been solved. Just the opposite seems to be true. As shown in Table 4-2, communities without structural protection were much more likely than those with protective works to believe that flooding was "not a problem" locally. In fact, the more different types of structural measures communities employed, the less likely they were to think flooding problems had been solved. The association between the presence of structural protection and the belief that flooding was a community problem continued when both past flood experience of the community and proportion of the community subject to flood damage were controlled statistically.[2]

By decreasing the costs of flooding, structural flood control works may increase the attractiveness of flood-hazard areas for urban development (Lind 1967). One of the primary criticisms of federal flood control policy has been the disassociation of the benefits of flood plain occupancy from the costs of protection, since "...it encourages uneconomic encroachment on the flood plain" (Krutilla 1966, 185). The rate of urban expansion into flood-hazard areas is estimated to be between 1.5 percent and 2.5 percent per year, and White (1975, xviii) has warned that structural flood control measures fostered by the federal government "...will be of little value if the reduction in damages that they accomplish is more than offset by new damage potential resulting from additional development in flood plains."

TABLE 4-2
Effect of flood control measures on community
land use management

	Percent of Communities, 1979			
	Riverine Community Uses Structural Measures[a]		Coastal Community Uses Structural Measures[a]	
Indicators	Yes	No	Yes	No
(Number of Communities)	(686)	(253)	(128)	(47)
Problem of Property Loss From Flooding in Community Rated:				
Critical/very serious	20	13	30	25
A problem, not serious	62	51	52	48
Not a problem	18	36	18	27
Flood Plain Encroachment				
Number of building permits issued for flood plain construction in 1978				
0	39	56	3	14
1-9	35	29	27	19
10 or more	26	15	70	67
Percent of building permits issued for flood plain construction in 1978				
0%	38	53	3	12
1-4%	44	32	28	30
5% or more	18	15	69	58

(continued)

TABLE 4-2 (cont.)

Indicators	Percent of Communities, 1979			
	Riverine Community Uses Structural Measures[a]		Coastal Community Uses Structural Measures[a]	
	Yes	No	Yes	No
Scope of Flood Plain Land Use Management Program[b]				
0-2 measures	10	14	5	10
3-5 measures	29	41	32	38
6-8 measures	34	29	34	31
9 or more measures	27	16	29	21

[a]Use of any of following measures in community: dams and reservoirs, small watershed projects, dikes or levees, channel improvements, or sea walls, groins, or jetties.
[b]See Table 3-2 for list of land use management measures.

Although structural protection is expected to encourage flood plain encroachment, no studies have documented that result. Earlier, White and his associates (1958) noted the increasing occupancy of flood hazard areas over the period 1936-1956, but reported, "...no direct correlation could be found between the degree of protection and rate of flood plain growth." Table 4-2 shows that such a correlation does exist. Among the national sample of communities studied, both the number of building permits issued in 1978 for construction in flood-hazard areas and percent of all permits issued that involved hazard-area construction were substantially higher in communities with flood control works in place than in communities that had not benefited from federal flood control assistance. The positive (and statistically significant) association between structural protection and new construction in the flood plain continued to hold true when the percent of the community land area located in the hazard area, extent of existing flood plain development, availability of nonhazard sites for development, and scope of the community land use management program were controlled statistically. Thus, structural protection is associated with continuing development of the flood plain.

Given the potential for structural protection assisted by federal programs to encourage flood plain development, disastrous results could occur if communities did not also take steps to employ land use management techniques to limit future flood losses. Before the advent of the National Flood Insurance Program, few communities made this necessary connection. According to Platt and McMullen (1979, 7-8),

> Remoteness of non-federal interests from flood control was magnified by the flood control Acts of 1936 and 1938. These acts and their successors established a national policy and program for the management of floods through massive engineering structures funded and implemented almost entirely by federal agencies. It follows that local communities, believing themselves to be adequately protected from floods through federal intervention, took little interest in the use of land within their own flood plains...The absence of any restriction upon the occupancy of downstream floodplains was to seriously undermine the entire federal flood control effort. (Also see White 1964.)

This problem has been resolved by the massive increase in community flood plain land use management spurred by the NFIP.

Communities are more (rather than less) likely to believe they have a flood problem when they have some form of structural protection in place. The bottom panels of Table 4-2 show that they are also more (rather than less) likely to have adopted a broad-gauged flood plain land use management program. It appears that communities no longer view structural protection and land use management as alternative flood-hazard mitigation approaches but instead as complementary means of coping with their flood problems. In this sense, progress is being made toward adoption of the integrated approach to flood problems that was called for in the U.S. Water Resources Council's "Unified National Program for Floodplain Management."

In summary, the data analyzed here show that the availability of federal assistance for the construction of flood control works has resulted in the widespread use of dams and reservoirs, channel alterations, dikes and levees, and other structural measures in communities across the nation. Contrary to previous reports, the adoption of structural flood control measures does not necessarily result in a sense of complacency regarding the community flood problem or reluctance to adopt local flood plain land use management measures. In fact, communities with structural

measures in place tend to be more concerned with the
flood problem and are more likely to have adopted an
array of land use management measures than communities
that lack structural protection. On the other hand, it
does seem to be true that structural protection
encourages urban use of flood hazard areas, which in
many circumstances may destroy natural attributes of
the flood plain and may increase the potential for
property damage in the event of catastrophic flood
events. Because of this, federal agencies such as the
U.S. Army Corps of Engineers must continue and
intensify their efforts to foster state and local land
use management as a key component of a comprehensive
flood-hazard management program.[3]

THE NATIONAL FLOOD INSURANCE PROGRAM

The National Flood Insurance Program (NFIP) is at
the center of the federal government's effort to
mitigate the national flood problem through the use of
nonstructural measures. Launched with passage of the
National Flood Insurance Act of 1968, the NFIP is
designed to accomplish two major ends.

The first is to reduce national flood losses by
requiring participating local governments to implement
land use regulations that will result in safe building
practices in flood-hazard areas. Noncomplying
communities are not eligible for the sale of subsidized
flood insurance and are subject to several additional
penalties. By charging actuarial rates for new construction in communities where Flood Insurance Rate
Maps have been prepared, the NFIP should also discourage the noneconomic increment of new development
that formerly located in flood-hazard areas, but gained
no particular locational advantages as a result.

The second major objective of the National Flood
Insurance Program is to shift the economic burden of
flood losses from the taxpayers in general (through
federal disaster relief programs) to the occupants (and
beneficiaries) of flood plain locations. It
accomplishes that by making flood insurance available
in participating communities and refusing to provide
anything but emergency federal disaster assistance in
nonparticipating communities.[4] Although insurance for
existing structures in participating communities is
subsidized at up to 90 percent of actuarial rates, as
soon as Flood Insurance Rate Maps are prepared,
insurance rates reflect the true costs of the flood-
hazard location.[5]

The National Flood Insurance Program was the

catalyst for a spectacular increase in community flood
plain land use management during the 1970s. Research
commissioned by the Federal Insurance Administration
indicates that as a result of local flood plain land
use regulations stimulated by the NFIP, the increase in
annual flood losses between 1975 and 1990 will be $46.4
million less than would have occurred without the regulations in place (Sheaffer and Roland, Inc.1981b).

The NFIP has been praised by many observers for
inducing communities to manage their flood-hazard
areas; and as shown later in this chapter, it is also a
major source of technical assistance for local communities. Fear has been expressed, however, that the
National Flood Insurance Program may confirm existing
development in hazard areas and, by providing insurance
against losses, lead to even greater development of the
flood plain. (Miller 1975; Miller 1977; Kusler 1982)
There also has been some concern that the minimum land
use management standards established by the NFIP may
stifle community efforts to develop broader local
management programs (Howells 1977, 198).[6] The data
summarized in Table 4-3 suggest that the first concern
may be justified, but that the latter is not. The NFIP
seems to have stimulated, not suppressed, communities'
adoption of broader land use management programs.

Three indicators of community participation in the
National Flood Insurance Program were selected for
these analyses. One, the year the community joined the
NFIP, was chosen to capture maturation effects of participation in the program. A second indicator,
participation in the regular versus the emergency phase
of the program, was chosen to gauge the effects of the
more stringent management standards and higher monetary
insurance coverage associated with the regular phase of
the program. The third indicator, the number of
insurance policies issued in a community, was selected
to gauge the effects of the insurance feature of the
program. Together, these three indicators capture most
of the salient elements of the National Flood Insurance
Program that might affect flood plain development and
community land use management.

The statistical tests summarized in the top panel
of Table 4-3 indicate that participation in the
National Flood Insurance Program is associated with
continued development of flood-hazard areas,
particularly in coastal communities.[7] In coastal areas,
communities that had been in the NFIP more years, that
were in the regular rather than the emergency phase of
the program, and that had more insurance policies in
effect tended to have a higher proportion of new construction in 1978 located in the hazard zone.[8] In

TABLE 4-3
Impact of national flood insurance program on
community flood plain land use management

Gamma Correlation Coefficients[a]

Program Indicator	Riverine	Coastal
	Flood Plain Encroachment[b]	
1. Year community joined NFIP	-.15*	-.47*
2. Participation in regular phase of NFIP	.02	.29
3. Number of flood insurance policies issued in community	.35*	.51*
	Scope of Flood Plain Land Use Management Program[c]	
1. Year community joined NFIP	-.32*	-.20
2. Participation in regular phase of NFIP	.35*	-.01
3. Number of flood insurance policies issued in community	.22*	.29*
	Annual Expenditures for Flood Plain Land Use Management	
1. Year community joined NFIP	-.30*	-.26
2. Participation in regular phase of NFIP	.19*	.30
3. Number of flood insurance policies issued in community	.40*	.43*

* = Chi-square significant at .05 level or less.

[a]Gamma is a nonparametric statistical measure of the
correlation between the variables, varying from -1 (+1)
indicating a perfect negative (positive) monotonic
association between two variables and zero indicating
the lack of any association. It requires an assumption
of ordinality in the measurement of two variables but

(continued)

TABLE 4-3 (cont.)

takes advantage of that assumption to provide more
consistent and readable results than chi-square, which
varies with sample size of table.
[b]Percent of total building permits in 1978 issued for
construction in flood-hazard area.

riverine areas, participation in the regular phase of
the program was not associated with new flood plain
development, but communities that had been in the program for more years and that had more insurance
policies in effect had a higher proportion of new
construction occurring in the flood plain. Data
collected in case studies of three riverine communities
(reported more fully in Chapter 7) also indicate
that the NFIP may have less impact on development of
riverine than coastal communities. Comparison of the
percent of development occurring in flood hazard areas
in representative years after the communities joined
the NFIP with the percent occurring in hazard areas
before joining the program showed no marked increase in
hazard area development after flood insurance became
available (see Burby and French 1981).

The statistical tests summarized in the bottom two
panels of Table 4-3 indicate that participation in the
National Flood Insurance Program has not stifled communities' flood plain land use management programs. In
fact, just the opposite seems to have occurred.
Communities that have been in the program for a longer
period of time, that have advanced to the regular phase
of the program, and that have more flood insurance
policies in effect tend to be those that also are using
the most flood plain land use management methods and
are spending the most money on managing their hazard
areas. The analysis summarized in Table 4-3 were per-
formed with data from our 1979 national survey.
Similar analyses using data from the 1983 survey
produced very similar results.

FLOOD PLAIN INFORMATION AND TECHNICAL ASSISTANCE

Doubts about the efficacy of flood control
structures as the sole means of addressing the national
flood problem surfaced in the 1940s. In 1953 the
Tennessee Valley Authority began to provide communities
with flood plain information as a means of discouraging
continued invasion of flood-hazard areas. In Section
206 of the Flood Control Act of 1960, Congress
authorized nationwide provision of flood-hazard information reports by the U.S. Army Corps of Engineers. In
the 1960s, however, it became apparent that more than
information would be needed if continued flood plain

invasion was to be slowed. Research by Kates (1962) and others, as well as experience in the Tennessee Valley (Wall 1969), showed that even after they were aware of the hazard, people continued to locate in flood plains. This realization led to a shift in the focus of flood plain information from individual property owners and managers to local officials and other community decision makers.

The U.S. Water Resources Council stressed that flood-hazard information is not an end in itself but is the foundation for the development of a community's flood plain management program. According to the Water Resources Council (1976, 15),

> The development of needed technical information and public education, especially of officials and planners who will have the major task of interpreting and applying it, are essential in an effective flood plain management program....Vital information includes the hydrology and hydraulics of small, large, and very large floods on the areas subject to inundation, on the flood plain's resource attributes, on the role of the flood plain within the region, and on the potential impact of land use decisions on flood potential.

Programs to provide this "vital information" have been developed by a number of federal agencies.

Two questions have arisen with regard to the provision of flood-hazard information: One, is information being provided to all communities that need it? Two, is the information provided adequate to meet communities' flood-hazard management needs? The U.S. Water Resources Council (1979, 27) observed that although information is available in many forms and from many sources, "Unfortunately, information is neither of uniform quality nor available for all areas." In the case of technical assistance from the National Flood Insurance Program, the Institute for Rational Design (1977, 29) suggested,

> Combining in one program the very complex functions of insurance and land planning requires tremendous administrative ability and is bound to cause some difficulties. HUD has delegated the planning function to localities, and has retained the insurance function and the responsibility for technical studies common to both. The problem is HUD's resultant concept of the program. The FIA, which administers the program, handles it as an insurance program, and is relatively insensitive to planning issues. There has been little useful

guidance or technical assistance to communities concerning flood plain management.

In addition, specific issues have been raised about the accuracy of flood plain maps (Vitek and Richards 1978; Dingman and Platt 1977; Daniel and Williams 1977; Shows 1977; and Kusler 1982). Most of these questions and issues were addressed in the present research by asking communities whether they had obtained technical assistance from various sources, whether adequate technical assistance had been obtained from the National Flood Insurance Program, and what additional assistance was needed.

Sources of Flood Plain Information and Technical Assistance

Most seriously flood-prone communities in the United States have now received some form of technical assistance in the preparation of a community flood-hazard management program. Communities' use of assistance from various agencies is summarized in Table 4-4. The major source of aid to communities in both 1979 and 1983 was the Federal Emergency Management Agency (National Flood Insurance Program), followed by the U.S. Army Corps of Engineers, the U.S.D.A. Soil Conservation Service, and the U.S. Geological Survey.

The primary role of the National Flood Insurance Program in providing flood-hazard information is illustrated further by the dates when communities were first provided information about the nature of their flood problem. Fewer than 10 percent of the 1,204 communities surveyed in 1979 had obtained flood-hazard information from the Corps of Engineers, the U.S. Geological Survey or the Tennessee Valley Authority prior to the initiation of the National Flood Insurance Program in 1968. During the five years following passage of the National Flood Insurance Act, however, almost two-thirds of the riverine communities and almost nine out of every ten coastal communities were given sufficient information about the nature of their flood hazard to inaugurate a local management program. Communities that were early (before 1974) recipients of technical assistance tended to have the most severe flood problems. They had a larger area of the community located in the flood plain, a greater number of residential and nonresidential buildings located in hazard zones, and had experienced more large floods than communities that first received flood plain technical assistance after 1973. Thus, the National Flood insurance Program clearly served as the vehicle through which communities became engaged in flood plain

TABLE 4-4
Sources of technical assistance received by communities

Source of Technical Assistance	Percent of Communities Using Sources	
	1979 Survey[a]	1983 Survey[b]
Federal Emergency Management Agency	81	42
U.S. Army Corps of Engineers	39	40
U.S.D.A. Soil Conservation Service	26	34
U.S. Geological Survey	12	14
Other Federal Agencies	(c)	14

[a]Question: Has your jurisdiction received technical assistance, such as model ordinances or help in plan preparation from any of these agencies?
[b]Question: Has your jurisdiction received help in matters related to flood hazard management from any of the following federal agencies during the past five years?
[c]Data not obtained in 1979 survey.

management, and the NFIP clearly focused its attention on communities with the more severe flood hazards. They tended to be communities where the demand for insurance was highest, as noted earlier, but they are not necessarily those where flood plain land use management is likely to be most effective. This dichotomy in the mission of the NFIP is explored further in the concluding chapter of this book.

Since 1979, the Federal Emergency Management Agency's role in providing technical assistance to local governments, relative to that of other federal agencies, has diminished, although in 1983 it remained the most frequent source of assistance cited by local governments. FEMA's reduced role may be due to the delegation of technical assistance functions to state governments, which accelerated in 1980 with initiation of FEMA's State Assistance Program. Also, in our 1983 survey we asked about assistance received during the past five years only. Since FEMA's main contact with communities comes when they enroll in the NFIP

emergency and regular phases, which occurred more than
five years prior to 1983 in many communities, its role
in providing technical assistance may be diminishing
over time.

Adequacy of Technical Assistance

About two-thirds of the communities surveyed in
1979 and 1983 believed that technical assistance provided by the National Flood Insurance Program was
adequate to meet their needs.[9] Riverine communities
were less satisfied with the technical information they
had received than were coastal communities. Among
riverine communities, those that participated in the
emergency phase of the NFIP (and that had not yet
received Flood Insurance Rate Maps and floodway maps)
were significantly less satisfied than communities
participating in the NFIP's regular phase.
Communities' assessments of the adequacy of technical
assistance provided by the NFIP were also examined in
relation to the size of the community, scope of the
community land use management program, and staff time
devoted to flood plain management. None of those
factors was associated with coastal communities'
assessments of technical assistance. In riverine
areas, however, as the size of the community and amount
of effort devoted to flood plain land use management
increased, communities were increasingly critical of
the adequacy of technical assistance received from the
NFIP. This finding runs counter to conventional wisdom
and congressional testimony (Senate Committee on
Appropriations, April 12, 1975), both of which assume
that smaller communities are those most likely to require assistance. While smaller communities may be
those most in need, communities that most want
assistance tend to be larger communities that also want
to pursue a vigorous flood plain management program.

Inadequacies in flood plain maps have received the
most attention in the literature and were of most
concern to the flood-prone communities we surveyed.
When asked what additional assistance they needed, 37
percent said better maps. Effective flood plain land
use management is highly dependent on maps that
delineate the flood-hazard area for floods with various
recurrence intervals and indicate the depths of
flooding that can be expected. This information is
provided by the Flood Insurance Rate Maps (FIRMSs)
provided to communities by the Federal Emergency
Management Agency. Because of the high costs involved
in preparing such detailed flood-hazard maps, as of
1983 fewer than half of the flood-prone communities in
the nation have flood hazard maps with enough detail to
enable them to regulate the elevation of new develop-

ment to be certain that it is free of flooding. In
addition, delays in detailed mapping reportedly have
caused uncertainties among flood-prone communities as
to whether they should move ahead with a management
program based on incomplete flood plain mapping or wait
for an indeterminate period of time for better maps
(Platt 1976).

Besides problems caused by unavailability of Flood
Insurance Rate Maps in many communities, questions have
been raised about the accuracy of even those detailed
maps furnished to communities for their flood plain
land use management programs. Because of the
relatively limited time period covered by most stream-
flow data on which flood frequency-magnitude relations
are based, the precision of most hazard-area maps is
somewhat questionable (Kennedy 1976; Dingman and Platt
1977). The accuracy of the maps also varies with the
type of flood hazard and the particular estimation
methodology used in the mapping (Shows 1977). Most
maps are based on existing hydraulic conditions, but
the frequency and magnitude of flooding in smaller
watersheds can increase many times over as the watershed changes from an undeveloped to a developed state
(Leopold 1968; Johnson and Sayre 1973). In addition, a
number of problems have been encountered in delineating
coastal flood hazards (see Kusler 1982).

Although communities do not need highly accurate
hazard-area maps to have a legally valid basis for
their flood plain regulations (Dingman and Platt 1977),
map inaccuracies may cause several problems. Various
inaccuracies tend to lessen a flood plain map's credi-
bility among local citizens (Institute for Rational
Design 1977). In Littleton, Colorado, for example, our
detailed case studies (see Chapter Seven) uncovered
confusion among some residents because two flood plain
maps with different delineations of the flood-hazard
area (based on different assumptions about watershed
development) had been circulated by public agencies. A
second problem arises from the incidence of the costs
and benefits from flood plain land use management. If
map inaccuracies lead communities to require some
property owners to install unneeded floodproofing
measures or fill to elevate their structures while
others who should take such precautions are relieved
from doing so because of map error, then the program
may produce costly inefficiencies. The substantial
magnitude of these possible costs was documented in a
hypothetical case study by Daniel and Williams (1977),
while Rettger (1977) noted their potential occurrence
in a study of flood hazard management in Binghamton,
New York. A third problem stems from the NFIP's concept
of the floodway and floodway fringe. The regulatory

floodway is defined as that portion of the flood plain
needed for the passage of the 100-year flood with no
more than a one-foot increase in the flood height. No
development is to be allowed in the floodway once it
has been delineated, but development in the remainder
of the flood plain (the "floodway fringe") may be
allowed as long as water does not rise more than one
foot as a result. The problem is that it is difficult
to calculate the "one-foot rise" and to determine, in
cases where each side of a stream is in a different
jurisdiction, which side can take advantage of the
allowable encroachment on the flood plain (Platt and
McMullen 1979; Kusler 1982).

Besides an expressed need for better maps, about
one in every five communities indicated a need for
assistance in calculating elevations at which new flood
plain development would be free of flooding (from the
100-year flood) and for better information on state and
federal programs that could be of use in community
flood plain management. Fewer communities wanted
additional assistance in designing enforcement procedures, designing public information programs, or
model ordinances. In each case, however, communities
participating in the emergency phase of the National
Flood Insurance Program were more likely than regular-
phase communities to want additional aid. Moreover,
among both emergency-and regular-phase riverine communities, the larger the community, the more likely it
was to want additional assistance from the NFIP.

To summarize briefly, it now appears that virtually
all flood-prone communities in the nation have the
minimum flood-hazard information needed to mount a
local flood plain land use management program. While
stimulating local flood plain land use management (and
making it technically feasible), the National Flood
Insurance Program has been slow to prepare sophisticated Flood Insurance Rate Maps that would enable
communities to adopt fully effective local programs.
In addition, a number of questions have been raised
about the accuracy of the maps used in flood plain
management. Communities tend to be satisfied with the
adequacy of technical assistance provided by the
National Flood Insurance Program, but a sizable
minority--more than one-third of the riverine and more
than one-quarter of the coastal communities surveyed in
1979 and 1983--are dissatisfied. Highest on their list
of additional assistance needs are better maps. Larger
communities and communities most interested in pursuing
a vigorous flood plain land use management program are
most interested in receiving various kinds of
additional assistance.

OTHER FEDERAL PROGRAMS AND FLOOD PLAIN
DEVELOPMENT/PROTECTION

Besides structural flood control measures, flood
insurance, and technical assistance, a number of other
programs pursued by federal agencies have the potential
either to promote further development and use of hazard
areas or to protect them from urban encroachment.
Those impacts may be direct, such as when a federal
agency acquires a flood plain for a nature preserve or
builds a facility within a flood-hazard zone; or they
may be indirect, such as when a federal facility in-
duces private-sector investment in the hazard area.
Current federal policy, as exemplified by Executive
Order 11988, is to avoid, if at all feasible, both
direct and indirect support of flood plain development.
Executive Order 11988 was issued in 1977 after it
became apparent that federal agencies were not complying adequately with Executive Order 11296, which had
been issued more than a decade earlier to require
agencies to avoid unwise and hazardous use of flood
plains in construction, land disposition, and in
administering grants and loans (see Comptroller General
of the United States 1975).

Evidence regarding adverse direct and indirect
effects of federal programs has been mounting in recent
years. According to the New England River Basins
Commission (1976, 200), for example,

We found numerous examples of federally funded
studies and structures in three case study areas
that imply little consideration for flood risk. A
substantial portion of flood damage is sustained
by public facilities.

A National Wildlife Federation study of wastewater
treatment facilities constructed with support from the
Environmental Protection Agency's `201' Program
indicated that the program subsidized urban development
in flood-hazard areas on a large scale (Bick, 1977).
The Research Group, Inc. (1978) investigated federal
program effects on flood plain development in a number
of communities and found that three programs tended to
encourage urban development in hazard areas--the `201'
Wastewater Treatment Works Program of the U.S. Environmental Protection Agency, the U.S. Department of
Transportations's Federal Aid Highway Program, and the
U.S. Army Corps of Engineers' Public Works Program
(levee and dam construction). Finally, Sheaffer and
Roland, Inc. studied barrier island development and
concluded, "Current federal programs support development, effectively leveraging private development money

by shifting to the public sector portions of the costs of bridges, roads, causeways, watersupply systems, wastewater treatment systems, shore protection, disaster relief, and flood insurance. (Sheaffer and Roland, Inc. 1981a, 6) The Federal subsidy of barrier island development was set at $25,570 per developed acre. (Also see Sheaffer and Rozakus 1980; Miller 1980-81.)

To provide an early reading on the effectiveness of Executive Order 11988 in reversing this trend, the authors asked regional councils of government across the country in 1979 whether federal programs operating in their areas were having a significant or insignificant effect on the development or protection of flood-hazard areas. The regional agencies' perceptions of federal program impacts are summarized in Table 4-5.

In most of the 583 regions responding, agency personnel did not believe that any federal program's effect in promoting flood plain development was significant. Nevertheless, in about one-third of the regions, four programs were viewed as having such an effect. Those programs, which should be monitored carefully to assure compliance with EO 11988, include structural protection works developed by the Corps of Engineers, the Soil Conservation Service, the Tennessee Valley Authority, and the Bureau of Reclamation; the Department of Transportation's Federal Aid Highway Program; the Farmer's Home Administration's Sewer and Water Facility Loan and Grant Program; and the Environmental Protection Agency's `201' Wastewater Treatment Works Program. For the most part, those are the same programs identified by earlier research as supporting continuing flood plain development and use.

In most of the regions, regional agency personnel also did not believe that federal programs were having a significant effect on the protection of flood-hazard areas. Nevertheless, from one-quarter to half of the agencies noted positive effects from six federal programs. They included the flood plain information programs of the Corps of Engineers, the Soil Conservation Service, and the Tennessee Valley Authority (cited by 45 percent of the regional agencies); the Department of Commerce's Coastal Zone Management Program (43 percent); the Heritage Conservation and Recreation Service's Land and Water Conservation Fund (36 percent); the Environmental Protection Agency's `208' Areawide Water Quality Management Program (34 percent); the Corps of Engineers' `404' Dredge and Fill Permit Program (33 percent); and the National Environmental

TABLE 4-5
Impacts of other federal programs on flood
plain development/protection

Federal Program	Percent of Regional Councils of Government Which Perceive Program's Impact as:	
	Significant	Insignificant
Federal Programs that can PROMOTE Flood Plain Development[a]		
Corps of Engineers, Soil Conservation Service (SCS), Tennessee Valley Authority (TVA), or Bureau of Reclamation dams, reservoirs and other structural protective works	49	51
Department of Transportation (DOT) Federal Aid Highway Program	34	66
Farmers Home Administration (FmHA) Sewer and Water Facility Loan and Grant Program	33	67
Environmental Protection Agency (EPA) `201' Wastewater Treatment Program	32	68
Department of Housing and Urban Development (HUD) Community Develop- Block Grant Program	19	81
Economic Development Administration (EDA) Public Works Facility Program	18	82
Department of Housing and Urban Development (HUD) Housing Programs	18	82

(continued)

TABLE 4-5 (cont.)

Federal Program	Percent of Regional Councils of Government Which Perceive Program's Impact as:	
	Significant	Insignificant
Department of Commerce Coastal Energy Impact Program	9	91
Federal Programs that can PROTECT Flood Plains from Development[b]		
Corps of Engineers, Soil Conservation Service (SCS), or Tennessee Valley Authority (TVA) Flood Plain Information Programs	45	55
Department of Commerce Coastal Zone Management Program	43	57
Heritage Conservation and Recreation Service (HCRS) Land and Water Conservation Fund	36	64
Environmental Protection Agency (EPA) `208' Areawide Water Quality Management Program	34	66
Corps of Engineer's `404' Dredge and Fill Permit Program	33	67
National Environmental Policy Act (NEPA)	26	74

[a]Question: Other federal programs have the potential to encourage flood plain development. For each of the following programs, would you estimate that its effect in promoting development of flood plains in your region has been significant or insignificant? Circle the appropriate response for each program; if a program has not been used in the region, circle N/A.
[b]Question: Some federal programs have the potential to aid in the protection of natural flood plains. For each of the following programs would you estimate that its effects in protecting flood plains in your region

(continued)

TABLE 4-5 (cont.)

has been significant or insignificant? Circle the
appropriate response for each program; if the program
has not been used in the region, circle N/A.

Policy Act (26 percent).

     Finally, regional agencies were asked to provide a
summary evaluation of the effectiveness of federal
efforts to protect flood plains in their regions. Six
percent of the agencies rated federal efforts as very
effective; 40 percent rated them as moderately
effective; 42 percent rated them as slightly effective;
and 12 percent indicated that federal programs were not
effective in protecting flood plains in their region.
These regional agency evaluations suggest that
Executive Order 11988 and other federal programs are
having some effect on the preservation of natural flood
storage and other environmental values often concentrated in flood plains, but that much additional
progress could be made.

SUMMARY

     Programs to deal with flood hazards have evolved at
all levels of government--federal, state, and local.
This chapter examined federal flood plain management
programs, not from the usual top-down perspective, but
from the perspective of local communities that have
been affected by various federal programs. The
distribution of federal program benefits among local
communities and the effects of federal programs on
continued flood plain development and communities' land
use management programs were described.

     Most flood-prone communities are receiving benefits
from a variety of federal flood plain management programs, including flood control works, various forms of
technical assistance, and flood insurance. In general,
the more serious the local flood problem, the more
likely communities are to have sought and received
federal assistance. Communities receiving help in
solving their flood plain problems tend to be making
active urban use of their flood hazard areas. Thus,
federal programs tend to be used not to preserve
natural flood plain values, but to make the flood plain
safe for continued urban development. For the most
part, federal programs are associated with and make
possible continuing urban encroachment on hazardous
areas.

     At the same time, it is clear that federal flood

hazard management programs have not stifled community flood plain land use management efforts. Just the opposite seems to be true. Communities that are making the most use of flood control structures, that were early recipients of technical assistance, and that were early participants in the National Flood Insurance Program tend to be those that have developed the broadest, most sophisticated flood plain land use management programs.

In making possible continued and even accelerated flood plain use, federal programs appear to be in line with community goals for their flood-hazard areas. As indicated in the preceding chapter, communities are much more interested in reducing flood losses than in protecting the natural environment in flood-hazard areas. Federal programs, such a assistance in the construction of structural flood control works and the National Flood Insurance Program, are helping communities achieve their loss reduction objectives by keeping flood waters away from people and damageable property (assistance with flood control works) and by keeping property out of the reach of flood waters by promoting elevation and floodproofing adjustments to the hazard and indemnification through insurance (through the National Flood Insurance Program) if the adjustments fail.

Federal programs that can help communities preserve environmental values and protect flood-hazard areas from urban encroachment are having an insignificant effect, according to a majority of 583 regional councils of government surveyed. When asked to provide a summary evaluation of the effectiveness of federal programs in protecting flood plains, most of those regional agencies rated the current federal effort either as only "slightly" effective or as not effective at all. Executive Order 11988 for the first time gives equal footing in federal flood-hazard management policy to environmental protection goals. The data and analyses summarized in this chapter highlight the need for a more balanced policy toward flood-hazard areas and to the potential difficulty in overcoming the built-in momentum of the continuing development of the nation's flood plains and coastal high hazard areas.

NOTES

1. Flood-storage reservoirs provide protection to broad areas by modifying flood flow rates, timing of the rise in waters, and extent of the area flooded. They may not, however, provide needed protection to specific local areas subject to flooding. Dikes,

levees, and floodwalls protect a specfic portion of the
local flood plain from damage. Channel alterations
accelerate the quantity and/or velocity of flow through
an area, allowing a stream to pass a greater volume of
water without flooding adjacent areas. Diversions
redirect excess flows away from developed areas through
the use of either natural or artificial channels. Land
treatment measures modify floods by increasing infil-
tration rates and/or slowing the rate and volume of
storm runoff. Each of these measures may be effective
up to specified design levels. Since it is usually not
economically feasible to design structural measures to
prevent all levels of flooding, however, structural
measures may fail to provide protection against
extremely rare catastrophic events. (See U.S. Water
Resources Council 1979.)

2. Of course, while local governments continue to
be aware of the flood problem, citizens within these
communities may believe that the structural measures
solved the flood threat, and, as a result, may continue
to expose themselves to flooding.

3. Although consultants and others have recommended greater Corps involvement in and support of land
use planning and regulation in connection with its
civil works programs, the Corps of Engineers
traditionally has viewed land management as contro-
versial and has not supported it aggressively. See
Dzurik 1980.

4. Property owners in participating communities
who do not purchase flood insurance and suffer damages
may receive federal disaster loans from the Small
Business Administration or Farmers Home Administration,
but as a condition for such aid they will be required
to purchase flood insurance.

5. In addition to subsidizing insurance rates for
existing structures in flood-hazard areas (to encourage
the purchase of flood insurance), rates are subsidized
for new construction in communities in the emergency
phase of the NFIP where actuarial rates have yet to be
determined.

6. For a discussion of other problems associated
with the standards for local land use regulation required by the National Flood Insurance Program see
Bosselman, Feurer, and Richter 1977, 92-111.

7. The association between program participation
indicators and continued flood plain development remained strong when a number of indicators of the
potential for flood plain use (including the proportion
of the community land area and population in the hazard
area, relative availability of hazard-free sites for
development, number of existing hazard-zone structures,
and scope of the community's flood plain land use
management program) were controlled statistically.

8. These data and the preceding findings regard-

ing high insurance sales in coastal areas lend some
credence to the contention that insurance premiums in
coastal areas are underpriced and, as a result, may
encourage uneconomic development in coastal hazard
areas (Shows 1977, 973; Heritage Conservation and
Recreation Service et al. 1979, 24).

9. This finding is comparable to the results
obtained in a survey of small (under 5,000 population)
jurisdictions conducted for the Federal Insurance
Administration, which indicated that 58 percent of the
responding communities were satisfied with the amount
of technical assistance they had received. (See
National Institute for Advanced Studies 1977.)

5
State and Regional Approaches to Flood Plain Land Use Management

In past years, there has been a tendency to regard flooding as a national or local concern and not as a problem to be addressed by state governments and sub-state regional agencies. The public works programs of the Corps of Engineers, Bureau of Reclamation, and Soil Conservation Service, for example, were designed to respond to local requests for help. The resulting federal-local partnership left little room for state or regional agencies to play more than minimal roles at the fringes of project decision making (see National Science Foundation, 1980). Initially, the nonstructural approach to flood plain management promoted by the National Flood Insurance Program followed a similar path. The NFIP was established as a federal-local effort with the states' role limited to providing program information to local governments. Regional councils of government and other substate agencies were ignored. As experience with non-structural flood plain management has accumulated, however, it has become apparent that the states and substate regional agencies need to pay more than residual bit parts if the national trend toward mounting flood losses is to be halted. This chapter describes flood plain management programs that have been adopted by states and regions and assesses their effectiveness in mitigating flood hazards at the local level.

STATE AND REGIONAL ROLES

Interest in greater state and regional agency involvement in flood plain management stems in part from three problems with local hazard mitigation programs: underinvestment in flood plain management; interjurisdictional spillovers from land use and hazard mitigation decisions; and fragmentation of management responsibilities. The underinvestment problem stems from the tendency, discussed in Chapter 3, for local governments to discount the serious- ness of potential flood hazards and, as a result, to devote little staff time on money to flood hazard mitigation. The Council of State Governments (1979, 11) observed that when a problem is "invisible" at the local level, it is unlikely that local public attitudes will support the use of community resources to deal with it. Flooding is just such a problem. Its probabilistic nature and infrequent occurrence lead officials in all but the most flood-prone communities to devote little attention to mitigating the potential hazard.

Underinvestment in hazard mitigation, particularly during the early stages of flood plain invasion and use, has serious consequences for the later viability of land use management as a means of limiting the hazard. Most land use management measures are de- signed to intervene early in the development process. They prevent future flood problems from occurring by limiting flood plain invasion and by requiring that new buildings locating in flood hazard areas be elevated or floodproofed. As will be shown in the next chapter, land use management is not particularly effective in dealing with the flooding problems of unprotected development that was allowed to locate in hazard areas before land use measures were adopted. Thus, there is a paradox. Land use management does not work very well after flood plain invasion has occurred, but before flood plain invasion occurs communities are not interested in managing flood hazard areas, since perceptions are that a flood problem does not yet exist (flood problems are not usually recognized until development is located in the flood plain to be flooded). One means of resolving the paradox is for state governments to become actively involved in flood plain management--either by undertaking their own management programs or by mandating the adoption of local flood plain regula- tions, setting standards for local programs, and pro- viding assistance so that local management efforts are effective in preventing flood-related problems from arising.

Spillover effects of flood plain development and hazard mitigation from one jurisdiction to another is a second problem stimulating increased interest in state and regional flood plain management (see Platt and others 1980). Potential adverse spillover effects are easy to imagine when jurisdiction share a river or stream. If one jurisdiction allows intensive development of the upstream portions of a watershed, for example, the severity of flooding downstream may be increased severalfold. If a jurisdiction on one bank of a river attempts to provide flood protection by erecting levees, it may increase flooding in the community on the opposite bank. Similarly, if one jurisdiction allows extensive filling in the flood-plain, the severity of flooding in adjacent jurisdictions bordering the same river may be increased. Not all spillovers are negative, however. For example, if one community relocates structures from the flood plain to a flood-free site, the increased flood storage provided may lessen the severity of flooding in nearby communities along the same stream.

As long as flood plain land use management is conducted solely at the local level, the spillover effects of land use and hazard mitigation decisions are likely to be ignored. One means of bringing a broader perspective to bear on management decisions and ensuring that factors of greater than local concern are taken into account is to involve regional agencies and state government in flood plain land use management decision making. Increased state attention to interjurisdictional spillovers from flood plain development and local efforts to mitigate the hazard is in keeping with the "quiet revolution" in land use management, which has seen more and more states develop new institutions and programs to deal with land use and environmental problems (see Bosselman and Callies 1972; Levin, Rose and Slavet 1974; Council of State Governments 1975; and Healy and Rosenberg 1979; DeGrove 1984).

The third problem justifying increased regional and state involvement in flood plain land use management has been the extreme fragmentation of responsibility for flood hazard mitigation and resulting lack of coordination of management efforts. Both the Congressional Office of Technology Assessment and U.S. Water Resources Council have commented on this problem. According to the Office of Technology Assessment (1979, 2),

> The integration of the socioeconomic, technical, and physical tools at all levels of government, but especially at the local level, is very weak. Continuing with poorly integrated management of flood hazards will incur very serious flood losses.

The U.S. Water Resources Council (1979, II-6) cited "fragmented and uncoordinated responsibility" for flood plain management as a major problem that had to be resolved before a unified national program for

108

flood plain management could be implemented. Among
the adverse consequences of fragmentation noted by the
Council were,

>...lack of consistency among public programs
designed to meet flood problems within and
between areas and among those plans designed to
meet the other needs of the affected areas. Fragmentation contributes to inadequately conceived
measures to solve flood problems. This results
in the destruction of resources that the public
values and generation of costs that are as unde-
sirable as the damages that they attempt to
relieve. Such inadequately conceived measures
are frequently accompanied by inadequate and
misdirected commitments of program resources.
(U.S. Water Resources Council, 1979, II-6)

There are a number of ways of overcoming the
lack of coordination and fragmentation of responsibility that have characterized flood plain management.
Two basic ones are to shift responsibility for management decisions to a higher level, such as state
government, and to promote greater interaction among
local agencies sharing a common watershed and flood
plain, such as through participation in a regional
council of governments or other substate regional
agency.

In 1979 the U.S. Water Resources Council (1979,
III-6) noted that only "A few states have vigorous and
comprehensive flood plain management programs..."
As the rationale for state government involvement in
flood plain management has become more evident, however, states have steadily expanded their efforts to
mitigate flood hazards. In the following section,
state approaches to flood plain management are
described in some detail and a review of state
program effectiveness from the perspectives of local
governments is provided. To aid in the diffusion of
more effective program components, key elements which
differentiate the most effective state programs are
isolated and described briefly. Following the
analysis of state programs, the chapter turns to an
examination of flood plain management activities being
pursued by substate regional agencies. Based on data
assembled from 583 regional agencies, the chapter
looks at the frequency with which regional agencies
employ various types of land use management measures,
and the effectiveness of regional programs. The
chapter concludes with a brief review of findings
regarding state and regional flood plain management.

THE STATES AND FLOOD HAZARD MANAGEMENT

State flood hazard management programs may involve the use of six types of measures (roughly paralleling local action instruments discussed in Chapter 2): (1) planning and coordination; (2) incentives; (3) regulations; (4) land acquisition and public investments; (5) public information and technical assistance; and (6) post-disaster assistance. Table 5-1 lists the potential components of state floodplain management programs. The remaining chapter subsections note the frequency and staffing of each component group across the fifty states, and provide descriptive information about the content of such programs.

Planning and Coordination

As flood plain management nationally moves away from its past focus on flood control projects to include a balanced mix of structural and nonstructural measures, the need for areawide planning and coordination has increased significantly. At the local level, "horizontal" planning and coordination are necessary to eliminate potential spillover effects noted above and to avoid conflicts among local jurisdictions sharing a common flood plain.[1] In addition, better coordination of federal programs ("vertical" coordination) affecting flood plain management is also needed. Federal flood related activities are spread across twenty-eight agencies and nine program purposes. (U.S. Water Resources Council 1979, VII-2) As was shown in the previous chapter, these programs may work at cross-purposes, with some promoting flood plain development and use while others are designed to discourage flood plain encroachment and protect natural values. State governments are close enough to the local scene to help with areawide (horizontal) planning and coordination and increasingly are being called upon to help coordinate federal programs related to flood hazard management.

Among seven broadly defined possible state roles listed in Table 5-2, hazard management officials in forty-five states (90 percent) rated planning and coordination and technical assistance to local government (86 percent) as the two most important roles for states in flood hazard mitigation. Five other broad potential state roles--public information/flood warning, regulation of hazard areas, post-disaster assistance, construction of flood control works, and relocation/land acquisition--ranked far behind. When asked in which two activities states were most involved, officials in thirty-eight states (74 percent)

TABLE 5-1
Potential components of state flood plain
management programs

PLANNING AND COORDINATION

Statewide comprehensive water resources planning
State comprehensive land use planning
Flood hazard management planning in cooperation with
local and federal governments
Review and coordination of public works projects
for flood protection
Review and coordination of highway construction
in light of flood hazard management needs
Disaster response planning

INCENTIVES

Property tax relief/incentives for open space/low
intensive use of flood hazard areas
Grants-in-aid for local shares of federal
matching requirements
Grants-in-aid for land use management programs
Grants-in-aid for land acquisition or relocation

REGULATIONS

State permits for dams, reservoirs, levees and
other flood control works and for fills, docks,
and other obstructions of navigable waters
State permits for buildings and other structures
located in either the floodway or the floodway
fringe
Wetlands protection/dredge and fill regulations
Sedimentation pollution stormwater management
regulations
Coastal management requirements and hazard
mitigation regulations
State standards for local regulation of flood
hazard areas
State requirements for local regulation of flood
hazard areas with provision for state regulation
if localities fail to act
Dam safety inspections
State monitoring of compliance with flood management
regulations
State mandate for participation in National Flood
Insurance Program

LAND ACQUISITON AND PUBLIC INVESTMENT

Acquisition of flood hazard areas for natural areas,
open space parks, and other uses
(continued)

TABLE 5-1 (cont.)

Acquisition and relocation of existing structures
in the floodplain
State construction of flood control works
State public facility location and design standards
with respect to flood hazard mitigation
Standards attached to grants-in-aid to local governments, specifying design criteria for structures
located within flood hazard areas

PUBLIC INFORMATION AND TECHNICAL ASSISTANCE

Floodplain mapping
Stream hydrology data services
Soil mapping
Wetlands delineation
Flood insurance studies
Flood warning system
Floodway/floodplain marking/posting system
Model ordinance development
Assistance to local governments with National Flood
Insurance Program
Assistance with backwater computations
Training and education programs for state and local
officials, bankers, lawyers, planners, and others
involved in floodplain development
Public education/awareness programs
Research on flood problems and hazard mitigation
strategies

POST-DISASTER ASSISTANCE

Interagency councils for response coordination
Central clearinghouse for relief funding information
Pre-disaster planning for reconstruction
Reconstruction technical assistance
Reconstruction of public facilities assistance
Restoration of private facilities assistance
Contingency funds

mentioned technical assistance, making it the most
commonly employed method the states are perceived to be
using to deal with flooding.

State governments may employ a number of different
methods in planning for and coordinating flood plain
management. One of the most basic is the development
of a statewide comprehensive water resources plan (or
planning framework study) and designation of a single
state agency to coordinate compliance with the plan
among different departments and local governments (see
Morse 1968, x). In addition, by formulating such a

112

TABLE 5-2
State officials' perceptions of state hazard
management roles

State Roles	Percent of States in Which Hazard Management Officials Perceive:[a]	
	Role is One of Two Most Important for States[b]	Role is One of Two in Which States Are Most Involved
1. Planning and coordination	90%	68%
2. Technical assistance to local governments	86	74
3. Public information/flood warning	56	56
4. Regulation of flood hazard areas	52	38
5. Post-disaster assistance	10	66
6. Construction of flood control works	10	20
7. Relocation/land acquisition	6	6
Number of states responding	(50)	(50)

[a]Role mentioned by one or more of five officials surveyed in each state.
[b] Columns add to more than 100 percent because officials were asked to indicate up to two roles.

plan or water resources framework, the states have a
logical basis for (1) working with the federal government and local communities in devising cooperative
pre- and post-flood hazard mitigation plans keyed to
the needs of specific communities (see Bloomgren 1980)
and for (2) reviewing and coordinating U.S. Army Corps
of Engineers, U.S. Soil Conservation Service and other
federal agencies' public works projects, both of which
are additional approaches the states may use to
coordinate flood plain management activities.
Finally, various measures discussed elsewhere in this
section, such as state standard setting for local
regulations and state public investment policies, may
also be used to achieve greater coordination and
uniformity in flood plain management.

Although the opportunity for a greater state role
in planning and coordination is present and a number
of studies have suggested the states need to become
more involved in water resources planning and intergovernmental coordination, the states' record to date
in this area is not very good. Over a decade ago, for
example, Morse (1968, 57) noted that thirty-five
states had designated separate state agencies to work
with each federal flood control agency in reviewing
federal project plans, but that the "...activities and
policies of these separate state agencies have not
been effectively coordinated..." Morse (1968, 14)
also found that in many states state review of federal
flood control projects was "perfunctory and cursory."
More recently, a study of national flood hazard
management policy conducted by the National Science
Foundation (1980, 86) concluded,

Generally, state input to the federal-local
partnership promoting structural solutions has
been minimal. States have not provided either
the legislative or the institutional framework to
accommodate or promote integration of the
structural solution into a more comprehensive
approach.

In addition to doing little to coordinate and
integrate federal public works projects related to
flood control, it also appears that the states have
had little effect on the coordination of local flood
hazard mitigation efforts. One of the principal means
the states have for improving local coordination is
the National Flood Insurance Program. Each state is
required by the NFIP to appoint a state coordinator to
assist local communities with the program, but in most
cases the states have treated this function very
lightly. A survey of state coordinators conducted in
1978 found that in twenth-nine states fewer than

fifteen person hours per month were devoted to the NFIP
and that in all but five states the state coordinators
worked less than full-time on flood-related matters.
(National Institute for Advanced Studies 1978, III-11)
Finally, a recent investigation of local intergovernmental flood plain management concluded, "...states
played relatively inconspicuous roles in most of the
case studies." (Platt, et al. 1980, 277)

Various reasons have been advanced for the states'
lackluster performance in planning and coordinating
flood plain management. Federal policy seems to be
one key factor. As noted above, until recently
federal agencies worked directly with local
governments and did not encourage state involvement in
project planning and implementation. With the federal
government dominating the field, few state legisla-
tures have been willing to provide adequate funding
for a centralized, vigorous state flood hazard management program. (U.S. Water Resources Council 1979,
VII-15) Instead, the states have usually followed an
ad hoc approach to hazard mitigation and flood plain
management. State programs related to flooding tend
to be dispersed across a number of state agencies,
creating difficulties in coordinating a state's own
programs and making coordination of federal or local
flood plain management programs virtually impossible.

Table 5-3 describes the current state-of-practice
for planning and coordination activities across
the fifty states. States typically engage in
five planning and coordination activities. All but
Indiana and Vermont (96 percent of all states) had a
recognized disaster planning program when surveyed in
1983. Nearly three-quarters of the states had programs
in comprehensive water resources planning (74 percent),vertically integrated flood hazard management
planning (76 percent), review and coordination of
public works projects for flood protection consequences (76 percent), and review and coordination of
highway construction in light of flood hazard management needs (72 percent). Just 14 percent of the
states, however, had some form of statewide land use
planning.

The planning and coordination activities in place
clearly depict the flood hazard management area concentrated in two broad areas of state government--
emergency management/disaster preparedness agencies and
water related agencies. The emphasis on planning
and coordination for disaster events and water policies
demonstrates a relative neglect of planning and
coordination among land use related activities which
are usually housed in state community development

TABLE 5-3
State planning and coordination programs in place,
1983

Program Component	Percent of States with Component, 1983	Mean Staff Size
Disaster response planning	96	12.4
Review and coordination of public works projects for flood protection	76	7.8
Flood hazard management planning in cooperation with local and federal governments	75	9.8
Statewide comprehensive water resources planning	74	16.1
Review and Coordination of highway construction in light of flood hazard management needs	72	9.0
Statewide comprehensive land use planning	14	3.3

agencies that have a clear-cut emphasis on local
technical assistance programs.

In addition to dispersing the planning and
coordination mechanisms across a number of program
areas, the personnel commitments to all of the
activities are small. Mean staff size for the programs
ranged from 3.3 persons full- and part-time for
statewide land use planning to 16.1 persons for comprehensive water resources planning. Mean staff size for
the programs are reported in Table 5-3.

Public Information and Technical Assistance

While large cities may have sizeable staffs to
work with flood related issues, to the small towns of
the nation flood management is one of many development
related concerns that have to be handled by a small

building inspection, public works, or planning department. Not infrequently, in very small places all
these matters are handled by one individual, the town
manager or clerk. As shown in Table 1-1, the average
population of the flood-prone jurisdictions included in
our 1983 random sample of communities participating in
the National Flood Insurance Program was only 3,221.[2]
If these small communities are to implement flood
management effectively, and if large communities are
to implement it consistently, public information and
technical assistance programs at the state level may
be essential. Among seven possible state roles listed
in Table 5-2, hazard management officials in forty-
three states (86 percent) rated technical assistance
as one of the two most important roles for states in
flood hazard mitigation. In addition, 56 percent
rated public information as one of the two most important roles. Only planning and coordination received
more attention than either of these, and four other
possible state roles--regulation of hazard areas,
post-disaster assistance, construction of flood control works, and relocation/land acquisition--ranked
behind. The state officials surveyed in thirty-eight
states (76 percent) also thought that technical
assistance was the most commonly employed method the
states use in dealing with flooding.

Table 5-4 classifies state technical assistance
programs into three groups: information collection,
information dissemination, and information use
assistance. An information use assistance program,
helping local governments with the National Flood
Insurance Program, is the most prevalent assistance
program in force, used in every state but California
and Washington (96 percent). This shows the intergovernmental focus of flood plain management, with the
states serving in the pivotal position in helping
implement a national program with mandates on local
governments. The second most frequent type of state
technical assistance is in the information dissemination category: training and education programs for
state and local officials and development officials
is in operation in 80 percent of the states. The
information collection category includes the third
most frequent type of technical assistance: 68 percent
of the states offer stream hydrology data services.

Technical assistance programs that are not widely
employed by the states are worth noting, since any
neglect by the states may have significant effects on
local governments, especially those small communities
lacking in expertise and other resources. Few of the
thirteen specific assistance activities listed in
Table 5-4, in fact, are employed by a majority of the

states. Two critical types of assistance--floodplain
mapping and flood insurance studies--are provided by
only 34 percent and 22 percent of the states, respectively. One useful nonstructural tool for flood
hazard management--floodway/floodplain marking/posting
systems--is generally neglected.

Staff sizes for all of the public information and
technical assistance programs were small. Mean figures
for all states for each activity ranged from 3.2 full-
and part-time persons (for flood warning systems) to
9.9 full- and part-time (for flood insurance studies).
(See Table 5-4.)

Incentives

The voluntary or local decision-based nature of
most land-use issues related to flood hazard management suggests that state initiated incentives and
disincentives are potentially important program tools.
When legal or political reasons make effective regulation impossible, tax incentives for low intensity land
use and fee simple acquisition of flood prone
properties may be the only feasible methods of
reducing potential flood damages. Our 1983 survey of
state officials, however, found no state officials who
believed incentives to be one of the two most
important roles for states.

Incentive program components may be classed as
tax relief and grants-in-aid. We examined three
grants-in-aid program components (grants for local
shares of federal matching requirements; grants for
land-use management programs; and grants for land
acquisition or relocation) and one tax relief program
component (for open space or low intensity use of
flood hazard areas). None of the incentive program
components was in common use, as shown in Table 5-5.
Mean staff sizes for the states with incentive
programs, however, were large compared to other
program components in the state flood hazard management system. That may in part be traceable to the
small number of states with incentive programs. Mean
staff size ranged from 33.5 full-or part-time
positions for land acquisition and relocation grants-
in-aid to 5.4 for local shares of federal matching
requirements grants-in-aid.

Regulations

As might be expected in a policy area involving
both land use and water resources policies, state

TABLE 5-4
State public information and technical assistance
programs in place, 1983

Program Component	Percent of States	Mean Staff Size
Information Collection		
Stream hydrology data services	68%	8.8
Research on flood problems and hazard mitigation strategies	46	4.1
Soils mapping	40	8.9
Wetlands delineation	40	4.0
Floodplain mapping	34	7.2
Flood insurance studies	22	9.9
Information Dissemination		
Training and education programs for state and local officials, and development officials	80	5.6
Public education/awareness programs	62	5.4
Flood warning system	26	3.2
Floodway/floodplain marking/posting system	8	3.7
Information Use Assistance		
Assistance to local governments with National Flood Insurance Program	96	6.5
Model ordinance development	60	3.4
Assistance with backwater computations	32	5.3

TABLE 5-5
State incentive programs in place, 1983

Program Component	Percent of States with Component, 1983	Mean Staff Size
Grants-in-aid for local shares of federal matching requirements	32	5.4
Grants-in-aid for land use management programs	16	10.9
Grants-in-aid for land acquisition or relocation	8	33.5
Property tax relief/ incentive for open space/low intensity use of flood hazard areas	6%	17.8

regulatory activities encompass a wide range of possibilities for state flood hazard programs. State agency officials ranked regulation fourth among the program areas in which they thought states should be involved (see Table 5-2). This may be due to the fact that the state regulatory role related to nonstructural flood hazard management is relatively new, compared to active regulation related to structural flood protection.

Table 5-6 classifies state regulatory programs as: (1) structural flood protection; (2) nonstructural flood protection; and (3) flood related environmental protection. Structural flood protection regulations, such as permits for flood control works and dam safety inspections are nearly universal, with 90 percent and 86 percent of the states reporting such activities. Not as common, but still used in roughly half of the states are flood related environmental protection regulations, such as wetlands protection and dredge and fill regulations (56 percent), sedimentation pollution control stormwater management regulations (54 percent), and coastal management requirements and hazard mitigation regulations (44 percent).

TABLE 5-6
State regulatory program components in place, 1983

Program Component	Percent of States	Mean Staff Size
Structural Flood Protection		
State permits for flood control works and/or obstructions of navigable waters	90%	6.5
Dam safety inspections	86	5.4
Nonstructural Flood Protection		
State monitoring of compliance with flood management regulations	50	8.2
State permits for buildings and other structures located in either the floodway or the floodway fringe	32	13.2
State standards for local regulation of flood hazard areas	32	7.9
State requirements for local regulation of flood hazard areas with provision for state regulation if localities fail to act	16	8.2
State mandate of participation in National Flood Insurance Program	8	3.2
Flood Related Environmental Protection		
Wetlands protection/dredge and fill regulations	56	9.0
Sedimentation pollution control/stormwater management regulations	54	8.5
Coastal management requirements and hazard mitigation regulations	44	10.8

Given that local governments bear primary
responsibility for land use regulations, it is not
surprising that none of the five nonstructural program
components listed on Table 5-6 are used by more than
half of the states. Fifty percent do monitor
compliance with local flood management plans and nearly
a third of the states (32 percent) require permits for
buildings in the floodplain and/or set standards for
local regulation of flood hazard areas (32 percent).
Much of the state technical assistance role is aimed
at enhancing the local capacity to develop and
implement local level nonstructural measures and regulations, both of which are cost effective in promoting
the idea that those who occupy flood hazard areas
should be responsible for paying the costs of disaster
events.

Flood related environmental protection program
components tend to have larger staffs than the other
regulatory categories, with mean staff sizes of 10.8
for coastal management, 9.0 for wetlands, and 8.5 for
sedimentation control. The mean staff size for the two
structural programs was 6.5 full- or part-time persons
for permitting and 5.4 full- and part-time persons for
dam safety. The larger and more diverse nonstructural
category has a mean staff size across the states
ranging from 13.2 full- or part-time persons for state
flood plain building permit programs to 3.2 full- or
part-time persons for programs that involved mandates
of participation in the National Flood Insurance Program.

Land Acquisition and Public Investment

In many cases, the most secure protection against
flood losses is direct public investment. Construction
of flood control works can provide reliable mitigation
of damages from the levels of flooding for which they
are designed. Fee simple acquisition of flood-prone
land by a state can ensure against development of that
land. But, land acquisition and public works projects
are very expensive, pricing most states out of such
programs. It is the national government that has
invested most in flood control works, leaving states
with the tasks of dealing with unique and/or localized
problems, and, perhaps, setting standards for other
public projects to reduce the threat of flood damage.
High capital outlays and maintenance costs make
structural projects difficult to implement for state
governments.

State flood hazard management officials in only 10
percent of the states rated construction of flood control works as one of the two most important roles for

any state, with officials in 6 percent of the states
identifying relocation or land acquisition as such (see
Table   . And, actual state practice in this area
suggests relatively low levels of state involvement,
compared to other possible state roles.

Five specific programs are grouped into two
categories, land acquisition and public investment in
Table 5-7 . Only one public investment strategy, state
public facility location and design standards, is used
by over half the states (54 percent). Standards
attached to grants-in-aid are used by 28 percent of the
states. All other programs are rare, with actual
acquisition and relocation of existing structures in
the floodplain pursued by only 6 percent of the states.

Given the nature of the activity, it is expected
that the mean staff size for state construction of
flood control works would be among the largest of all
state flood program components, 17.5 full- and part-
time persons. The mean staff sizes for other public
investment and land acquisition programs range from
11.8 to 2.0 persons full- and part-time.

Post-disaster Assistance

Although the state officials in the 1983 survey of
state practices perceived the states to be very
actively involved in post-disaster assistance programs,
few thought this was one of the most important state
roles (Table 5-2). The state-of-practice summary
provided in Table 5-8 depicts three classes of post-
disaster assistance programs employed by the states:
(1) planning and coordination, including pre-disaster
reconstruction planning and interagency councils for
response coordination; (2) technical assistance, including a clearinghouse for relief funding information
and technical assistance for reconstruction; and (3)
financial assistance, including funds for restoration
of public and private facilities, as well as
contingency funds for flood relief.

Many states make an effort to plan and coordinate
disaster response via an interagency council (66 percent) and a clearinghouse for relief funding information (68 percent) but only 36 percent offer pre-
disaster planning for reconstruction. While 58 percent
provide contingency funds and 56 percent provide funding for restoration of public facilities, less than a
fourth (24 percent) offer funds for restoration of
private facilities. Only 42 percent offer reconstruction technical assistance.

TABLE 5-7
State land acquisition and public investment programs
in place, 1983

Program Component	Percent of States	Mean Staff Size
Public Investment		
State public facility location and design standards with respect to flood hazards	54%	5.3
Standards attached to grants-in-aid to local governments, specifying design criteria for structures located within flood hazard areas	28	2.5
State construction of flood control works	18	17.5
Land Acquisition		
Acquisition of flood hazard areas for natural areas, open space parks, and other uses	18	11.8
Acquisition and relocation of existing structures in the floodplain	6	2.0

EVALUATING STATE PROGRAMS

What difference do state flood hazard management programs make? From the earlier discussion of state program components in flood hazard management it is clear that the state role is primarily one of informing, aiding, and coordinating local flood management efforts. It is difficult to assess the effectiveness of such a secondary or background role except through the perceptions of local government personnel and indirectly by association with the scope and effectiveness of local government programs. We use both of these approaches. First, we present data on local officials' use of state programs and opinions of the adequacy of state efforts. Then we use survey data from state and local officials to examine the

TABLE 5-8
State post-disaster assistance programs in place, 1983

Program Component	Percent of States	Mean Staff Size
Planning and Coordination		
Interagency councils for response coordination	66%	14.8
Pre-disaster planning for reconstruction	36	7.7
Technical Assistance		
Central clearinghouse for for relief funding information	68	11.8
Reconstruction technical assistance	42	7.0
Financial Assistance		
Contingency funds	58	5.5
Reconstruction of public facilities	56	3.9
Restoration of private facilities	24	3.2

relationships between state programs and local program scope and effectiveness.

Local Government Experience with State Programs

It is not surprising, given the limited resources states are committing to flood hazard management, that a majority of local government officials (52 percent) we surveyed in 1983 reported they were not familiar with their state's flood hazard management programs. Of those that claimed to know something about their state's program, only 11 percent reported they were very familiar with state efforts in this area.

A majority of local officials, on the other hand, had had some contact with state technical assistance programs during 1982-1983. Types of contact, which

are summarized in Table 5-9, varied from correspondence, the most frequently mentioned type, to
receipt of state-government-originated technical
reports on some aspect of flood hazard management,
which was mentioned least often.

Table 5-9 also summarizes types of assistance
local governments reported receiving from their state
between 1978 and 1983. The successful efforts of
state NFIP coordinators are clearly evident. A
majority of local governments reported receiving
information about the NFIP from state sources and
almost a majority (49 percent) cited the state as
their source for flood plain maps. Relatively few
local governments, however, had received other types
of assistance from state government. Between 1978 and
1983, only one of every six had received help with
disaster preparedness planning and fewer had had help
in administering local floodplain regulations or had
used state hydrological data aservices. Less than one
in ten local governments had received technical
assistance with storm drainage, even though 80 percent
reported storm drainage problems. State grants or
loans for flood control works and floodplain property
acquisition were the least common forms of assistance
received, reflecting the relative absence of grant and
loan programs at the state level, shown in Table 5-5.

Communities most likely to be seeking out state
assistance and that were in contact with state
programs during 1982-1983 tended to be those facing
the most severe flood hazards. In comparison with
local governments that were not in touch with state
programs, those seeking assistance: (1) already had
allowed extensive development of flood hazard areas;
(2) were experiencing more floodplain development
currently; (3) were more likely to subjectively rate
flooding as a community problem and to have actually
experienced serious flood damage over the preceeding
decade; but were expecting even more hazard-area
development over the next five years. However, they
were also significantly more likely to be taking
a variety of steps to deal with the hazard.
Communities that received state flood hazard management assistance, between 1978 and 1983, in comparison
with those not getting help, had already used
structural measures to control flooding, had adopted a
wider variety of nonstructural hazard management
measures, and were devoting more local resources to
solving the flood problem.

Types of assistance sought and received by local
governments also varied to some extent with the nature
of the local flood hazard. Communities with the most

126

TABLE 5-9
Local government experience with state flood hazard
management programs

Indicator	Percent of Local Governments[a] (N=956)
Contact with State Flood Hazard Management Program During 1982-1983	
No contact	42%
Some contact	58
Type of Contact	
Corespondence regarding flood hazard management	35
Telephone calls dealing with flood hazard management	32
Personal visits (face-to-face)	26
Received flood hazard management newsletter	15
Received flood hazard management technical reports	8
Flood Hazard Management Assistance Received from State Between 1978 and 1983	
National Flood Insurance Program Information	53%
Flood plain maps	49
Disaster preparedness planning assistance	16
Help in administering flood plain regulations	14
Hydrologic data	13
Help with storm drainage problems	9
Grants or loans for construction of flood control works	6
Grants or loans for flood plain property acquisition	<1

[a]Column adds to more than 100 percent because local
governments may have had more than one type of
contact/received more than one type of assistance.

severe flood hazard problems were no more likely than those with less severe hazards to have received help with nonstructural management. Reflecting the greater threat of losses of life and property they faced, however, they also were significantly more likely to have received state grants for flood control works over the past five years and state help with disaster preparedness planning as well.

For the most part, local governments were satisfied that state flood hazard management programs were capable of meeting their needs. When asked to rate the adequacy of their state's programs, 63 percent of those venturing an opinion thought it was adquate, 16 percent rated the state effort as barely adequate, and 21 percent wanted more help than was available. (These percentages exclude a relatively large proportion of local governments, 38 percent, which did not know enough about state assistance programs to offer an opinion.)

Possibly because of limited staffing, there were no statistically significant correlations (r's) between the availability of state assistance programs and local governments' rating of program adequacy (see Table 5-10). On the other hand, local governments that had actually used state programs tended to be more positive, as indicated by the strong positive correlation coefficients (r's) between ratings of program adequacy and direct contact with state programs (personal visit, telephone, and correspondence), receipt of help with the NFIP, receipt of help with local flood plain regulations, and the total number of different forms of help obtained.

Effects of State Programs on Scope and Implementation of Local Programs

In order to determine the effect of state programs on the scope and implementation of local programs we examined the relationship of two dimensions of state programs, (1) direct state floodplain regulation and (2) community use of local assistance programs, with three local program scope and implementation variables: (1) number of local components adopted to protect property from flood damage, (2) number of local program components adopted to protect the natural value of flood hazard areas, and (3) administrative priority of efforts to implement the measures. The effects of a number of other variables that might

TABLE 5-10
Association between selected state program components
and local governments' evaluation of the adequacy
of state programs

Selected Program Indicators	Correlation with Program Adequacy Rating (simple r)
Program Availability/Staffing	
Floodplain mapping	
Availability	ns
Staff size	ns
Model ordinances	
Availability	ns
Staff size	ns
Assistance with NFIP	
Availability	ns
Staff size	ns
Training and education programs	
Availability	ns
Staff size	ns
Public education/awareness programs	
Availability	ns
Staff size	ns
Programs Used by Local Governments	
State program contacts within past year	
Personal visit	.58
Telephone	.60
Correspondence	.46
Technical Report	.42
Newsletter	ns
Assistance Received During Past Five Years	
Floodplain maps	ns
Help with NFIP	34
Help with administration of local regulations	.65
State grants of loans for construction of flood control works	ns
State grants or loans for acquisition of hazard area property	ns
Number of different types of assistance used	.49

NS = Not significant at .05 level of confidence

be expected to also influence the scope and implementation of local programs, including federal programs,
regional programs, and community background variables,
were also included in the analysis. The results of
multiple regression analysis are shown in Table 5-11.
(These analyses extend the regression results
reported in Chapter 3, Table 3-7, but the results
are similar.)

The first dependent variable examined concerns
local government programs to protect property from
flood damage. (This variable was measured as the number of twenty-two flood hazard management program
components adopted by local governments). Federal
program variables, population of the jurisdiction and
the availability of hazard-free sites for development
had the strongest effect on the scope of local
programs to protect property from flood damage. Both
state program variables--state flood plain regulation
and community use of local assistance programs--had
statistically significant effects as well.

The second dependent variable was measured by
summing the number of program components local governments had adopted to preserve the natural value of
flood hazard areas. It includes density controls,
such as zoning, subdivision regulations, erosion and
sedimentation regulations, dredge and fill
regulations, and similar measures. Again, the strongest effects are from federal program variables, population of the jurisdiction, and availability of
hazard-free sites for new development (Table 5-11).
Direct state regulaton is a strong and significant
variable, but community use of state local assistance
programs is not.

The third dependent variable is the administrative
priority given to flood hazard management. It was
measured in terms of local governments' responses to a
survey question asking them to assess the priority
given to flood hazard management by the staff member
responsible for the program in comparison with other
responsibilities of that person. The seriousness of
the flood problem had the strongest effect on administration priority. Both state program variables, community use of state assistance programs and direct
state floodplain regulation, had significant positive
effects on the degree of administrative priority local
governments gave to flood plain management.

In summary, we find that state flood hazard
management programs are instrumental in stimulating
local programs to protect property and preserve the

TABLE 5-11
Relative importance of policy and background variables
in explaining scope and implementation of local
government flood hazard management programs, 1983

Standardized Regression Coefficients

Policy and Background Variables	Measures to Protect Property[a]	Measures to Preserve Environment[b]	Administrative Priority[c]
Federal Programs			
Years in NFIP	.20*	.20*	.03
NFIP status (regular/ emergency phase)	.20*	.14*	.05
Community use of local assistance programs	.19*	.19*	.04
State Programs			
Direct state flood-plain regulation	.12*	.12*	.06*
Community use of local assistance programs	.09*	.04	.13*
Regional Programs			
Council of governments active in flood hazard management	.02	.01	.08*
Special districts active in flood hazard management	-.02	-.03	.00
Background Variables			
Population of jurisdiction, 1980	.27*	.24*	.06
Size of jurisdiction (acres)	.03	.02	.01
Flood hazard areas: Acreage	-.01	-.07*	-.07*

(continued)

TABLE 5-11 (cont.)

Standardized Regression Coefficients

Policy and Back- ground Variables	Measures to Protect Property[a]	Measures to Preserve En- vironment[b]	Admini- strative Priority[c]
Percent developed	-.01	-.07*	-.04
Number of structures	-.03	.04	.26*
Single-family residential	.09*	.09*	.04
Multi-family residential	.07*	.01	.01
Commercial (stores, offices)	.03	.07*	-.01
Industrial	.10*	.06*	.05
Current development pressure	.04	-.07*	.08*
Estimated future development pressure	.01	.03	.10*
Availability of hazard-free sites for development	.19*	.20*	.06*
Flooding:			
Serious flood in past ten years	-.06*	-.04	.07
Frequency of damage due inadequate storm drainage	.06	.08*	.08*
Community concern with flooding:			
Perceived serious-ness of flood problem	.04	-.01	-.16*
Public interest in flood problem	.02	.00	-.02
Local officials' interest in flood problem	.08*	.08*	.08*
R^2	.362	.324	.202

(continued)

132

TABLE 5-11 (cont.)

Standardized Regression Coefficients

Policy and Back-ground Variables	Measures to Protect Property[a]	Measures to Preserve En-vironment[b]	Admini-strative Priority[c]
F-value significance	.0001	.0001	.0001

*Coefficient statistically significant at .05 level of confidence.

[a]Number of twenty-two flood hazard management measures adopted by local government: protection of future development from flooding is local goal; plan exists for flood hazard areas; use of up to six structural flood control measures: dams, reservoirs; small watershed projects; dikes, levees; channel improvements; diversions, bypasses; seawalls, groins; use of up to six nonstructural measures: elevation requirements, floodproofing requirements, special flood hazard areas ordinance, zoning regulations, subdivision regulations, building code; public infor-mation about hazard; land acquisition, relocation of development, location of public facilities outside of hazard areas; allowance of higher density elsewhere on property in exchange for low density use of hazard area; and preferential taxation to encourage open space land uses for hazard areas.
[b]Number of thirteen environmental management measures adopted by local government: protection of natural values is local goal; plan exists for flood hazard area; prohibition of floodway development; zoning regulations; subdivision regulations; land acquisition; relocation of development; public facility location outside of hazard area; erosion/sedimentation regulations; dredge and fill regulations; sand dune protection regulations; allowance of higher density elsewhere on property in exchange for low density use of hazard areas; and preferential taxation to encourage open space land use in hazard areas.
[c]Based on local government response to following survey question: "In comparison with other responsibilities assigned this person (person with lead responsibility for flood hazard management), would you say that flood hazard management has highest priority, high priority, low priority, or no priority?"

environment, and they are instrumental in increasing the local administrative priority of flood hazard management.

REGIONAL AGENCIES AND FLOOD HAZARD MANAGEMENT

Regional flood hazard management program components may be classified into four groups: (1) planning and coordination; (2) regulations; (3) land acquisition; (4) information and technical assistance. Table 5-12 shows the percent of the regional agencies responding to our 1979 survey of regional agencies that were using each of those program components.

Planning and technical assistance program components were common. Eighty-three percent of the regional agencies provided technical assistance to local governments; 75 percent included flood hazards in regional planning; 62 percent discouraged public investments in flood hazard areas; and 61 percent provide public information about flood hazards. Land acquisition and regulatory program components were rarely used, however. In general, regional agencies devoted little staff time to flood hazard management. The overwhelming portion of the agencies, 84 percent, spent less than one half person day per week on flood hazard management; only 4 percent had assigned one or more persons full time to dealing with flooding problems.

Regional agency personnel generally felt their flood hazard management programs were moderately or slightly effective in preventing increases in flood losses: 7 percent rated their programs very effective; 33 percent, moderately effective; 42 percent, slightly effective; and 18 percent, ineffective. Table 5-13 shows the relationship between the various regional program components and the regional agencies' evaluation of program effectiveness. Regulations were most strongly associated with effectiveness, followed closely by open space acquisition. Information and technical assistance components were less closely associated with program effectiveness, and planning and coordination components had little effect. Referring to Table 5-11, we found that multipurpose regional agencies had a significant effect on local administrative priority given to solving flood problems.

Table 5-14 identifies obstacles to expansion of regional roles. The most serious obstacles identified by regional agency personnel were lack of financial support and lack of public support. Other obstacles

TABLE 5-12
Regional activities in flood plain management[a]

Regional Roles	Percent of Regional Agencies (N = 585)
Planning and Coordination	
Discouraging public investments from locating in flood hazard areas through A-95 review process	62%
Include flood hazards in regional planning	75
Coordinate local flood plain management programs	44
Regulations	
Regulate flood hazard areas	11
Land Acquisition	
Acquire flood hazard areas for open space	7
Relocate existing development	2
Information and Technical Assistance	
Provide technical assistance to local government	83
Provide public information about flood hazards	61
Monitor and evaluate local programs	24
Designate flood hazard areas	20

[a]Question: With which of the following flood plain management roles is your agency currently involved? (Circle all that apply)

TABLE 5-13
Association of measures used in regional flood plain management with program effectiveness in preventing increased flood losses

Program Components	Association with Effectiveness	
	Gamma[a]	Chi-Square Significance
Regulating flood hazard areas	.60	.0001
Acquire flood hazard areas for open space	.51	.0016
Provide public information about the flood hazard	.40	.0001
Designate flood hazard areas	.35	.0004
Provide technical assistance to local governments	.35	.0001
Monitor and evaluate local flood programs	.33	.0001
Include flood hazards in regional planning	.33	.0001
Coordinate local flood plain management programs	.26	.0004
Discourage public investments from locating in flood hazard areas through A-95 review	.19	.0018

ns = Not significant at the .05 level of confidence.

[a]Gamma is a nonparametric statistical measure of the correlation between the variables, varying from -1 (+1) indicating a perfect negative (positive) monotonic association between two variables and zero indicating the lack of any association. It requires an assumption of ordinality in the measurement of two variables but takes advantage of that assumption to provide more consistent and readable results than chi-square, which varies with sample size and size of table.

TABLE 5-14
Obstacles to expanded regional flood plain management
programs

Obstacles	Percent of Regional Agencies Rating Obstacles:		
	Serious	Moderate	Minimal
Lack of financial support	53	31	16
Lack of public support	30	46	24
Member agency resistance to implementation of areawide policies	25	39	36
Role legislated by state government	21	28	51
Lack of interest by policy board	20	42	38
Flooding not perceived as a regional problem	19	40	41
Lack of appropriate professional personnel	18	32	50
Legal restraints in state law	14	25	61
Lack of technical assistance from state agencies	13	37	50
Lack of technical assistance from federal agencies	11	35	54

seen as serious by at least one in five respondents
were member agency resistance to implementation of
areawide policies, the role legislated for the agency
by state government, and a lack of interest by the
agency's policy board.

SUMMARY

This chapter has examined the scope and effectiveness of state and regional programs for flood hazard
management. The data show that the fifty states have
engaged in a wide variety of activities dealing with
flood hazards, and that those programs have had some
effect on the scope of local governments' flood plain
management programs. Regional agency programs were
more focused, but were only moderately effective.

State programs ranged broadly over areas of planning and coordination, incentives, regulations, land
acquisition and public investment, public information
and technical assistance, and post-disaster
assistance. Planning and coordination and technical
assistance were the two most prevalent state
activities. Resources devoted to all state programs
areas were generally slight, however. State program
variables had small but significant effects on the
scope and intensity of local government flood hazard
management programs, most notably on measures to protect property and local administrative priority given
to flooding issues. Regional agency programs may
encompass planning and coordination, land acquisition,
regulations, and information and technical assistance.
Planning and coordination and technical assistance
activities were the focus of most regional agency
involvement. Few resources were devoted to most regional
agencies' flood management programs. Regional
programs were viewed by their administrators as being
only slightly to moderately effective. Regulations
and flood hazard area acquisition were viewed by
regional administrators as the most effective program
components. Regional agencies were instrumental in
advancing the priority given to flood hazard management by local government program administrators.

NOTES

1. Platt and others (1980) have enumerated a
number of potential intergovernmental conflicts in the
management of flood-prone areas, including "...(1)
adoption versus non-adoption of any floodplain management measures whatsoever; (2) structural versus nonstructural approaches; (3) levels of protection to be

achieved through either structural or nonstructural means; (4) management of natural flood storage areas lying in more than one jurisdiction; (5) coordination of regulations; (6) coordination of acquisition and relocation; or (7) exercise of extraterritorial powers."

2. As part of our 1983 survey of local communities, we asked who was in charge of flood hazard management. In over a third of the communities, flood hazard management was handled by the chief executive officer (25 percent) or someone other than a department head (legislative body, 7 percent; planning board, 2 percent; town clerk, 1 percent; regional or state agency, 1 percent).

6
How Well Are Local Flood Plain Land Use Management Programs Working?

This chapter evaluates how well local flood plain
land use management programs are working and identifies
community and program characteristics that are
associated with effective efforts.

As discussed in Chapter 1, three different
indicators of program effectiveness are applicable to
an assessment of flood plain management: (1) avoidance
of hazard zone locations; (2) protection of property
from flood damage; and (3) program impacts on other
objectives, such as protection of the environmental
value of flood plains. Each indicator is investigated
in this chapter.

Avoidance of hazard area locations by new urban
development was measured in terms of the number of
flood plain building permits issued by communities in
1978 and 1982 and by the proportion of total community
development occurring in nonhazardous locations in
those two years. Table 6-1 shows the average and
median values for those two variables in 1978 and 1982.
The large difference between the mean and median values
indicates that the distributions are skewed with a few
extreme cases having very high values. Communities
participating in the regular phase of the National
Flood Insurance Program (NFIP) had issued a larger
number of permits for flood plain development and had a
lower percentage of new development occurring on
hazard-free sites.

To measure the effectiveness of programs in protecting property from flood damage and in preserving
the natural value of flood plains, in 1979 and in
1983 local officials were asked to rate their own
programs in terms of program effects on the exposure of
existing development to flooding, exposure of future
development to flooding and encroachment on natural
areas.[1] Respondents rated their programs using a

139

140

TABLE 6-1
Number and percent of flood plain permits

| | Status in National Flood Insurance Program | | | |
| | Regular Program | | Emergency Program | |
	Mean	Median	Mean	Median
1979 Survey				
Number of flood plain building permits issued in 1978	54	2	32	1
Percent of new construction located outside the flood plain, 1978	91%	99%	99%	99.6%
1983 Survey				
Number of flood plain building permits issued in 1982	16	0	5	0
Percent of new construction located outside the flood plain, 1982	93%	100%	95%	100%

three-point scale (very effective, moderately effective, not effective) in 1979 and a five-point scale (0 - not effective to 4 - very effective) in 1983.

Flood plain land use management was most effective in dealing with the exposure of future development to flooding, as shown by the data summarized in Table 6-2. Where that was a potential problem, 58 percent of the communities surveyed in 1979 and 48 percent of those surveyed in 1983 rated their program very effective. Far fewer programs were rated as very effective in dealing with the exposure of existing development to flooding. That difference occurs because many land use management methods intervene early in the development process and are not very useful in remedying mistakes in development after they have been made. It is perhaps also indicative of the respondents' optimism.

TABLE 6-2
Local rankings of program effectiveness

Goal	Percent of Jurisdictions[a]		
	Very Effective	Moderately Effective	Not Effective
Reduce exposure of existing development to flooding			
1979 Survey	15	52	33
1983 Survey	21	42	37
Reduce exposure of future development to flooding			
1979 Survey	58	38	4
1983 Survey	48	37	15
Reduce encroachment on natural areas[b]/ preserve natural values of flood hazard areas[c]			
1979 Survey	27	52	21
1983 Survey	33	42	25

[a]In the 1979 survey, effectiveness was measured on a three-point scale (very, moderately, not effective), while a five-point scale was used in 1983 (4 - very effective to 0 - not effective). For the comparisons reported here, 1983 scores of 0 and 1 are scored as not effective; 2 and 3, as moderately effective; and 4, as very effective.
[b]Wording in 1979 survey.
[c]Wording in 1983 survey.

These figures compare with 27 percent in 1979 and 33 percent in 1983 who thought their communities' programs were effective in dealing with encroachment on natural areas and the protection of the natural value of flood hazard areas.

In terms of impacts, most communities were issuing few building permits for construction in flood hazard areas, but in some cases the number and percent of permits was quite large. Flood plain land use management appears to be most successful in dealing with exposure of future development to flooding and preserving natural areas. One third (slightly more in 1983) of the 1979 respondents rated their own programs as ineffective in dealing with the flood problems of existing development. The remainder of this chapter will investigate reasons for variation in impacts from one community to another. The analysis proceeds in three stages. First, we identify key community characteristics and other contextual factors that were related to variation in program impacts. More specifically this analysis tests the importance of contextual factors alone in determining communities' success in limiting flood plain development and explaining variation in program effectiveness. In the second stage, the role of program composition and implementation in determining program impacts is tested. Finally, the impacts of different programs in different contexts are investigated in an effort to find out which flood plain land use management programs were most effective in specific local situations.

COMMUNITY CONTEXT AND PROGRAM EFFECTIVENESS

Initially, the direct relationship between contextual factors and program impacts is investigated by using product moment correlation coefficients to show the strength and direction of empirical associations. Only four of the impact measures discussed earlier are used in this stage of the analysis. These measures are (1) the number of flood plain permits issued in 1978 and 1982; (2) the percent of total new development locating outside of flood hazard areas in 1978 and 1982; (3) perceived effectiveness in preventing flood damage to future development; and (4) perceived effectiveness in preventing encroachment on natural areas. Few contextual factors were found to be related to effectiveness in dealing with exposure of existing development to flooding. Where such relationships exist, even though weak, they will be reported.

Physical Factors

The relationship (simple r) between the variables which comprise the physical context and the four program impact measures are shown in Table 6-3.

As the table shows, the number of flood plain permits and the percent of new development locating outside of flood hazard areas were strongly related to several physical factors. The number of flood plain permits issued by the community was positively related to the proportion of the community in the flood plain, coastal location, extent of flood plain development, and more intensive flood plain land uses, such as multiple-family residences and commercial development.

TABLE 6-3
Relation of physical factors to program impacts

Physical Factors	Number of Flood Plain Building Permits	Percent of New Development Located Outside Flood-Hazard Areas	Effectivness in terms of: Future Development	Natural Areas
Severity of risk				
1979 Survey	.12	-.17	ns	-.10
1983 Survey	.07	-.11	-.11	-.22
Number of recent floods				
1979 Survey	ns	ns	ns	ns
1983 Survey	.10	-.07	ns	-.10
Flood plain development				
1979 Survey	.23	-.30	-.08	-.07
1983 Survey	.08	-.24	ns	-.12
Flood plain uses				
Multiple-family				
1979 Survey	.27	-.27	ns	-.07
1983 Survey	.17	-.17	ns	-.08
Commercial				
1979 Survey	.24	-.24	ns	-.07
1983 Survey	.15	-.21	ns	ns
Industrial				
1979 Survey	.13	-.14	ns	ns
1983 Survey	.14	-.08	ns	ns
Proportion of community in flood plain				
1979 Survey	.42	-.45	-.08	ns
1983 Survey	.04	-.39	-.07	-.08
Flood control works used				
1979 Survey	ns	ns	ns	ns
1983 Survey	ns	ns	ns	ns
Coastal location				
1979 Survey	.34	-.34	ns	ns
1983 Survey	.07	-.15	ns	ns

Correlation Coefficients (simple r)

(continued)

TABLE 6-3 (cont.)

Physical Factors	Number of Flood Plain Building Permits	Percent of New Development Located Outside Flood-Hazard Areas	Correlation Coefficients (simple r) Effectivness in terms of: Future Development	Natural Areas
Supply of non-hazard sites				
1979 Survey	-.14	.28	.10	ns
1983 Survey	ns	.19	.21	.21

NS = Not significant at the .05 level of confidence.

This suggests that existing flood plain development may act as a magnet attracting still further urban development. Once significant public and private investment in the flood plain is made, it provides added incentive to develop. For the most part, the correlations between physical factors and flood plain invasion were stronger among the communities studied in 1979 than among those studied in 1983. Those differences (see Table 6-3) are probably due to the larger size, on average, of the communities studied in 1979 and correspondingly greater development pressure.

The other measure of communities' success in limiting flood plain invasion, the percent of total new development locating outside of flood hazard areas, showed similar relationships with the proportion of the community in the flood plain, coastal location and the extent of flood plain development. This impact measure also showed a moderately strong negative association with intensive flood plain land uses, particularly multiple-family and commercial development. Fairly strong positive relationships between the supply of non-hazardous sites for new development in a community and the proportion of new development locating outside the flood hazard areas were also found.

These relationships suggest that development is attracted to flood hazard areas by natural amenities such as the seashore or by proximity to existing development. The amount of development locating in the flood plain also varies inversely with the supply of alternative sites for new urban growth. Thus, the problem is intensified when there are few development sites outside the hazard area. Physical factors did

not, however, prove to be strongly associated with the
effectiveness measures based on local officials' perceptions of program impacts. The signs of these
associations are in the expected direction, with
programs rated as less effective in communities where
the risk of flood damage is greater, but as shown in
Table 6-3, the relationships are in many cases not
statistically significant.

A comparison of the flood plain invasion measures
obtained in both 1979 and 1983 for coastal and riverine
communities demonstrates that the amount and rate of
flood plain invasion was, indeed, much greater in
coastal communities. Table 6-4 shows the average number
of building permits and percent of total permits
located in the flood hazard area for coastal and
riverine communities.

Further analysis of only riverine communities also
lends support to the hypothesis that structural
solutions encourage invasion of the flood plain, as
discussed in Chapter 4. Table 6-5 shows the average
number of flood plain building permits and the average
percent of new development locating in the flood plain
for the non-coastal communities in the 1979 and 1983
samples. The difference between the mean number of
flood plain permits in communities with and without
structural protection are statistically significant for
both samples. The differences between the percent of
development in the flood plain of communities with and
without structural protection are statistically
significant as well. Thus, in non-coastal communities,

TABLE 6-4
Coastal location and flood hazard area development

Average Values

Location of Community	Number of Flood Hazard Area Building Permits	Percent of New Development Located in Hazard Area
Coastal communities		
1979 Survey	182 (N=150)	22% (N=139)
1983 Survey	35 (N=44)	18% (N=44)
Riverine communities		
1979 Survey	24 (N=891)	5% (N=804)
1983 Survey	10 (N=770)	6% (N=765)

TABLE 6-5
Structural protection and flood plain
invasion in riverine communities

Average Values

Availability of Structural Protection	Number of Flood Plain Building Permits	Percent of New Development Located in Hazard Area
No structural protection		
1979 Survey	5 (N=248)	3% (N=209)
1983 Survey	3 (N=260)	5% (N=260)
Some form of structural protection		
1979 Survey	31 (N=648)	6% (N=695)
1983 Survey	15 (N=539)	7% (N=534)

structural protection clearly seems to encourage
further flood plain invasion.

The effects of different types of structural
measures were also investigated. The influence of
dikes and levees is particularly noticeable. Table 6-6
shows the mean values in 1979 and 1983 for the two
measures of flood plain development for communities
with and without dikes and levees. The difference
between the two means for number of permits and two
means for percent of flood plain development are
statistically significant for both the 1979 and
1983 samples. No other structural measure showed as
strong an influence, suggesting that, while structural
protection in general encourages flood plain development, communities with dikes and levees are even more
likely to experience invasion of the flood plain.

Structural protection was also one of the
contextual factors found to be correlated with the
effectiveness of flood plain management programs in
dealing with existing flood hazard area development,
but the association was weak (r=.10). Effectiveness in
dealing with existing development was negatively
associated with intense flood plain land uses,
particularly commercial development.

This stage of the analysis indicates that the
physical characteristics of a community, and
particularly the flood hazard area, are related to the
impact measures based on the location of development
(number of flood plain building permits issued/percent

TABLE 6-6
Dikes and levees and flood plain development

Average Values

Use of Dikes or Levees	Number of Flood Plain Building Permits	Percent of New Development Located in Hazard Area
No dikes or levees		
1979 Survey	17 (N=684)	4% (N=612)
1983 Survey	7 (N=637)	6% (N=636)
With dikes or levees		
1979 Survey	48 (N=201)	8% (N=188)
1983 Survey	26 (N=163)	10% (N=159)

of new development outside of hazard area). A coastal location or structural protection in a riverine community were both related to continuing flood plain invasion. The proportion of the community in the flood plain and the extent of existing flood plain development were also positively related to the flood plain invasion measures. While physical factors were strongly associated with the two measures of flood plain invasion, they showed very little relation to the measures of program effectiveness based on local officials' perceptions of impacts.

Governmental Factors

Table 6-7 shows the relationships (simple r) between governmental factors and program impacts. These relationships are somewhat weaker than those of the physical factors just examined, but reveal some important information, nonetheless.

Direct state regulation showed a slight association with both the number of flood plain permits and the percent of new development locating outside of flood hazard areas among the communities surveyed in 1979 (but not for those surveyed in 1983). Direct state regulation was also positively associated with effectivensss in protecting future development from flood damage and preventing encroachment on natural areas. Direct state regulation was the only governmental factor positively related to effectiveness in dealing with exposure of existing development (not shown in Table 6-7).

Table 6-7
Relation of governmental factors to program impacts

		Correlation Coefficients (simple r)		
		Percent of New Develop- ment	Effectivness in terms of:	
Governmental Factors	Number of Flood Plain Building Permits	Located Outside Flood- Hazard Areas	Future Develop- ment	Natural Areas
Concern for Problem				
Priority of flood problems				
1979 Survey	.12	-.15	ns	ns
1983 Survey	.15	-.08	.23	.12
Lack of political support not an obstacle				
1979 Survey	.07	ns	.24	.17
1983 Survey	ns	ns	.24	.18
Intergovernmental Factors				
Enrollment in regular phase of NFIP				
1979 Survey	.07	-.11	.16	.08
1983 Survey	.07	ns	.15	.15
Direct state regulation of hazard area				
1979 Survey	-.16	.13	.09	.15
1983 Survey	ns	ns	.15	.14
Problems caused by neighboring jurisdictions				
1979 Survey	ns	ns	ns	ns
1983 Survey	ns	ns	ns	-.08

(continued)

TABLE 6-7 (cont.)

Governmental Factors	Number of Flood Plain Building Permits	Percent of New Development Located Outside Flood-Hazard Areas	Effectivness in terms of: Future Development	Natural Areas
Correlation Coefficients (simple r)				

Land Use Management Experience

	Number of Flood Plain Building Permits	Percent of New Development Located Outside Flood-Hazard Areas	Future Development	Natural Areas
1979 Survey	ns	ns	.19	.19
1983 Survey	(a)	(a)	(a)	(a)

NS = Not significant at .05 level of confidence.

[a]Data not obtained in 1983 survey.

The priority attached to the solution of flood plain problems was positively related to the number of flood plain permits issued. That is the opposite of the originally expected sign of the relationship. One possible explanation is the existence of some type of feedback which causes communities experiencing more rapid invasion of the flood plain to place a higher priority on solution of flood problems.

Several other factors were found to be related to the measures of program effectiveness. As expected, political support was positively related to effectiveness in terms of preventing flood damage to future development and to effectiveness in terms of preventing encroachment on natural areas. Previous experience with land use management was also positively related to both of those measures of program effectiveness. Enrollment in the regular phase of the National Flood Insurance Program was positively related to effectiveness in dealing with the exposure of future development to flood damage and encroachment on natural areas.

Socioeconomic Factors

Table 6-8 shows the relationship between several socioeconomic factors and program impacts. As could be expected, population was positively related to the number of flood plain permits issued by communities. It was not related, however, to officials' perceptions of program effectiveness. Both measures of the

TABLE 6-8
Relation of socioeconomic factors to impacts

Correlation Coefficients (simple r)

Socioeconomic Factors	Number of Flood Plain Building Permits	Percent of New Development Located Outside Flood-Hazard Areas	Effectivness in terms of: Future Development	Natural Areas
1979 Survey				
Population	.32	ns	ns	ns
Growth rate, 1970-75	.07	.07	.11	ns
Median family income	ns	ns	.13	.19
Median housing value	ns	ns	.16	.18
1983 Survey				
Population	.25	ns	.08	ns

NS = Not significant at .05 level of confidence.

standard of living were positively associated with the measures of program effectiveness. The median housing value was somewhat stronger than median income in that regard. The community's growth rate also showed a positive association with effectiveness, but the association was weak.

Regression Models for Flood Plain Invasion

Multiple regression models to explain the number of permits and the percent of new development locating outside of the flood plain were developed using the contextual factors as independent variables. Table 6-9 shows the results of regressing key contextual factors on the number of building permits issued by communities in 1978 and 1982 for development in flood hazard areas.

This regression model indicates that the proportion of the community in the flood plain was the most important factor in determining the number of flood plain

TABLE 6-9
Regression of context on number of building permits

Variables	Standardized Regression Coefficients	
	1979 Survey	1983 Survey
Proportion of community in flood plain	.30	ns
Population	.23	.22
Coastal location	.23	ns
Direct state regulation	-.07	ns
Multiple-family residences located in hazard area	.05	.09
Priority of flood problems	ns	.11
R^2	.33	.11
F-Value significance	.0001	.0001

NS = Not significant at .05 level of confidence.

permits issued in 1978, while population size was the key factor in 1982. Population was also found to be strongly related to the number of permits issued in 1978 as well, as was coastal location.

Table 6-10 shows the results of a similar model which regresses contextual factors on the percent of all new development locating outside of the flood hazard area. There is a marked similarity to the regression model for the number of permits issued, except population size is no longer an important factor.

The proportion of the community in the flood plain was found to be the most important contextual factor. Exposure to coastal flooding was negatively related to the percent of new development locating outside of the hazard area among the 1979 sample of communities. Communities with an ample supply of non-hazard development sites tended to have a larger proportion of new development occurring in non-hazardous locations. The extent of current flood plain development and the existence of commercial land uses in the flood plain

TABLE 6-10
Regression of context on percent of total new
development occurring outside of hazard area

Variables	Standardized Regression Coefficients	
	1979 Survey	1983 Survey
Proportion of community in flood plain	-.27	-.34
Coastal flooding	-.18	ns
Supply of non-hazard sites	.16	.10
Extent of previous flood plain development	-.08	-.09
Direct state regulation	.07	ns
Commercial uses located in hazard area	-.05	-.10
Priority of flood problems	.05	ns
R^2	.29	.21
F-Value significance	.0001	.0001

NS = Not significant at .05 level of confidence.

were negatively related to the percent of new development locating outside of flood hazard areas. The
priority placed on flood problems was significant among
the 1979 sample of communities, but showed the opposite
sign of the expected relationship. That may suggest
the priority assigned to solving flooding problems is
determined by flood plain invasion rather than being a
determinant of it, as noted earlier.

While considerable unexplained variation remains,
these models demonstrate the expected relationships
between several contextual factors and the measures of
flood plain invasion. Three physical factors were
found to be quite important for communities sampled in
both 1979 and 1983: (1) the proportion of the community
subject to the flood hazard; (2) location of intensive
land uses in flood hazard areas; and (3) the supply of
alternative development sites. The strong role of

these contextual factors indicates that the causes of
flood plain invasion have strong roots in the local
setting and may not be easily changed by manipulating
public policy. While not significant in the regression
models, closer analysis of the role of structural protection revealed that it also has substantial influence
in encouraging flood plain invasion, but mostly in
riverine communities.

Similar regression models using contextual factors
to explain variation in the perceived effectiveness of
local programs were not successful. In each model the
amount of variance explained (R^2) was less than .10.
The simple correlations between several governmental
and socioeconomic factors were, however, interesting.
Political support and previous experience with land use
management were both positively associated with perceived effectiveness.

Two explanations can be given for the fact that
contextual factors were related to the location of new
development, but not to any of the perceived effectiveness measures. First, effectiveness is more complex
than indicated simply by the amount of new development
occurring in hazard areas or even the percent of new
development locating there. A better indicator of
effectiveness may be changes in those variables over
time in a particular community rather than their level
as measured at a single point in time. Also, local
officials may view programs as effective even though
flood plain invasion continues to occur, if new
development in hazard areas is protected from flood
damage by being elevated or floodproofed.

PROGRAM CHARACTERISTICS AND PROGRAM EFFECTIVENESS

In this second stage of the analysis the relationship of program factors to impacts is investigated.
Table 6-11 shows the relationship between impacts and
three types of program variables for both the 1979 and
1983 samples: (1) measures of program scope and focus;
(2) four dummy variables indicating adoption of
particular classes of programs; and (3) three measures
of program implementation. The measures of program
scope and focus reported in Table 3-4 are
used in this analysis. Class 1 programs employ subdivision and zoning regulations; Class 2 programs use
elevation requirements or floodway regulations; Class 3
programs include land acquisition; and Class 4 programs
include relocation of development. While contextual
factors were found to be related to the measures of
flood plain invasion, program composition and implementation factors had little effect on the amount of new

TABLE 6-11
Relation of program to impacts

Correlation Coefficients (simple r)

Program	Number of Flood Plain Building Permits	Percent of New Development Located Outside Flood-Hazard Areas	Effectivness in terms of: Future Development	Natural areas
Program scope				
1979 Survey	ns	ns	.32	.21
1983 Survey	.15	ns	.39	.35
Program focus				
1979 Survey	ns	ns	.30	.23
1983 Survey	ns	ns	.36	.29
Class I program				
1979 Survey	ns	ns	.18	.17
1983 Survey	ns	ns	ns	ns
Class 2 program				
1979 Survey	.07	ns	.26	.09
1983 Survey	ns	.12	.15	ns
Class 3 program				
1979 Survey	ns	ns	.15	.23
1983 Survey	ns	ns	.20	.21
Class 4 program				
1979 Survey	ns	ns	ns	ns
1983 Survey	ns	ns	ns	ns
Level of funding				
1979 Survey	.15	-.11	.10	.07
1983 Survey	(a)	(a)	(a)	(a)
Staff time				
1979 Survey	.16	-.10	ns	ns
1983 Survey	.28	-.09	.17	.08
Qualified personnel				
1979 Survey	ns	ns	.26	.14
1983 Survey	ns	.09	.17	.19

NS = Not significant at .05 level of confidence.
(a) = Data not collected in 1983 survey.

flood plain development taking place. Program composition and implementation, however, did tend to be closely associated with the measures of perceived program effectiveness.

Both program scope and program focus were positively related to effectiveness in protecting future development from flood damage. Both measures of program composition were also positively related to effectiveness in preventing encroachment on natural areas, but to a lesser degree. In terms of specific program composition, the elevation and floodway regulations which comprise Class 2 programs were strongly related to effectiveness in terms of exposure of future development. Class 3 programs, which use land acquisition, were most strongly associated with effectiveness in dealing with encroachment on natural areas. Class 1 programs (those using subdivision and zoning) were positively associated with both of these effectiveness measures among the communities surveyed in 1979 but not among those surveyed in 1983. This difference may reflect the movement between 1979 and 1983 in communities with more effective programs into the regular phase of the National Flood Insurance Program, which requires the use building elevation requirements (a Class 2 program).

The most surprising finding is that the program composition variables were not strongly related to the two measures of flood plain development. While the signs of the correlation coefficients for Class 1 and Class 4 programs were in the expected directions, the relationships were not statistically significant. To this stage of the analysis, only physical factors have exhibited a strong association with the number of building permits issued for flood plain development and the percent of new development locating outside of flood hazard areas. Most other contextual factors and the program variables were not strongly related to these two measures. The findings indicate that programs which are considered effective by local officials do not necessarily reduce flood plain invasion. The programs may be viewed as effective because building and site design measures reduce the risk of property damage from flooding and because valuable natural areas are protected, even though portions of the flood hazard area are developed in urban uses.

With the exception of the qualifications of the staff, the implementation variables did not show the expected relationship with program effectiveness. Rather, funding and staff time were positively related to the number of flood plain building permits issued and negatively associated with the percent of permits issued by the community for development in non-hazardous locations. That is similar to the unexpected positive relationship reported earlier between priority and the invasion measures, which again suggests that flood plain invasion has a feedback effect on the implementation of local programs. Paradoxically, those communities which experience substantial flood plain invasion seem to undertake the most serious implementation efforts.

Class 4 programs (those using land acquisition and relocation) were positively related to effectiveness in dealing with the exposure of _existing_ development to flooding. The level of funding was also positively associated with that impact measure, which suggests that some land use management methods can produce desirable impacts in dealing with existing flood plain development.

Regression models using only program factors to explain impacts were developed based on the correlation analysis. The model for effectiveness in terms of exposure of future development to flooding was successful in explaining a moderate proportion of the variance in that variable. Table 6-12 shows the results of the regressions for both the 1979 and 1983 samples.

Most of the explained variation in this model is accounted for by two variables: the number of methods in use (program scope) and the qualifications of the implementation staff. The elevation and floodway regulations of Class 2 programs and the subdivision and zoning of Class 1 programs were significant in the model run on the 1979 data, but did not exert as much influence as the other two variables. With the 1983 data, Class 1 programs were associated with less effective results and the Class 2 program variable was not statistically significant. Apparently, the explanatory power of the program class variables in 1983 was captured by the program scope variable. While program focus showed a fairly strong bivariate relationship with effectiveness in dealing with future development, it was not included in the model because the number of methods (program scope) accounted for the same portion of variance in the dependent variable.

This stage of the analysis indicates that program composition and implementation alone have a moderate influence on program impacts. While several of the program variables showed strong bivariate associations with impacts, they are only able to explain about one-fifth of the total variance in any of the effectiveness measures. That indicates it is necessary to consider

TABLE 6-12
Regression for effectiveness in reducing damage to
future development

Variables	Standardized Regression Coefficients	
	1979 Survey	1983 Survey
Program scope	.20	.30
Qualified personnel	.23	.14
Class 2 program	.10	ns
Class 1 program	.06	-.22
R^2	.17	.20
F-Value significance	.0001	.0001

NS = Not significant at .05 level of confidence.

the interaction of program and context rather than
looking at those factors separately.

COMPLETE MODELS FOR EXPLAINING EFFECTIVENESS

In this section contextual factors are combined
with program variables to form a complete regression
model to predict impacts. These overall models
summarize the preceding analysis and provide a means of
determining the relative strength of the various relationships depicted by the conceptual model presented in
Chapter 1.

The complete models for the number of flood plain
building permits and percent of new development
occurring outside of hazard areas are very similar to
those presented in the section on contextual factors,
except they have been simplified by the substitution of
a community typology for two of the key physical
factors. Those two variables are: (1) the extent of
existing flood plain development; and (2) the supply of
non-hazardous development sites. The two variables are
expected to exert considerable influence on the
economics of flood plain development in the local community. Table 6-13 shows the correlation of the two
variables with other physical factors. The extent of
development was positively correlated with the
severity of risk. Communities with more urban develop
ment exposed to flooding perceived greater flood risk.
The extent of flood plain development was also

TABLE 6-13
Correlation among key physical factors

| | Correlation Coefficients (Simple r) | | | |
| | Extent of Flood Plain Development | | Supply of Alternative Development Sites | |
	1979 Survey	1983 Survey	1979 Survey	1983 Survey
Severity of risk	.29	.44	ns	-.10
Recent floods	ns	.26	ns	-.09
Flood plain land uses				
Multi-family	.40	.44	-.11	-.09
Commercial	.40	.44	ns	-.10
Industrial	.23	.24	ns	ns
Proportion of community in flood plain	ns	.15	-.23	-.18
Structural protection	.09	.23	.10	ns
Coastal location	.23	.12	-.07	ns

NS = Not significant at .05 level of confidence.

positively related to intensive flood plain land uses (multi-family residential, commercial, industrial), and to a coastal location. The supply of alternative development sites was negatively related to the proportion of the community in the flood plain. It was also negatively related to some intensive flood plain uses. It is important to note that alternative non-hazardous sites tended to be most often available in communities with less developed flood plains and with generally less serious flood problems.

Based on these two variables a "two-by-two" typology of communities was developed. Figure 6-1 shows the number of communities of each type in the sample. The two largest categories are Type 1 and Type 4 communities. In other words, a majority of communities had either little flood plain development and readily available alternative sites or moderate to

	Little Flood Plain Development	Moderate to Heavy Flood Plain Development
Alternative Sites Readily Available	TYPE 1 1979: N=452(38%) 1983: N=412(44%)	TYPE 2 1979: N=211(18%) 1983: N=110(12%)
Alternative Sites Limited or Unavailable	TYPE 3 1979: N=202(17%) 1983: N=230(24%)	TYPE 4 1979: N=311(26%) 1983: N=188(20%)

FIGURE 6-1: A typology of communities

heavy flood plain development with limited or unavailable alternative development sites.

Since this typology does not include all the relevant contextual variables which may affect flood plain land use management programs and their impacts, a number of other variables must be retained in the analysis in addition to the extent of flood plain development and supply of non-hazardous sites. The initial analysis used both individual contextual variables and the community typology. Table 6-14 shows the complete model for explaining the number of flood plain building permits issued.

Among the communities surveyed in 1979, the proportion of the community in the flood plain, the size of its population and coastal location were most strongly associated with the number of flood plain building permits issued by communities. All three of those factors were positively related to the number of permits issued. Among the communities surveyed in 1983, population and an intensive flood plain land use, multi-family residences, were significantly associated with the number of flood plain building permits issued.

Table 6-15 shows the factors related to the percentage of new development located outside of the flood plain. The key variables in both 1979 and 1983 were two physical characteristics of the community: the proportion of the community's land area in the flood plain and if it was a Type 4 community (with limited alternative development sites and moderate to heavy flood plain development). Among the 1979 communities, if the community was located in a coastal area, a lower proportion of permits were issued in nonhazardous

TABLE 6-14
Complete model for number of flood plain
building permits

	Standardized Regression Coefficients	
	1979 Survey	1983 Survey
Proportion of community located in flood plain	.28	ns
Population	.28	.17
Coastal location	.26	ns
Type 4 community	.13	ns
Direct state regulation	-.08	ns
Multi-family use of flood hazard area	ns	.13
R^2	.33	.09
F-Value significance	.0001	.0001

NS = Not significant at .05 level of confidence.

locations. Direct state regulation was significantly,
although weakly, associated with a higher proportion of
development in non-hazardous locations. Among the 1983
sample communities, state programs did not have a
significant impact, but the proportion of development
occurring in non-hazardous locations was positively
associated with the scope of local flood plain management programs.

The regression model for effectiveness in dealing
with future development improved somewhat with the
addition of several contextual factors. Compare Table
6-16 with Table 6-12. Among the communities surveyed in
1979, the important variables in the expanded model
shown in Table 6-16 are program composition and implementation variables: program scope, political support,
and qualified personnel. Lack of qualified personnel
was, as expected, negatively related to this measure of
program effectiveness. Lack of support by public
officials was also negatively related to program
effectiveness. Class 2 programs, which include elevation and floodway regulations, were positively related
to effectiveness in dealing with potential flood damage
to future development. Among the communities studied in

TABLE 6-15
Complete model for percent of new development
located outside of flood plain

	Standardized Regression Coefficients	
	1979 Survey	1983 Survey
Proportion of community located in flood plain	-.24	-.32
Type 4 community (extensive existing hazard area development/limited alternative sites for new development)	-.21	-.15
Coastal flood hazard	-.20	ns
Direct state regulation	.08	ns
Dikes and levees	.08	ns
Commercial uses in flood plain	ns	.10
Program scope	ns	.12
Staff time	ns	-.08
R^2	.28	.22
F-Value significance	.0001	.0001

NS = Not significant at .05 level of confidence.

1983, program scope and political support were key
factors associated with program effectiveness in
preventing damage to future development. Thus, program
variables and governmental factors seem to have a substantial influence on effectiveness. Note also that
Type 1 communities were more effective (in 1979 and
1983) and coastal communities were less effective (in
1979 only) in dealing with future development. Among
the communities studied in 1983, severity of risk was
negatively associated with program effectivenes. The
impact of this factor among the communities studied in
1979 may have been captured by the coastal flooding
variable, with which it was related.

The models for explaining effectiveness in terms of
preventing encroachment on natural areas left most of

TABLE 6-16
Complete model for program effectiveness in
reducing damage to future development

	Standardized Regression Coefficients	
	1979 Survey	1983 Survey
Program scope	.17	.22
Qualified personnel	.14	.06
Lack of political support	-.19	-.19
Class 2 program (elevation and floodproofing)	.10	ns
Type 1 community (little or no existing flood plain development/non-hazardous sites readily available)	.09	.09
Coastal location	-.12	ns
Enrollment in regular phase of NFIP	.06	ns
Flood problems caused by neighboring jurisdictions	-.08	-.06
Class I program	.08	ns
Median housing value	.07	(a)
Severity of risk	ns	-.17
State regulations of flood plain	ns	.06
Priority of flood hazard management	ns	.11
R^2	.23	.31
F-Value significance	.0001	.0001

NS = Not significant at .05 level of confidence.

[a]Data not collected in 1983 survey.

the variation in the dependent variable unexplained
among the communities studied in 1979, but was more
successful in explaining effectiveness among the communities studied in 1983 (see Table 6-17). Among the
1979 communities, the most important variable is a
program composition measure: the adoption of a Class 4
program which includes land acquisition and relocation.
However, with the exception of Class 1 programs and
availability of qualified personnel, the rest of the
significant variables are governmental and socioeconomic factors. Among the communities studied in
1983, program scope and focus were both positively and
strongly associated with program effectiveness in preserving the natural value of flood hazard areas.
Because the measures of Class 4 programs and program
focus are similar, the results with the 1979 and 1983
data are generally comparable.

A similar regression model using program and
contextual factors to explain effectiveness in terms of
existing development could not account for even one-
tenth of the variation in this dependent variable.
This plus the fact that one third of the survey respondents rated their own programs "not effective" in
dealing with the problem of exposure of existing
development to flooding suggests that flood plain land
use management is not the most appropriate solution to
that problem.

The regression models for effectiveness in terms of
future development and encroachment on natural areas
imply that a combination of program and contextual
factors determine program effectiveness. While a
greater number of contextual factors seem to be important, the influence of program variables (as indicated
by the standardized beta coefficients) is generally
stronger.

FITTING THE PROGRAM TO THE CONTEXT

The preceding analyses suggested to us that perhaps
context and program factors cannot be considered
separately, but rather impacts are produced by
the interaction of the two types of factors. Table 6-
18 shows that impacts varied by type of community in
both 1979 and 1983. Flood plain land use management
programs were much more effective and there was
less flood plain invasion in Type 1 communities in
both years. The Type 4 communities showed a much
greater number of flood plain permits and lower percent
of development in non-hazardous locations than the
other types of communities in both years. As might be
expected, flood plain land use management programs were
rated less effective when used in that context.

TABLE 6-17
Complete model for program effectiveness
in reducing encroachment on natural areas/
protecting natural values

	Standardized Regression Coefficients	
	1979 Survey	1983 Survey
Class 4 program (relocation)	.18	ns
Previous experience with land use management	.12	(a)
Median housing value	.12	(a)
Class I program (zoning and subdivision regulations)	.09	ns
Flood problems caused by neighboring jurisdictions	-.13	-.06
Qualified personnel	.08	.10
Direct state regulation of flood plain	.12	.07
Severity of risk of flooding	ns	-.25
Lack of political support	ns	-.11
Program scope	ns	.27
Program stringency	ns	.40
Type 2 community	ns	.08
R^2	.14	.26
F-Value significance	.0001	.0001

NS = Not significant at .05 level of confidence.

[a]Data not obtained in 1983 survey.

The relationship between program variables and the
effectiveness measures was found to vary considerably
among types of communities when each type of community
was analyzed separately. The relationship between
program and impacts was much stronger in Type 1
communities than in the other types of communities.

TABLE 6-18
Impacts by type of community

Type of Community	Number of Flood Plain Building Permits		Percent of New Development Outside of Hazard Area	
	1979 Survey	1983 Survey	1979 Survey	1983 Survey
Type 1: Limited existing development/ extensive alternative sites	15	6	98%	98%
Type 2: Heavy existing development/extensive alternatives sites	58	18	98%	94%
Type 3: Limited existing development/limited alternative sites	20	11	95%	95%
Type 4: Heavy existing development/limited alternative sites	107	20	82%	70%

	Percent Very Effective for:			
	Future Development		Natural Areas	
	1979 Survey	1983 Survey	1979 Survey	1983 Survey
Type 1: Limited existing development/extensive alternative sites	65%	54%	32%	38%
Type 2: heavy existing development/extensive alternative sites	58%	46%	25%	38%
Type 3: Limited existing development/limited alternative sites	53%	47%	29%	32%
Type 4: Heavy existing development/limited alternative sites	49%	39%	23%	20%

Table 6-19 compares the positive association between program variables and the two effectiveness measures for Type 1 and Type 4 communities. In general (seven of eight comparisons), scope and focus of methods used showed a stronger positive relationship with effectiveness in Type 1 communities than in Type 4 communities, which have considerable flood plain development and a limited supply of alternative sites. The relationships in the other two types of communities (Type 2 and Type 3) fell between the two extremes found in Type 1 and Type 4 communities.

The relationship between several program variables and the effectiveness measures also varied considerably depending on the presence of structural protection. Program scope, program focus and particularly Class 4 programs (those using land acquisition and relocation) were more strongly related to effectiveness in communities which had some form of structural protection.

This analysis suggests that program composition is in fact quite important in certain community settings. In riverine communities which have little existing flood plain development and readily available alternative development sites, program composition seems to be strongly related to effectivness. Further analysis showed that even Class 1 programs, which rely on subdivision regulations and zoning, were quite effective in dealing with exposure of future development in Type 1 communities. More focused programs that included land acquisition increased effectiveness still further.

TABLE 6-19
Relationship of program to effectiveness by type of community

	Correlation Coefficients (simple r)			
	Reduce Losses to future Development		Protect Natural Values/Reduce Encroachment	
	Type 1 Community	Type 4 Community	Type 1 Community	Type 4 Community
Program Scope				
1979 Survey	.35	.25	.23	.17
1983 Survey	.38	.42	.36	.29
Program Focus				
1979 Survey	.41	.20	.29	.21
1983 Survey	.34	.28	.28	.14

In an effort to identify the best flood plain land use management strategy for each type of community, we examined the percent of communities rated "very effective" in reducing damage to future development and preventing encroachment on natural areas for each combination of community type and program class. Table 6-20 shows the percent of "very effective" communities for various combinations of program and context.

Table 6-20
Effectiveness by community type and program class

| | Percent Very Effective for: | | | |
| | Reducing Loss to Future Development | | Protecting Natural Values/Reducing Encroachment | |
	1979 Survey	1983 Survey	1979 Survey	1983 Survey
Type 1 communities with:				
Class 1 program	48	15	33	11
Class 2 program	68	56	33	37
Class 3 program	86	63	50	50
Class 4 program	86	63	29	38
Type 2 communities with:				
Class 1 program	55	29	23	17
Class 2 program	61	47	24	33
Class 3 program	58	60	22	58
Class 4 program	90	(a)	25	(a)
Type 3 communities with:				
Class 1 program	36	18	20	23
Class 2 program	61	58	33	38
Class 3 program	63	72	37	20
Class 4 program	66	(a)	46	(a)
Type 4 communities with:				
Class 1 program	38	25	16	19
Class 2 program	55	37	12	16
Class 3 program	56	58	39	17
Class 4 program	57	(a)	0	(a)

[a]Insufficient number of cases (less than 5) to calculate percentage.

The most obvious feature of this table is that all
types of communities considered their program more
effective in protecting future development than in
preserving natural areas. Type 1 and Type 2
communities were generally rated more effective than
the other two types in this regard, indicating the
importance of the supply of alternative development
sites for effective flood plain land use management.
Almost half of the Type 1 communities were rated very
effective in 1979 in reducing losses to future
development when using only subdivision and zoning
(Class 1 programs), but Class 1 programs were not rated
as highly among the communities studied in 1983. Of
those using Class 2 programs, 68 percent were rated
very effective in 1979 and 56 percent in 1983. That
percent climbed to 86 percent of the Type 1 communities
using land acquisition (Class 3 programs) in 1979 (and
to 63 percent among those surveyed in 1983).

In Type 3 and Type 4 communities, Class 1 programs
using subdivision and zoning were rated very effective
by a much lower proportion of communities than those
with programs using elevation and floodway regulations
(Class 2) or land acquisition (Class 3).

In terms of preventing encroachment on natural
areas, only 50 to 60 percent of the communities in the
best combinations of context and program were rated
very effective in 1979 and 1983. Among the communities
studied in 1979, the most effective programs were in
Type 1 communities (little existing development and
readily available alternative sites) using Class 3
programs, which include land acquisition. Programs
using land acquisition (Class 3 programs) were rated
highly in type 1 communities in 1983 as well, but Class
3 programs were also judged to be effective in
preserving natural values among Type 2 communities in
1983.

Based on this analysis and the earlier parts of
this chapter, the following combinations of program and
context seem most likely to be effective:

Type 1 (Little Development, Readily Available
         Alternative Sites)

Class 2 (Elevation and Floodway Regulations)
         and if encroachment is a problem,
Class 3 (Land Acquisition)

Type 2 (Moderate to Heavy Existing Development,
         Readily Available Alternative Sites)

Class 2 (Elevation and Floodway Regulations) and

Class 3 (Land Acquisition or
Class 4 (Relocation of Existing Development)

Type 3 (Little Development, Few Alternative Sites)

Class 2 (Elevation and Floodway Regulations) and
        if encroachment is a problem,
Class 3 (Land Acquisition)

Type 4 (Existing Development, Few Alternative Sites)

Structural Protection, in conjunction with
Class 2 (Elevation and Floodway Regulations) and
Class 3 (Land Acquisition)

In Type 1 and Type 2 communities, where alternative
sites are readily available, the flood plain land use
management program should emphasize land use allocation
methods to influence the location of new development.
In Type 1 communities fairly simple methods, such as
those contained in Class 1 and Class 2 programs, may be
effective (the 1983 findings cast some doubt on that),
but the community should be particularly careful about
the location of intensive uses. Since intensive uses
such as commercial development and multiple-family
residences seem to attract additional flood plain
invasion, communities also may want to use the location
of public facilities and comprehensive planning to
guide those uses away from the flood plain. In Type 2
communities the emphasis is still on land use
allocation methods, but existing flood plain development can be expected to compound the problem by
attracting additional development. The program must,
therefore, be more concerned with protection of any
structures that do locate in the flood plain and, if
possible, relocating some of the existing development
to available alternative sites. Structural protection,
especially dikes and levees, should not be used in
communities which have alternative development sites
available.

In Type 3 and Type 4 communities where alternative
sites are limited or unavailable, the flood plain land
use management program must rely primarily on construction methods to influence the form of new development.
Since Type 3 communities have little existing development, the program should focus on elevation and
floodway regulations (Class 2 programs) with selective
land acquisition to protect valuable natural areas. In
Type 4 communities, some form of structural protection
is probably necessary. That structural protection
should only be used, however, in conjunction with Class
2 and Class 3 land use management methods. Those land

use management methods can reduce the risk associated
with any flood plain invasion induced by the structural
measures and can protect the natural values of at least
part of the flood plain.

By fitting the flood plain land use management
program to the local context as suggested here, it
should be possible to concentrate the limited
resources available for land acquisition, relocation
and structural protection where they are most needed.
Appropriate flood plain land use management methods are
prescribed for those communities where this analysis
has indicated they have a reasonable chance of success.
By consciously fitting the program to the local context
in this way, it should be possible to improve the
current performance of flood plain land use management.

SUMMARY

Local flood plain management programs currently in
place seem to be most effective in protecting future
development from flood damage. They are less effective
in protecting existing flood plain development. This
analysis found very little relationship between program
composition and flood plain invasion. Flood plain
invasion seems instead to be determined by contextual
factors, particularly those related to the size,
development and structural protection of the flood
hazard area. Program effectiveness, at least as perceived by local officials, was explained in part by the
composition and implementation of the local flood plain
land use management program. The number of methods
used in the program (program scope), elevation and
floodway regulations, and land acquisition seemed to be
particularly important program components in terms of
protecting future development. Land acquisition is a
necessary program component for program effectiveness
in preventing encroachment on natural areas. Further
gains in effectiveness seem to be most dependent on
tailoring programs to meet specific local conditions.
Analysis of program effectiveness in communities with
varying physical constraints suggests that different
mixes of program components will work best in
different types of communities. While significant
variation in program composition now exists, this
analysis suggests that encouragement of still
more diversity is necessary to produce really effective
local flood plain land use management programs.

NOTES

1. In 1983, the latter measure was phrased "preserve natural values of flood hazard areas."

7
Flood Plain Land Use Management Under the Microscope

To add depth to the analysis based on survey data reported in Chapter 6, flood plain management programs in three communities were studied in greater detail in 1979. Those three communities are Raleigh, North Carolina; Jackson, Mississippi; and Littleton, Colorado. In each of the communities local property tax and building permit records were investigated and a series of interviews was conducted in 1979. Flood plain landowners and occupants, real estate agents, developers, public officials and others concerned with flood plain land use were included in the interviews. Although the three communities do not represent the full range of programs or contextual situations examined in Chapter 6, the information collected provides additional insights concerning the impacts and effectiveness of flood plain land use management and the economic forces which may lead to flood plain development.[1]

Raleigh is a fairly typical medium-sized city with a moderately severe flash flood hazard on Crabtree and Walnut Creeks. Jackson is a somewhat larger city with severe backwater flood problems along the Pearl River and extensive structural modifications of the flood plain. Jackson experienced a major flood in the spring of 1979.[2] Littleton, a suburb of Denver, Colorado, is exposed to flash flooding along the South Platte River and several of its tributary watersheds. Littleton has combined regulation and large scale land acquisition with structural measures to mitigate the flood hazard. Selected characteristics of the three communities are summarized in Table 7-1.

RALEIGH, NORTH CAROLINA

Raleigh is the capital of North Carolina. It is located near the "fall line" which separates the

171

TABLE 7-1
Characteristics of case study communities, 1979

Characteristics	Raleigh, North Carolina	Jackson, Mississippi	Littleton, Colorado
Land area (sq.mi.)	48.30	64.30	10.30
Population (1975)	134,231	166,512	28,125
Growth rate (1970-75)	9.3%	2.5%	6.5%
1974 median income	$4,904	$4,514	$5,503
1970 median housing value	$19,673	$13,858	$22,994
Date of last flood	1973	1979	1965
Type of hazard	Flash	Riverine	Flash
NFIP program status	Regular	Emergency	Regular

Piedmont from the coastal plain region of the state. The city's population in 1979 was 156,727, but for planning purposes the city also controled an extra-territorial area with roughly 30,000 additional residents. Raleigh experienced substantial growth during the 1970s due to the expansion of activities related to state government and the development of the neaby Research Triangle Park as a prime location for major research-oriented facilities.

As shown in Figure 7-1, Raleigh and its immediate environs are located on two watersheds, Crabtree Creek and Walnut Creek. Both of those water-courses are tributaries to the Neuse River which lies to the east of the city. Because of the location of urban development in and around Raleigh with respect to the creeks, flood hazards were most severe in the Crabtree Creek watershed. That watershed drains approximately 150 square miles with most of the drainage area located upstream from the city. The primary flood threat was from intense local storms over the watershed; there was

little threat of backwater flooding from the Neuse
River. A lesser hazard existed along Walnut Creek, a
mostly undeveloped watershed of 46 square miles which
lies predominantly within the city. Little flood
problem existed along the Neuse River within the
vicinity of Raleigh since development in that flood
plain had been very sparse.

The flood hazard developed in Raleigh after 1955
as the city grew north into the Crabtree Creek flood
plain. Damaging floods were first experienced in 1957,
when a storm flooded 50 homes, the Farmer's Market, and
an area of industrial development, causing more than
$100,000 in damages. More severe events, however,
occurred in 1973: a February storm resulted in $750,000
in damages, while a summer storm reportedly caused
damages amounting to $350,000.

Approximately 16 percent of Raleigh's planning area
fell within the 100-year flood plain. It was estimated
that over 45 percent of Crabtree Creek watershed was
developed in 1979. Under those development conditions,
average annual flood damages were estimated by the
Corps of Engineers in 1977 to be $1,020,900. In
addition, some potential for flooding existed along
Walnut Creek; however, no studies had been undertaken
to assess the extent of the danger. Judging from the
absence of past flood damages in that watershed, it

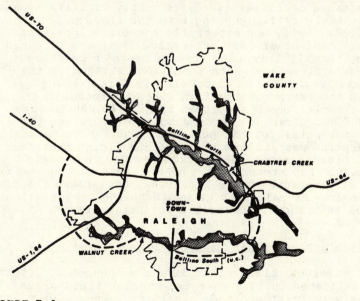

FIGURE 7-1
Raleigh study area

appears that flood problems in Walnut Creek were small.
Development induced by a new limited access beltway,
however, may change that situation in the future.

In its 1979 annual report to the federal Flood
Insurance Administration, the city estimated that 662
buildings, or approximately 1.7 percent of the
structures within its jurisdiction, were located in the
100-year flood plain. There were approximately 12,000
acres subject to flooding in Raleigh.

Development Decision Making on Raleigh's Flood Plain

Most people building or buying property in the
flood plain were aware of the potential for flooding
(although they seemed to discount its seriousness) and
what they had to do to satisfy flood plain building
regulations before they made a final decision to locate
there. Individuals involved in various residential and
commercial developments were interviewed. They had
taken a number of factors into consideration before
deciding where to put their buildings. The potential
for flooding was recognized, but it was given low
priority as a locational feature to be considered when
selecting a site.

It was found that increased building costs
associated with elevating flood plain structures
eliminated developers who were poorly capitalized and
most single-family housing from the flood plain. New
multiple family and especially commercial projects
found flood plain land attractive if it was situated
along heavily travelled streets or in an existing
business area. When such conditions existed in the
flood plain, commercial developers were willing to
spend the extra construction costs to locate there.
For example, one businessman spent $100,000 to elevate
a $900,000 structure because no other location had as
much potential for his business. Another commercial
enterprise was willing to lease a building that had
been flooded repeatedly because it was on a major
highway. The storekeeper found it advantageous to risk
flooding because of the locational advantages for his
business. He said that he would be there even without
flood insurance to cover his potential losses.

Raleigh's Flood Plain Land Use Management Program

Raleigh's flood plain land use management program
was initiated in 1973 when two overlay flood plain
zones were first adopted. In 1978 it underwent major
revisions when the city took steps to comply with the

requirements of the regular phase of the National Flood Insurance Program. Those two events represented the most important milestones in the Raleigh flood plain land use management program when the Raleigh case study was conducted.

The flood plain land use management program consisted of five component parts: (1) flood plain and floodway regulations; (2) land acquisition under the Greenway Program; (3) subdivision regulations; (4) sedimentation and erosion control regulations; and (5) zoning.

Of the five parts of the flood plain program, flood plain regulations were most important. The regulations required a flood permit for all new construction or additions within the 100-year flood plain. The regulations prohibited development within the floodway and required elevation or floodproofing in the floodway fringe. All requirements of the flood plain regulations had to be certified by a licensed engineer before a new structure was approved for occupancy. Certain activities, such as the storage of toxic or hazardous materials in the flood plain, were prohibited by the regulations.

The Greenway Program was active in acquiring land for open space and recreation along major creeks. By the summer of 1979 roughly 300 acres had been acquired. Of the total acreage acquired, 55 acres were purchased at the current market price, and the remainder was dedicated by land developers. Voluntary dedication was encouraged because developers of multiple family or cluster development could transfer density from flood plain areas to adjacent parts of the site. That decreased the program's negative economic impact on developers and the owners of vacant land.

The subdivision ordinance required that all lots have a buildable (i.e., non-floodway) site before they could be platted. Streets and culverts had to be certified by an engineer to meet special construction requirements and water and sewer systems had to be made flood resistant in flood plain areas.

Sedimentation and erosion control regulations required that development could not increase the velocity of runoff beyond a certain point. Retention ponds designed to contain flood waters generated by a ten-year storm were required until June, 1979. That requirement was dropped because such ponds were considered unsightly, too expensive, and ineffective in protecting development from major storms. In fact, the retention ponds were criticized for increasing flood crests of major storms by storing up and releasing runoff just when peak flows from upstream areas reached the city.

Originally, zoning was the basis for the flood plain regulations. In 1973 two overlay flood plain zones were adopted to control development: one for the floodway and one for the floodway fringe. In order to qualify for the regular phase of the National Flood Insurance Program, the city had to modify its ordinance somewhat. Since even minor modifications to the flood plain maps required lengthy notice and a public hearing as a zone change, Raleigh decided to replace the overlay zones with specific flood plain regulations. By 1979, zoning in the flood plains differed little from that in other parts of the city. It set zoning limits on the type and density of permissable development. It should be noted, however, that in 1979 most major new developments in the flood plain would have required rezoning prior to application for a flood permit. That acted as a damper on flood plain development. The zoning ordinance also included a conservation buffer zone which had been used in several areas to protect flood plains and lakeshore areas.

In addition to land use controls, a number of small scale structural measures were being undertaken to reduce flood problems in Raleigh. Eleven dams were being built by the U.S. Soil Conservation Service and Wake County in the Crabtree Creek Watershed to take some property out of the 100-year flood plain and reduce the amount of land in the floodway. The Army Corps of Engineers estimated that once all eleven structures were in place, average annual flood damages in Raleigh would be reduced to $175,800 (a reduction of over 80 percent).

An early flood-warning system for Crabtree Creek had been established, as a result of the 1973 floods. A number of commercial establishments had developed emergency floodproofing procedures which were triggered by the warning system.

Flood plain land use regulations were implemented by Raleigh's Planning, Inspections, and Engineering departments. The Planning Department reviewed requests for subdivisions and zoning changes, and administered the Greenways Program. All flood plain regulations were enforced through the Conservation Engineer's Office in the Inspection's Department. The Engineering Department played a minor role in the flood plain program; it was responsible for seeing that all streets and public utilities were built to flood plain standards.

Most of the Planning Department's expenditures on flood plain management were in planning and administering the Greenways Program. Approximately $40,000 each year was spent for the purchase of land. The Inspections Department spent roughly $100,000 a year to implement the regulatory parts of the program. That figure covered salaries, transportation, and other costs associated with enforcing the flood plain regulations. The program costs to the Engineering Department were too small to estimate.

Table 7-2 shows the total building activity in Raleigh and an estimate of flood plain development before and after the program. In 1978 the construction industry in Raleigh was enjoying one of its best years for new building starts. However, the absolute level of flood plain construction appears to have remained about constant over the period studied.

Most people owning flood plain property first became aware of flood plain regulations when they went to the Inspections Department to request a building permit. Early in the building permit process, it was standard procedure for inspectors to check a flood plain map to see if the applicant's property was subject to flooding. Raleigh did not attempt to directly inform the owners of vacant flood plain property of the building restrictions that had been imposed on their land except through public hearings held when the regulations were adopted. Although most lenders required

TABLE 7-2
New construction projects in Raleigh: 1971, 1974 and 1978

Year	Total Permits Issued	Units Built	Value of New Construction	Flood Permits Issued
Post-Program:				
1978	1,277	1,967	$101,064,330	8
1974	965	1,070	42,176,625	8
Pre-Program:				
1971	1,275	5,413	88,067,958	8

Source: "Monthly Summary of Building Permits," Raleigh Building Department. Flood permit estimates based on map location of 25 percent sample of building permits.

someone buying or constructing a building in the flood
plain to purchase flood insurance, that method of
informing potential owners of the flood program did not
appear to be foolproof. Several ways that a person
could buy flood plain land without being aware of the
hazard were brought to light by interviews with people
owning flood plain property.

It was normal practice for a potential buyer to
have his lawyer check deeds and tax records for "liens
and encumbrances," but there may have been no routine
check to discover potential flooding problems. A
lender did not require flood insurance unless (1) the
lot was or would be improved with a structure and (2)
the loan on the purchase was backed by the federal
government. In some cases, particularly when the
transaction involved raw land, personal savings were
used and a lender was never contacted.

In one large development where space was being
leased and rented, the realtor handling the project was
unaware that it was in the flood plain. The owner,
architect, engineer, builder and public officials had
all considered and complied with flood plain building
requirements, but except for the owner, no one had the
responsibility to inform the real estate agent of the
flood hazard. Not having been told of the flood
problem, the realtor did not inform his customers or
their lenders. As a result, flood insurance was not
purchased.

The Impacts of Raleigh's Program

Raleigh's flood plain land use management program
has had many different types of impacts; however, none
of them has been major. The program's impacts through
1979 are summarized in Table 7-3. The program seems to
have reduced private property damage through flood
flood plain building regulations. The regulations also
held down the price of some vacant flood plain property.
Flood plain regulations increased construction costs,
thereby precluding almost all new residential development from the flood plain. The availability of flood
insurance increased the value of existing flood plain
development and may have been an important consideration in some decisions to locate commercial operations
in the flood hazard area. The program's effect on
annual public property damages and tax revenues
generated by flood plain land, as well as program
administration costs, were quite small. Impacts on
environmental quality were also minor since only a
small amount of land had been included in the Greenway
System and most of the flood plain could be developed
if structures were elevated in compliance with the

TABLE 7-3
Summary of net program impacts

Category of Impacts	Impacts
Economic Impacts	
Annual private property damage	Slight decrease
Losses of production, stocks and wages	Slight increase
Land values	Slight decrease
Construction costs	Increased
Locational effects	Major
Fiscal Impacts	
Annual public property damage	Slight decrease
Program administration costs	Minimal
Property tax revenues	No impact
Environmental Impacts	
Open space	Slight increase
Natural resources protection	Increased
Water quality	Undetermined
Social Impacts	
Health and safety	Slight increase
Recreation	Slight increase
Equity	No impact

regulations. Health and safety and recreational
opportunities increased, resulting in some positive
social impacts.

Flood plain land use management had not adversely
affected Raleigh's economy. Most economic consequences
of the program were beneficial (i.e., reduced flood
losses), except in particular instances where land
values were depressed and construction costs increased.

No direct measurement of expected flood losses was
possible as a part of this study; however, changes in
expected losses could be inferred from the program
performance data. The small amount of flood plain
development after the program was initiated and the
requirement that all new development be elevated or
floodproofed probably kept annual damages below the
level that would have been reached without the program.

Raleigh's flood plain program may have actually
increased damages due to interruptions of production,

180

perishable stocks, and lost wages. Relocation of
existing commercial development was not a part of the
program; therefore, developments such as the Farmer's
Market which suffered large losses in the past were
likely to experience future damages. Although it was
likely that the owners and occupants of those
businesses were protected by insurance against
structural damages and losses to stock, they were not
reimbursed for lost income during flood events. In
addition, employees of flood-struck establishments
would likely be laid off while repairs were being made.
Since most new development in the flood plain was
commercial, a major storm would likely cause
considerable losses in wages and production.

Table 7-4, derived from a sample of vacant flood
plain and nonflood plain parcels, indicates that flood
plain land was not increasing in value as fast as
nonflood plain property. A similar analysis of a
limited sample of vacant parcels located entirely in
the floodway showed that their values had actually
decreased by about 5 percent between when the program
was initiated and 1979. Similar impacts were probably
not widespread, however, because most parcels platted
in Raleigh had buildable sites outside the floodway.

Construction costs increased substantially due to
the elevation and floodproofing requirements of the
program. It was not possible using existing public
records to determine the percentage by which costs had
risen; however, developers and city officials estimated
increases in construction costs of 10 to 20 percent.
Those additional expenditures did not appear to have
slowed construction activities in the city, but they
did seem to have affected development patterns somewhat. Flood permits issued for new construction since

TABLE 7-4
Assessed value per acre of land in Raleigh,
1968 and 1978

Type of Parcel	Number of Parcels	Average Values 1968	1978	Percent Change
Flood Plain Property	11	$833	$1,740	+108.2
Nonflood Plain Property	11	$896	$2,493	+178.2

Source: Wake County Tax Department records.

Raleigh entered the regular phase of the National Flood Insurance Program in 1978 were all for commercial development. Several realtors and developers attributed that to increased site development costs which they thought precluded residential development as an economic use of flood plain land.

Fiscal impacts associated with flood plain land use management in Raleigh were minimal. Annual public property damage from flooding was not decreased greatly by the program. Property tax revenues derived from flood plain property were kept stable by the availability of flood insurance. In addition, the costs of administering the program and constructing public facilities in a manner that complied with special flood plain requirements were low.

Little impact on property tax revenues collected from flood plain parcels was evident. As mentioned previously, flood plain land did not increase in value as fast as nonflood plain properties. Therefore, some additional tax revenues might have been collected if it were not for the program; however, two other influences of the program offset those losses. One, higher construction costs resulting from flood plain regulation increased the amount of real property subject to city taxes. In addition, the availability of flood insurance assured that existing developed properties would maintain their values even if they were flooded, thus further strengthening the city's tax base. The impacts of the program on tax revenues were minimal.

Implementation expenditures for administering and enforcing the program in 1979 amounted to only .002 percent of Raleigh's overall operating budget. Those expenditures represented only 10 percent of the total cost of the building inspections program.

Another facet of Raleigh's flood plain management program, the acquisition of flood plain land for inclusion in its Capital Area Greenways System, was also only a small proportion of municipal expenditures. The Greenways Program's operating budget and land acquisition appropriations amounted to only .003 percent of the general operating budget. The total expenditures on the Greenways program could not be attributed to flood plain management because it provided an array of other benefits, such as recreational and educational opportunities, which were, in fact, its principal objectives. Since costs associated with program implementation and public facility construction were relatively low and property tax revenues have remained stable, it appears that Raleigh experienced only minor fiscal impacts in managing its flood plains.

Almost all of the land included in the Greenways System was flood plain property which was protected from future urbanization, but the overall impact of this program on environmental quality was minor. Only 10 percent of the Raleigh flood plain was included in the system and most of that property was located in sections of the city where development pressures were not great.

Enforcement of flood plain construction regulations seemed to be carried out in a consistent and equitable manner. Professional engineers had to certify that building heights and floodproofing requirements were satisfied, thus providing an assurance of compliance. Field checks of building sites throughout the city found no violations and revealed enforcement to be equitable among all income groups and sections of the city.

JACKSON, MISSISSIPPI

Jackson is a medium-sized city of approximately 205,000 people. It is the capital of Mississippi and serves as a distribution center for the Deep South. In the period between 1970 and 1977, Jackson's population grew by 33.2 percent compared to a 14.2 percent increase for the entire metropolitan area. Most of that growth occurred in the northern sections of the city below Ross Barnett Reservoir. See Figure 7-2. There were six other jurisdictions in the Jackson area: Rankin County, Madison County, Hinds County, and the Towns of Pearl, Richland, and Flowood.

Most of Jackson is situated within the Pearl River Basin, although some western and northern portions of the city are located in the basin of the Big Black River. Eight tributaries to the Pearl River pass through the city. All were subject to flooding from two sources: (1) direct runoff from intense local storms; and (2) backwater from the Pearl River caused by storms over upper reaches of the river basin.

Much of the older portion of the city is located within the Town Creek watershed, and periodic flooding of portions of the Central Business District was of long-standing concern. Flooding of the other creeks was a growing problem as development encroached on the flood plains along those streams. Large floods on Purple Creek were recorded in 1953, 1962, and 1966 with little property loss, but by 1979 similar floods would have caused considerable damage to recent development. Similar situations existed along Lynch Creek and Cany Creek.

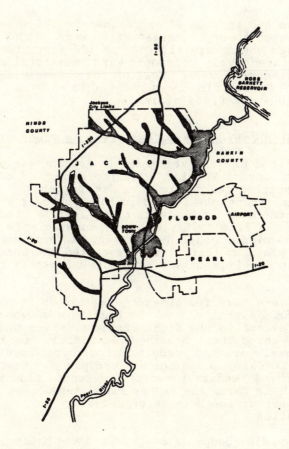

FIGURE 7-2
Jackson study area

There were a number of major floods on record for the Pearl River at Jackson. The most severe occurred on Easter weekend in 1979. Flood stages of more than twenty-five feet above normal were recorded. The 1979 Easter flood caused up to $500 million in damages in the Jackson area, compared to the $1.2 million in losses which resulted from the previous major flood on the Pearl River.

In 1971 the Army Corps of Engineers estimated that $68.8 million of private property was located in Jackson's 100-year flood plain. In addition, it calculated that a 100-year frequency flood would cause damages of $7.3 million. Although Jackson grew rapidly between 1971 and 1979, more recent studies of expected damages had not been conducted.

Jackson had an area of approximately 105 square miles of which about 11 square miles were in the flood plain. Over one square mile of the 100-year flood plain was intensively developed with commercial and residential development. Most of the property damaged by the 1979 Easter flood was located in and just outside the 100-year flood plain.

Development Decision Making on Jackson's Flood Plain

Most flood plain development in Jackson was single-family residential housing, with the exception of several shopping and office park developments. Moderate income people living in the Hightower area were once the main inhabitants of the city's flood plain. By the late 1970s, however, considerable wealthy and middle class development had encroached on the flood plain so that it characterized the hazard area. That development was severely damaged by the Easter flood.

There were very few absentee landowners in the flood plain. Almost all of the housing was owner-occupied, except in the Hightower area, where most residents rented their housing. In addition to land-owners, developers and lenders had been involved in decisions to develop Jackson's flood plain. Most developers and lenders incurred few losses from the 1979 flood; in fact, the Easter flood stimulated lending and construction because of necessary rehabilitation.

Flood plain occupants bought land and houses, and chose to stay there after being flooded in 1979, for a number of reasons. Factors that influenced locational decisions can be grouped into two categories: those that affected the initial phase of flood plain property development and those that persuaded flood victims to remain within the reach of the river. Jackson's flood plain program had little influence on initial decisions to locate in the flood plain; however, it had some impact on flood victims' ability to relocate.

Three sets of factors contributed to the growth and development of flood plain property in Jackson: (1) ignorance of the flood hazard; (2) attractiveness of the flood plain for development; and (3) structural measures undertaken to reduce future flood damage.

Ignorance about flood hazards was a significant factor contributing to flood plain development in Jackson. The flood plain in Jackson was deceptive. In many cases no water was in sight. Unwitting buyers had

to rely on the city, the developer or the banker to
determine if a particular area was flood-prone. Even
in areas which experienced as much as eight feet of
flooding, many homeowners interviewed claimed to have
been completely unaware that their property was subject
to flooding. In those instances, information about
flood insurance and flood plain building regulations
never reached the property owners even though much of
it had been available from the Corps of Engineers for
some time. Therefore, the risk of flooding was often
not even considered in the selection of a place to
live.

The physical attractiveness of the floodplain was
another major reason for extensive flood plain development in Jackson. Many of the city's more wealthy
neighborhoods and more prosperous businesses were
located in the flood hazard area because of the
proximity of the flood plain to the Jackson Country
Club and Colonial Country Club. Desirable schools,
stylish shopping centers, and several major highways
also served to attract development to the flood hazard
areas.

Structural measures to reduce the potential for
flooding may also have induced some flood plain
development. A levy built to protect the downtown
section of Jackson encouraged people to develop there
and to forgo the purchase of flood insurance. Some
Jackson residents mistakenly thought that the Ross
Barnett Reservoir was meant to provide flood control,
while others believed that its flood reduction
capacities would keep their property from being
flooded. Neither the dam nor the levee offered significant protection during the Easter flood.

Very few people who were flooded during Easter,
1979 chose to relocate during the year following the
flood. A number of factors, such as the provision of
flood insurance and disaster relief loans, may have
encouraged people to rebuild in the flood hazard area,
and in some cases may have discouraged relocation.
Where insurance was inadequate to cover flood damages,
flood victims were left with the choice of either
securing a disaster relief loan and rebuilding, or
moving and losing much of the investment in their
property. Most of those who were flooded found it
financially advantageous to stay in the flood plain.

This phenomenon can be best summed up by examining
the plight of one homeowner. He was unaware that his
home was in the flood plain until the water started
rising in his yard. He had no flood insurance at the
time of the flood, but was required to purchase it

after the flood to qualify for a disaster relief loan. The disaster relief loan with an interest rate of 3 percent was used to pay a $45,000 repair bill on his $65,000 home. Although this flood victim did not want to remain in the flood plain, he said that he had to rebuild so that he could protect his investment. If property values ever return to the pre-flood levels in his neighborhood, he hopes to sell and move to another section of the city.

In sum, decisions to locate and remain in the flood plain in Jackson resulted from: (1) a lack of knowledge of the flood hazard; (2) a desire to live in good neighborhoods; (3) an attractive business climate; and (4) institutional arrangements that gave flood victims no alternative but to return to their flooded properties. The Easter flood served to highlight those factors.

Jackson's Flood Plain Land Use Management Program

In response to frequent past flooding, Jackson initiated steps to decrease the exposure of new development to the flood hazard in 1973. The flood plain land use management program, as amended in 1979, required newly constructed buildings to be elevated to the level of the 100-year flood as defined by the Corps of Engineers and later by the Federal Insurance Administration. While those requirements were more stringent than the minimum required for participation in the emergency phase of the National Flood Insurance Program, they were somewhat less stringent than those in place in Raleigh and Littleton during their participation in the emergency phase.

In April 1973, the Jackson City Council passed a resolution that instructed the Director of the Building Department to, "...review all building permit applications to determine if the proposed construction is consistent with the need to minimize flood damage" and "...to make recommendations for construction in all locations which have flood hazards." After 1974 those provisions were interpreted to mean elevating all new structures to the level of the 100-year flood. Jackson received its Flood Hazard Boundary Maps in November 1978 and moved into the regular phase of the National Flood Insurance Program in 1980.

Jackson's flood plain land use management program consisted of other features in addition to elevation requirements. These included: (1) a site Plan Review Committee to make technical recommendations on new subdivision and multi-family projects; (2) sewer manholes elevated to 100-year flood level; (3) purchase of Mayes Lake Park (located in the flood plain) for recreational use; and (4) eventual flood plain zoning.

The elevation requirements applied to new structures and not to additions or remodeling. Field surveys or an engineer's certification of "as built" elevation was not required. Filling was used almost exclusively as the method of elevation. Most structures used "slab on grade" construction. By 1979 no structures had been floodproofed and only one had been elevated on piles.

The Site Plan Review Committee reviewed the technical aspects of all new subdivisions and multi-family complexes. This review included a comparison of the lowest contour on the site with that of the 100-year flood. Developers had to agree to elevate all structures in the flood hazard area to the level of the 100-year flood. Inspection for compliance was part of the routine building inspection process.

All new manholes were required to be elevated for protection against floods. Other public facilities were not necessarily elevated or floodproofed. For example, streets were not required to be elevated to the 100-year level. In 1978, a new $70 million dollar sewage treatment plant was located in the flood plain. The plant was protected by a dike which afforded protection against the 100-year flood event; however, the plant suffered $40 million in damages in the Easter flood when this dike was overtopped.

The city also purchased one large tract of flood-prone land in the Mayes Lake area. That property was used as a natural area. The city did not, however, have an ongoing program for the acquisition of flood plain land and had not focused land acquisition on the purchase of property likely to be developed.

In addition to those land use management activities, Jackson was involved in other flood plain activities. The city was directly responsible for two structural remedies applied to flood problems: (1) the construction of a tube to carry the 100-year flood event on Town Creek; and (2) clearance of debris and undergrowth from drainage ditches. In addition, Jackson worked with other units of government to control flooding. Levee protection for the downtown and the fairgrounds area was obtained by working with the Corps of Engineers. The Ross Barnett Reservoir, designed for flood reduction in addition to its water supply and recreation functions, was financed through a joint effort with the state of Mississippi. However, none of those structural measures provided a complete cure for the city's flood problem.

The responsibility for implementing the flood plain land use management program was split among various departments within the city. Building elevations were regulated by the building department; the city engineer was responsible for the floodproofing of manholes; and the director of planning was the local flood insurance coordinator. All three departments were represented on the Site Plan Review Committee.

Implementation costs of the program could only be estimated because it was handled as a part of the building permit and subdivision approval process. The planning director estimated that about 3 to 5 percent of the staff time devoted towards approving building applications in 1977 was spent on flood related activities. That represented a commitment of city revenues somewhere between $10,000 and $24,000 per year. In addition to money spent for enforcement and inspections, the city had expended $100,000 to buy flood plain land (Mayers Lake Park).

Table 7-5 lists the number of new construction projects in Jackson for selected years between 1970 and 1978. The table indicates that new construction was at an all time high for the decade in 1978 and that flood plain development had reached its lowest point. However, while the proportion of new development locating

TABLE 7-5
New construction in Jackson: 1970, 1973, 1976, and 1978

	Total Number of Permits Issued	Number of Permits Sampled	Number of Sampled Permits Located in the Flood Plain	Estimated Percent of Total Permits in the Flood Plain
1970	410	41 (10%)	8	26.8
1973	540	135 (25%)	38	28.1
1976	370	37 (10%)	8	21.6
1978	800	80 (10)	9	11.3

Source: Jackson Building Department permit records.

in the flood plain in 1978 was less than half the 1973 high, it was still over 10 percent of all new development, which was quite high.

Awareness of the flood plain land use management program among the general public, flood plain residents, lenders and developers in Jackson was rather limited for several reasons. One factor that kept people from being informed about the program was that banks and other lending institutions neglected to require some of their clients to purchase flood insurance. One banker even admitted that, prior to the Easter flood, it was not a standard procedure to check if a house was in a flood plain. Furthermore, some lenders and insurance agents seemed to have been confused about who could qualify for flood insurance. One homeowner was told he was in the 500-year flood plain and, therefore, could not get insurance.

In addition, interviews indicated that some structures within the 100-year flood plain were not required to meet flood plain elevation requirements even though they were constructed after the flood plain program was initiated. That type of inconsistent enforcement resulted in people buying flood-prone houses without knowing it. Also, there were other residents who remained uninformed about the program because they failed to check flood hazard maps before buying land or renting buildings. There were even instances where the flood insurance purchase requirement was bypassed by the use of private funding for construction.

It is apparent that no one governmental body or private institution felt the responsibility of informing all people about the flood hazard and the flood insurance program in Jackson. The Easter flood abruptly and abusively filled that void. The disaster encouraged banks and the city to take a closer look at flood plain development and to enforce the provisions of the National Flood Insurance Program more actively.

The Impacts of Jackson's Program

During the period of Jackson's program studied (1973-1979), the proportion of development locating in the flood plain declined. The elevation of new construction and floodproofing of some public facilities decreased potential public and private flood damages slightly. Since the regulations were not applied to commercial and industrial development, the program did not affect potential losses in production stocks and wages. Construction costs probably increased slightly due to elevation requirements, but those requirements

190

did not produce significant locational effects. Program administration costs were quite small and no reduction in tax revenues resulted from the program. The program had negative environmental impacts, if any, due to massive flood plain filling. Some positive impact on recreation opportunity could be attributed to the program. Table 7-6 summarizes program impacts.

Annual flood losses to private property may have been reduced somewhat by the city's elevation requirements on new flood plain construction. However, the actual extent to which damages were reduced was impossible to determine. An accurate assessment of the magnitude of property damage reductions due to flood plain land use management would require field measurements of the elevation of all flood plain construction that occurred while the program was in operation since no certification of as-built elevation was required in Jackson. Instead, inspectors from the Building Department checked compliance with elevation requirements through visual inspection ("eyeballing") of new

TABLE 7-6
Summary of net program impacts

Category of Impact	Impact
Economic Impacts	
Annual private property damage	No impact
Losses of production, stocks and wages	No impact
Land values	No impact
Construction costs	Slight increase
Locational effects	Not evident
Fiscal Impacts	
Annual public property damage	Slight decrease
Program administration costs	Undetermined
Property tax revenue	No impact
Environmental Impacts	
Open space	Slight increase
Natural resources protection	Undetermined
Water quality	Undetermined
Social Impacts	
Health and safety	No impact
Recreation	Slight increase
Equity	Slight decrease

TABLE 7-7
Assessed value per acre of land in Jackson,
1973 and 1978

Average Values

Parcel Type	1973	1978	Percent Change
Total			
Outside 100-Year			
Flood Plain (n=30)	$2,380	$2,442	2.6
Flood Plain (n=33)	2,189	2,148	-1.9
Vacant Properties			
Outside 100-Year			
Flood Plain (n=20)	4,031	4,023	-0.2
Flood Plain (n=23)	1,865	1,971	5.7
Developed Properties			
Outside 100-Year			
Flood Plain (n=10)	6,700	6,983	4.2
Flood Plain (n=10)	8,351	8,071	-3.7

Source: Jackson Tax Department files.

The estimated expenditure of between $10,000 to
$24,000 a year to implement Jackson's flood plain pro-
gram obviously did not represent a significant tax
burden on the city's 205,000 residents. The costs of
flood plain land use management may have been even less
than estimated, because most of the steps taken to
implement the program would have been done anyway
during the building permit process. For that reason,
the implementation expenditures for flood plain management were very small, indeed.

While Jackson's program did not cost much to
operate or significantly affect overall tax revenues,
it also had very little positive impact in terms of
reducing flood damages to public property. The Easter
flood, although considerably greater than the 100-year
event, illustrates the negative fiscal impacts of
flooding. Table 7-8 lists the damages that were incurred by public facilities. The costs of emergency
relief and emergency services to city taxpayers was not
ascertained, but were thought to be significant. Furthermore, damages to private property (see Table 7-9)
reduced property tax revenues because the assessed
values of flooded houses were lowered by an average of

TABLE 7-8
Damage to municipal facilities caused by
1979 Easter flood

Type of Damage	Amount of Damages
Debris clearance	$ 279,112
Flood control structures	45,640
Road system	832,481
Public buildings	65,943
Public utilities	2,036,541
Other	12,067
Total	$3,271,784

Source: Compiled using estimates obtained from the
City of Jackson and the State of Mississippi.

TABLE 7-9
Private property damaged by the 1979 Easter
flood in Jackson

Structure Type	Number Flooded
Single family and duplex structures	1,902
Apartments	372
Mobile homes	40
Commercial and industrial businesses	730

Source: Jackson City Planning Board by aerial
photography taken at the time of crest (April 7, 1979).

$16,674 (reduced from #35,218 to $18,544). While the
flood plain land use management program had little
fiscal impact, the Easter flood had considerable fiscal
impact, some of which might have been prevented by a
more aggressive program.

It is also apparent, based on the orientation of Jackson's flood plain program, that it did not preserve the natural environment. Construction in the flood plain was generally built on fill. That form of development destroys the storage capacity of the flood plain, increases the amount of sedimentation in runoff, inhibits groundwater recharge and may degrade surface water quality. The removal of fill also leaves unsightly pits where mosquitos may breed. Because Jackson was not actively involved in other types of flood plain management, and the demand to develop the flood plain was high, the rate and extent of flood plain filling was quite substantial. As a result, the overall environmental impact of the program would seem to have been negative.

The Jackson program may have had a negative affect on equity. Enforcement of flood plain regulations may not have been equitable because of inconsistent application. Some of the interviews conducted with owners of structures in the 100-year flood plain indicated that there were cases where no elevation or flood-proofing was required on structures built after flood plain building standards were in force. Those flood-prone buildings included both new commercial and new residential development. Thus, some builders and occupants were forced to follow flood·plain requirements while others were not. There were probably two reasons for this inconsistent enforcement: (1) the visual inspection technique; and (2) poor mapping. If all new construction was required to have its height or its floodproofing certified by a licensed engineer, the room for error between similarly located properties would have been reduced. The mapping problem resulted from the city using several maps of the flood plain. For example, one 20-acre parcel was shown on a 1980 Flood Insurance Rate Map (FIRM) as being completely within the 100-year flood plain, while it was completely outside of the flood plain on maps previously used by the city and lending institutions. Another property outside of the 500-year flood plain on several maps (including the FIRM) was flooded in both 1961 (a twenty-five year flood) and 1979. The quality of mapping the flood hazard area might have led to some oversights regarding projects located on the fringe of the flood plain.

LITTLETON, COLORADO

Littleton is a small, affluent suburb located south of the City and County of Denver. Its 1979 population was 34,300. Littleton is the county seat of Arapahoe County, which contains seven other suburban cities and extensive unincorporated development (Figure 7-3). The city's downtown serves as a retail trade center for Denver's south suburban area and predates much of the other development in the southern portion of the Denver metropolitan area. Littleton and the rest of the Arapahoe County have experienced rapid growth, mostly in the form of single-family housing, shopping centers and office parks.

As shown on the larger map (Figure 7-4), in 1979 Littleton's flood hazard area consisted of roughly 1,200 acres along the South Platte River and four smaller tributary watersheds. While the tributary watersheds were small, they were substantially urbanized and subject to flash flooding from urban runoff. The steep gradient of the South Platte as it descends from the mountains made flash flooding the principal hazard for its flood plain as well. Over 150 acres (12.5 percent) of the flood plain in Littleton

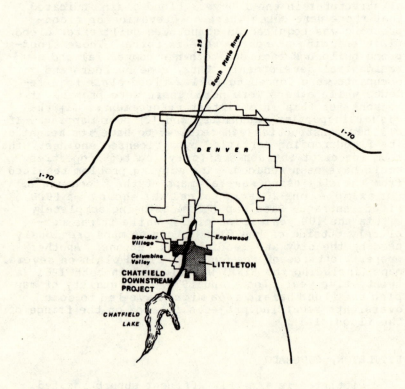

FIGURE 7-3
Littleton vicinity map

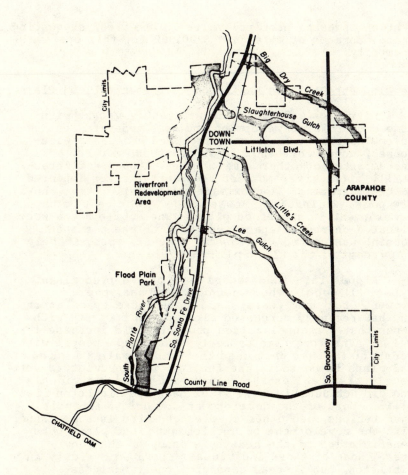

FIGURE 7-4
Littleton study area

was developed, mainly with small businesses, warehouses, the Centennial Race Track, and some low-to
moderate-income housing. Mostly single-family
residences bordered and encroached on the flood plains
of the tributaries. Eyewitnesses described the 1965
flood as a 25-foot-high wall of water that came
crashing down the South Platte from the mountains.
That flood was reported to have taken 13 lives and
caused $300 million in damages. In 1973 another sub-
stantial flood occurred, destroying property valued
at $100,000. The Army Corps of Engineers estimated
expected annual damages at $300,000 for the entire
South Platte flood plain between Chatfield Dam and
Denver. Littleton accounted for approximately 75 per-

cent of assessed property value in the area, suggesting annual damages of more than $200,000 for this one small community.

Development Decision Making on Littleton's Flood Plain

Littleton's flood plain was mostly vacant with some commercial development and some moderate- to low-income housing. Businesses included wholesale warehouses, motorcycle shops, gas stations, motels, restaurants and other similar uses. Though not necessarily attractive, most of those enterprises appeared to be prospering. Approximately 80 mobile homes and a few poorly maintained houses made up the rest of the development in the flood plain. The mobile homes were situated on rented spaces and most of the permanent housing was rented or leased. However, approximately 90 percent of the flood plain was vacant.

Flood plain land owners were of two predominant types: (1) people who owned or lived near their property for many years; and (2) absentee speculators who had recently purchased flood plain property with hopes that a channelization project would increase its value. The long time property owners were people with moderate incomes that used the land to make a living or had plans to do so in the future. The speculators were developers, real estate agents, and other individuals who did not usually live in or near the Littleton flood plain. Most of the development community, financial institutions, and other people connected in some manner with the development of Littleton's flood plain were beneficiaries of the healthy economy of the Denver area. None of those individuals operated strictly in Littleton, but instead conducted their business throughout much of the Denver metropolitan area.

Several economic factors served to attract people to the Littleton flood plain. Close proximity to major thoroughfares such as South Sante Fe Drive, made the area attractive for business uses. One shopping center developer and his tenants reported locating in the flood plain because up to 20,000 cars passed the site each day. In addition, flood insurance provided protection against large economic losses and reduced the risk of residing in the flood hazard area. One homeowner, for example, said he bought his house only after finding that flood insurance was available to cover any future losses.

The availability of less expensive housing in the flood plain also made it an attractive place to live for low- to moderate-income people. All three mobile home parks in Littleton were situated in or very near the flood plain. A history of flooding made the area less desirable as a place to live. As a result, land values and rents remained relatively low. Higher land values and rents were found in higher areas which had a good view of the Rocky Mountains and the metropolitan area.

Interviews revealed that many flood plain properties were being purchased for investment purposes. Buyers had become interested in flood plain land because of a proposed channelization project. They foresaw the potential for land being put to more profitable uses once the flood hazard was reduced or eliminated.

Perceptions of the flood hazard also had an influence on many flood plain location decisions. It appeared that Chatfield Dam, completed in 1973, encouraged development in the flood plain. Almost everyone interviewed who owned flood-prone property below the dam said that they felt confident their flood problems were solved. Additional improvements scheduled for the river channel had people convinced that another destructive flood would never happen. Those convictions were firm despite the fact that the properties in question would have remained within the 100-year flood plain until channelization was complete.

Littleton's Flood Plain Land Use Management Program

Littleton had a long history of involvement in flood plain land use management. The most important milestones in the city's program were the adoption of a flood plain overlay zone in 1971 and entrance into the regular phase of the National Flood Insurance Program in 1978. Initially, the flood plain land use management program was directed only at the South Platte River, because little information was available for the tributary watersheds. In 1978 the tributaries were included in the program and provisions for (1) mobile home tiedowns; and (2) floodproofing of all utilities were added to the regulations to bring them into compliance with the requirements of the NFIP regular program.

The flood plain land use management program had five major components: (1) zoning; (2) subdivision regulations; (3) land acquisition; (4) river-front redevelopment; and (5) a moratorium on building permits within 200 feet of the proposed South Platte channel.

The main thrust of Littleton's regulatory effort

was channeled through its zoning process. Any development within the designated 100-year flood hazard area
required a special exception permit. That permit
allowed certain uses in the floodway fringe provided
that prescribed criteria for flood plain development
were met. A detailed site plan and elevation profiles
had to be submitted with the application for the
special exception permit. All development in the
floodway was prohibited. The lowest habitable floor of
a structure had to be one foot above the elevation of
the 100-year flood and public facilities had to be
designed to withstand flooding. An "as built"
certificate of compliance was required before a
structure could be occupied. That was to ensure that
actual construction followed the plans submitted to
obtain a special exception permit.

Littleton's subdivision ordinance required dedication of land or, in lieu of dedication, payment of
fees for open space. Every developer had to dedicate
10.5 acres for each 1,000 residents in a proposed
subdivision or pay $505 per single-family unit and $360
per multi-family unit. That dedication provision and
the in-lieu fees were often used to acquire flood plain
land in the tributary watersheds. Additional requirements of the ordinance called for on-site retention of
10-year storm runoff and minor channel improvements
where necessary. The subdivision ordinance also
attempted to increase public awareness of the flood
hazard by requiring the delineation of the 100-year
flood plain on all final plats.

Littleton was also very active in land acquisition
through purchases along the South Platte. In 1971 the
city proposed to buy the South Platte flood plain as an
alternative to channelization as proposed by the Corps
of Engineers. By 1979 approximately 200 acres had been
purchased in the 2.7 miles immediately downstream from
Chatfield Dam. That land, when combined with an
additional 550 acres that was still to be acquired,
would have comprised the Littleton Flood Plain Park.
(Channelization was, however, proceeding for the 5.3
miles of the South Platte downstream from the park.)
The major 200-acre acquisition combined with land acquired through dedication and various public facility
holdings provided Littleton with approximately 300
acres of flood plain in public ownership.

Littleton formulated a riverfront redevelopment
plan using a U.S. Department of Housing and Urban
Development Small Cities grant. The plan called for
substantial new retail, office and multi-family
development within the existing flood plain adjacent to
the downtown area. The plan was predicated on the

channelization of the South Platte River which would
remove 150 acres from the 100-year flood plain. In
1979 the city took the first step toward implementing
the riverfront redevelopment plan by rezoning 90 acres
in that area. Significant economic and fiscal benefits
were expected to result from the planned redevelopment
of the riverfront area.

Finally, Littleton had been enforcing a moratorium
on building permits within 200 feet of the centerline
of the proposed South Platte Channel since 1973. That
part of the flood plain land use management program was
designed to keep property near the river undeveloped in
order to ease acquisition of the channel right-of-way
and eventual channel construction. Thus, Littleton's
flood plain land use management effort was designed to
complement the structural protection provided by Chatfield Dam and the pending channelization project.

In addition to those local flood plain land use
management activities, there were a number of related
activities at the metropolitan and other levels of
government that significantly affected the Littleton
flood plain. In response to flood losses in Littleton
and downstream in the remainder of the Denver area, the
U.S. Army Corps of Engineers authorized the Chatfield
Dam project in 1970. The project consisted of two
complementary phases: (1) the dam itself; and (2) the
channelization of the South Platte River from the dam
to the southern boundary of Denver (approximately 8
miles). The dam was completed in 1973 (just _after_ the
last substantial flood) at a cost of $80 million. The
dam alone, however, did not reduce the flood plain in
Littleton because continued urbanization on the
tributary watersheds increased runoff over the same
period.

In the Denver metropolitan area the Denver Urban
Drainage and Flood Control District mapped flood
hazards and provides technical assistance to local
communities. It also had the power to regulate flood
hazard areas if localities failed to act, but never
exercised that option. Urban Drainage and Flood
Control had provided Littleton with detailed maps of
its four tributary watersheds. Those maps, however,
differed substantially from maps provided by the
Federal Insurance Administration (FIA). The difference
resulted from the fact that the Urban Drainage and
Flood Control District based its mapping on the
assumption of complete development of small urban
watersheds. That assumption resulted in larger flows
than those mapped by FIA, which based its maps on the
level of watershed development that existed when the
maps were prepared.

Littleton was also involved with small channel-ization and channel maintenance projects which cost the city approximately $100,000 a year. Those were generally aimed at correcting flood and drainage problems through vegetation clearance and small-scale structural modifications of the tributary streams.

Littleton's flood plain land use management program was concentrated within the city's Department of Community Development, although the Engineering Section of the Public Services Department was also involved in its implementation. The city spent about $20,000 between 1973 and 1979 ($4,000 per year) enforcing its flood plain program regulations.

Acquisition of flood plain land required a major expenditure of public revenues. The total cost of the Littleton Flood Plain Park was expected to be $3,590,270. Much of the funding came from state and federal sources, but the park also required passage of a $400,000 local bond issue. Table 7-10 lists sources of funding and expenditures for the project. As of 1979, 200 acres had been acquired at a cost of $1,125,000. Several other small flood plain parks had been acquired with funds from the parks and open space provisions of the city's subdivision ordinance and through private donations.

Table 7-11 shows the total nunmber and value of building permits issued by Littleton from 1970 to 1979. Over the first 10 years of the program, only 11 special exception permits were granted to allow construction in floodway fringe areas. No record was kept of the number of permits that were denied; a number of field checks uncovered no violations of the permit require-ment. The projects for which special exception permits were issued seemed to be in compliance with the conditions of their permits. Interviews with developers and landowners revealed several individuals had been refused building permits because their property was in the floodway or within 200 feet of the centerline of the proposed South Platte Channelization project.

Littleton's flood plain land use management program qualified its citizens for flood insurance under the National Flood Insurance Program. As of October 31, 1978, 89 flood insurance policies were in effect.

Residential policies were valued at $2,215,600 and policies for other types of structures were valued at $549,300. Each policy provided up to $100,000 in coverage, since the city was in the regular phase of the NFIP.

TABLE 7-10
Funding and estimated development costs for
Littleton's flood plain park

Funding		Development Cost	
Funding Agency	Amount	Use	Amount
Bureau of Outdoor Recreation and Department of Housing and Urban Development	$ 234,646	Land	$2,241,770
		Reclamation of Mining Pits	1,150,000
Corps of Engineers	2,286,478		
		Recreation	198,000
City of Littleton			
-Bond Issue	400,000		
-Tax Revenues	54,000		
State of Colorado	146,000		
Additional Monies Needed	469,146		
Total Cost of Acquisition	$3,590,270	Total	$3,590,270

Source: Littleton Department of Community Development.

Most Littleton residents were only familiar with
the city's flood plain program indirectly through the
recreational opportunities it provided. Given the
public support for the bond issue to purchase the flood
plain park, it appears that most voters supported the
program. However, it is doubtful that those who did
not deal with the flood plain building regulations were
familiar with that aspect of the program.

Examples of the lack of public knowledge regarding
the requirements of the flood plain land use management
program were found while interviewing flood plain landowners. One owner received a letter and attended
meetings about the flood plain program, but did not
understand that the program restricted all development
on his floodway land until informed by a prospective
buyer. Most lenders and developers were generally well
aware of Littleton's efforts to manage its flood

TABLE 7-11
Building permits: total number and value for
new construction since 1970

Year	Number of Permits Issued	Change From 1970	Value of of Permits Issued	Change From 1970	Flood Plain Permits Issued[a]
1979[a]					
1978	239	+40	$15,998,770	$3,511,085	2
1977	227	+28	15,549,768	3,062,153	3
1976	142	-57	9,906,708	-2,580,907	1
1975	117	-72	10,053,246	-2,434,369	0
1974	98	-101	3,489,786	-8,988,829	0
1973	115	-74	5,271,840	-7,215,775	2
1972	351	+152	12,743,031	-255,416	0
1971	240	+39	8,074,990	-4,412,625	0
1970	190	-	12,487,615	-	0

[a] Three flood plain permits had been issued in 1979
through May.

Source: Littleton building permit files.

plains. However, interviews did reveal one occasion
when flood insurance was not required on the purchase
of a new house in the flood plain. This oversight
occurred because of poor mapping of a tributary flood
plain. Confusion existed about the location of those
flood plains because the Federal Insurance Administration (through the Corps of Engineers) and the Urban
Drainage and Flood Control District used different
baseline data in preparing maps of the flood hazard
area. The two conflicting sets of maps in the hands of
many lenders and developers tended to cause confusion
as to the actual location of the flood plain.

The Impacts of Littleton's Program

Littleton's flood plain land use management

program had a number of noticeable impacts. The program reduced potential public and private flood damages and increased the health and safety of the population by displacing a significant amount of new development which would have otherwise located in the flood plain. The program preserved a large part of the flood plain ecosystem in its natural state and provided open space and recreation amenities. Those amenities may have increased nonflood plain land values enough to offset reductions in the property taxes derived from flood plain land. The program had significant implementation costs, especially for land acquisition. If the riverfront redevelopment part of the program is successful, it wil have positive fiscal impacts by creating substantial new tax base. Table 7-12 summarizes these impacts.

Strict enforcement of flood plain regulations lowered property values in flood hazard areas. Analysis of assessed values of a random sample of vacant parcels in the city showed that property located outside of the flood plain was increasing in value at a higher rate than flood plain property (Table 7-13). An interview with the county tax assessor affirmed that finding. He reported that at the request of landowners, flood plain parcels could be reassessed downward. The restrictions on development generally reduced the assessment 25 to 50 percent below previously established land values. While the effects of the flood hazard and the flood plain program significantly reduced the value of flood plain land, several developers felt that land values outside of the flood plain had probably been increased due to the added amenities provided by the flood plain park. Thus, the net impact on land values in Littleton may have been positive overall if reductions in the flood plain were compensated by offsetting increases elsewhere.

Development costs were increased as a result of the flood plain program due to increased construction costs, as well as the expense of hiring a licensed engineer to meet the requirements of the special exemption permit. Local developers, builders, lenders and public officials estimated that development costs had increased by 10 to 25 percent in the flood hazard area.

It should be noted that in some cases those additional costs were offset by lower land prices. One lender explained that occurrance by saying, "Flood plain regulations are a two-edged sword. On the one hand they increase building costs, but on the other they reduce the price of land." He said he had financed one development in the flood plain which had

TABLE 7-12
Summary of net program impacts

Category of Impact	Impact

Economic Impacts

Annual private property damage	Decreased
Losses of production, stocks and wages	Slight decrease
Land values	Decreased
Construction costs	Increased
Locational effects	Major

Fiscal Impacts

Annual public property damage	Slight decrease
Program administration costs	Significant
Property tax revenue	Decreased sightly

Environmental Impacts

Open space	Increased
Natural resources protection	Increased
Water quality	Undetermined

Social Impacts

Health and safety	Increased
Recreation	Increased
Equity	No impact

TABLE 7-13
Assessed value of vacant land in Littleton,
1971 and 1978

	Average Values		
Type of Parcel	1971	1978	Percent Change
Flood Plain Property	$2,702	$2,881	+6.2
Nonflood Plain Property	$2,953	$4,881	+61.8

Source: Arapahoe County tax records.

saved 25 to 50 cents per square foot on total development costs because it was built on inexpensive flood plain land.

Local officials and the development community in Littleton agreed that without Littleton's flood plain land use management program the flood plain of the South Platte would have seen more commercial and industrial development. Also, without the program the tributary watersheds would probably have experienced more encroachment by residential development. With the program in place, much of that land remained undeveloped and available for open space or redevelopment after the river was channelized.

Property tax revenue derived from flood plain property decreased because of Littleton's flood plain program. The available evidence indicates that assessed values were reduced by 25 to 50 percent because of use limitations and increased construction costs imposed by the program. Although all flood plain parcels were eligible for revaluations, that was done only at the owner's request. South Platte flood plain land in Littleton was valued at $5,375,568 prior to the program. The value of private property in the flood plain was expected to decline to $3,133,798 after all of the flood plain park was acquired. That $2,241,770 reduction would have cut property tax revenue to the city by $17,934, based on the 1979 Littleton tax levy of 8.00 mils. A 50 percent decrease in the assessed value of private property remaining in the South Platte flood plain would cause an additional loss of $12,535 in tax revenues. Those estimates amount to nearly 4 percent of Littleton's tax revenues. The figures do not account for lost revenue associated with revaluations of flood plain land around the South Platte's four tributaries. The calculations also ignore possible increases in revenue derived from nonflood plain land that may be attributed to increased amenities provided by the program.

Most flood plain parcels were expected to rise in value (up to ten times) once the South Platte River was channelized. Those higher values would more than compensate for taxes lost from acquisition of the flood plain park. That positive fiscal impact was important in motivating both the city and the state to support the channelization project.

Administrative costs of the flood plain program amounted to 1.5 percent of the $270,000 budgeted to operate the city's Department of Community Development in 1979. That commitment of tax revenues for flood plain management represented a relatively small tax burden on Littleton's 34,000 residents.

Expenditures for flood plain land acquisition, although totaling nearly $4 million, represented a smaller commitment of local tax revenues than might be expected. Littleton spread the costs of buying flood plain land among federal, state and local levels of government. In addition, it financed the local portion of land costs through a $400,000 bond issue and from dedication fees collected through the subdivision ordinance. In that way the city was able to acquire flood plain land and hold down its tax rate. In fact, Littleton's mill levy was the eighth lowest of the ten municipalities in Denver's south suburban area.

In those areas of the South Platte flood plain not acquired, development was expected to intensify as the result of channelization and riverfront redevelopment. That land would likely be developed more intensely under the riverfront redevelopment plan than if it were developed without the program. Thus, the program may have some negative long range environmental impact on the portion of the flood plain being redeveloped, but the magnitude of those impacts is uncertain. On balance, however, flood plain management in Littleton seemed to have enhanced environmental quality. The benefits associated with the 750-acre flood plain park should outweigh the harm to the natural environment caused by channelization and redevelopment project.

Recreational and educational opportunities also increased through the acquisition of flood plain land for public parks. A survey of Littleton's residents completed in 1978 showed that only 2.6 percent were dissatisfied with local recreational facilities (Table 7-14). Since most of the city's parks were established as part of the flood plain program, it appears to have made a major contribution towards meeting the recreational needs of the community. In addition, educational facilities constructed in several of the parks took advantage of the natural terrain to provide an environmental education experience.

A COMPARISON OF PROGRAMS

It is now possible to compare the three communities' flood plain management programs. For example, both Raleigh and Littleton had adopted most of ten goals communities may pursue in flood plain management. (See Table 7-15.) Littleton's program was somewhat wider in scope, since it included the goal of economic development. The Jackson program consisted of only

TABLE 7-14
Satisfaction with Littleton parks and recreation
facilities

Rating	Percent
Excellent	36.6
Good	42.9
Acceptable	11.2
Poor	2.6
Don't Know	6.2
No Answer	0.2

Source: Littleton Mini-Census, 1978.

three of the most widely adopted goals regarding protection of the population and reduction of flood
losses.

In terms of the methods being used, Raleigh and
Littleton were both using a total ot ten of the seven-
teen methods studied by this research (see Table 7-16).
Raleigh's program emphasized elevation and floodway
regulations, while the Littleton program emphasized
land acquisition in addition to strict elevation and
floodway requirements. The Littleton program also
included plans to redevelop a considerable part of the
flood plain adjacent to the existing downtown in conjunction with the channelization of the South Platte
River by the Corps of Engineers. The Jackson program
consisted of elevation requirements administered
through the subdivision and building permit process.
No official floodway had been established for Jackson,
so there were no floodway regulations. Jackson's lack
of separate elevation and floodway regulations is
typical of the situation found in many NFIP emergency
program communities.

In terms of implementation, Littleton seemed to be
making the most effort. While Littleton was spending
only $4,000 annually on implementing its regulations,
land acquisition costs were expected to total nearly $4
million, of which $400,000 would come from local bonds.
Raleigh spent about $140,000 per year on program imple-
mentation. Of that total, $40,000 was for land acqui-
sition and $100,000 for enforcement and inspection

TABLE 7-15
Goals adopted by each community

Goals	Raleigh, North Carolina	Jackson, Mississippi	Littleton, Colorado
Reduce property loss	x	x	x
Protect safety of the population	x	x	x
Encourage economic development			x
Preserve natural areas	x		x
Reduce erosion and sedimentation	x		x
Distribute costs of program fairly			
Maintain water quality	x		x
Preserve open space	x		x
Reduce flood damage to public property	x	x	x
Minimize fiscal impacts of flooding	x		x

The figure for inspection may be somewhat mis-
leading because it combines implementation of
the flood plain regulations with implementation of the
sedimentation and erosion control ordinance which
primarily generated environmental benefits. Jackson
officials estimated impelmentation costs of $10,000 to
$24,000 annually, but exact figures were not available
because the program was implemented as a part of other
functions. Thus, the case studies indicate that implementation and spending levels are related to
effectiveness.

A key weakness was found in the implementation of
the Jackson program. The program did not require "as

TABLE 7-16
Methods adopted by case study communities

Management Methods	Raleigh, North Carolina	Jackson, Mississippi	Littleton, Colorado
Floodway regulations	x		x
Zoning	x	x	x
Subdivision regulations	x	x	x
Elevation requirements	x	x	x
Floodproofing requirements	x		x
Sedimentation and erosion control	x		x
Land acquisition	x		x
Wetlands protection			
Location of public facilities	x	x	x
Relocation of existing development			
Preferential taxation			
Density transfers	x		x
Comprehensive planning	x	x	x
Public information	x	x	x

built" certification of the elevation of new flood plain structures as did the other two programs. Instead, inspectors visually checked the amount of fill as a part of their building inspection procedure. As a result, there was no way of knowing whether any given structure was in compliance with the elevation requirements of the program.

All three programs had been in operation for at least five years, so there was enough time for them to generate measurable impacts. In general, the Littleton program seemed to generate the most noticeable impacts.

While the rate of flood plain invasion in Jackson was by far the highest, it should be noted that it had been cut roughly in half over the life of the program, while the rate of flood plain development in each of the other communities had stayed roughly constant. Table 7-17 shows the number and percent of total permits locating in the flood plain of each community in 1978.

Interviews with knowledgeable people indicated that the Littleton program was very effective in protecting future development and in protecting natural areas. The Raleigh program was considered very effective in protecting future development and somewhat effective in preserving natural areas. Knowledgeable local people rated the Jackson program somewhat effective, at best, in protecting future development and not effective at all in protecting natural areas. Of the three only the Littleton program significantly affected existing flood plain development: its redevelopment activities would displace some of the existing uses and replace them with more intensive uses once channelization of the South Platte was completed.

The physical characteristics of the flood plains in these three communities appear to have influenced the rate and amount of flood plain development. The size of the flood plain and the availability of alternative sites played particularly important roles. Jackson's large wide flood plain appeared to be much more difficult to manage than the smaller hazard areas found along the creeks and tributaries of the other two communities. In Raleigh many flood problems had been avoided by designing lots so that the flood plain falls in backyards. Other types of projects were allowed to transfer density from the flood hazard area to other

TABLE 7-17
Flood plain invasion in the case study
communities in 1978

	Number of Flood Plain Building Permits	Percent of Total New Development
Raleigh	8	0.6
Jackson	90	11.3
Littleton	2	0.8

parts of the development site not subject to flooding.
In Jackson these types of solutions were precluded by
the width of the flood plain which generally
encompassed an entire development site. In general,
there were no alternative sites nearby in Jackson.

The nature and extent of existing flood plain
development also appeared to be important. Jackson had
the most developed flood plain of the three
communities. The Jackson flood plain contained several
high income residential areas, shopping centers,
schools and had other locational advantages which
encouraged still further flood plain development. In
Raleigh the main impetus for development in flood
hazard areas was a favorable location for business
activity due to existing shopping facilities and
heavily traveled highways in and near the flood plain
of Crabtree Creek. In contrast, the Littleton flood
plain was considered one of the least desirable areas
for new development; lower land values made the flood
plain attractive primarily for marginal businesses and
low-income residences. Much of the Littleton flood
plain was vacant. Thus, once flood plain development
occurred it clearly seemed to attract additional flood
plain development and hindered the implementation of
land use management in the case study communities.
Apparently land use management must be implemented
before substantial development occurs if it is to be
effective.

All three of the communities had some type of
structural protection in place. Upstream from Raleigh
there were a number of small watershed dams
built by the Soil Conservation Service. The Corps of
Engineers built the Chatfield Dam to protect Littleton
and other downstream communities and was undertaking
channelization of the South Platte River. Downtown
Jackson was supposedly protected by a levee and the
channelization of Town Creek. The only clear evidence
of encroachment encouraged by structural protection was
in the area protected by the Jackson levee. That area
was severely damaged in the Easter Flood of 1979.

Political support for flood plain land use management also seemed to be an important factor. In both
Raleigh and Littleton the flood plain land use management program enjoyed widespread community support from
all parts of the population, including land development
interests. That was not the case in Jackson. There
was little knowledge of the land use management program
or support for that approach to the solution of the
flood problem. Both disaster relief and structural
protection enjoyed more political support than land use

management in Jackson. Development interests were particularly critical of the land use management approach.

In addition to political factors, intergovernmental relations were found to be important in determining the effectiveness of flood plain land use management programs. Jackson is a classic example of the problems caused by cross-river competition between jurisdictions. Jackson was reluctant to adopt restrictive controls which might have caused flood plain development to locate in Rankin County (the jurisdiction across the Pearl River). That would have hurt Jackson in two ways: (1) the city would have lost valuable tax revenue; and (2) flooding would have been worse as the result of increased filling on the other side of the river.

The case of Raleigh provides an interesting contrast. Much of the development in Raleigh was protected by the small watershed dams which Wake County had been instrumental in developing. Here cooperation between upstream and downstream jurisdictions had helped solve the flood problem. Littleton also had a good deal of cooperation from neighboring jurisdictions in arranging the funding used for the land acquisition and channelization projects.

In terms of socioeconomic characteristics, Jackson had the slowest growth rate and the lowest standard of living. Its program was also the least effective. This parallels the positive relationship between standard of living and program effectiveness found in the analysis of cross-sectional survey data reported in Chapter 6.

In summary, the case studies suggest that physical factors are related to flood plain invasion, particularly the size, configuration and development of the flood plain. Political support, enrollment in the regular phase of the National Flood Insurance Program, and problems caused by neighboring jurisdictions also seem to be related to program effectivenss. Communities with a higher standard of living seem to be more effective in flood plain land use management. The two communities which had adopted the largest number of goals and methods (programs with the greatest scope) were also the most effective. Land acquisition seems to be effective in preventing exposure of development to flooding and encroachment on natural areas, but it is extremely expensive. Elevation and floodway regulations can be effective at a reasonable cost, but they must be adequately implemented to ensure compliance.

In the case study communities none of the land use management programs was completely effective in dealing with the flood problems of existing development.

NOTES

    1. For a larger, though somewhat less detailed, set of case studies see Kusler (1982).

    2. For an excellent account of the 1979 flood, see Platt (1982).

8
Summing Up: Policies for Improving Flood Plain Land Use Management

Community flood plain management must be viewed as part of a system of hazard adjustments that includes not only land use measures, but also structural measures, emergency warnings, flood insurance and disaster relief. The recommendations presented in this chapter focus on land use management, but linkages with other types of adjustments require that policy recommendations address a full range of adjustments where appropriate. Reflecting the approach taken in earlier chapters, policies for improving community flood plain management are analyzed from a bottom up perspective. Policy recommendations are made for each of the governmental levels discussed earlier--federal, state, regional and community--but they are offered on the basis of their contribution to achieving local goals for flood plain use and for improving the performance of local programs rather than their contribution to goals at other levels of government. Thus, the focus here is on enhancing flood plain management at the local level. This reflects a belief that it is at the local level that flood plain land use management must ultimately occur. In some cases recommendations will focus on incremental adjustments to existing programs; in other cases new directions or entirely new programs may be warranted.

TOWARD MORE EFFECTIVE COMMUNITY PROGRAMS

At the local level two facts stand out. First, local political support is critical to program success. Second, a community's flood plain management program must be tailored to fit the local setting.

Both the case studies and the surveys of local communities make it clear that a community's political support for flood plain management is a key determinant of program effectiveness. While political

216

support is a critical ingredient, the surveys reported
in Chapter 3 and similar work by other researchers
clearly show that flooding is usually not considered a
serious problem by local political leaders. Given the
low level of concern with flooding in most communities,
lack of political support for programs aimed at solving
flood problems is not surprising. Paradoxically, the
political support necessary for effective flood plain
land use management is most often present in communities with large, heavily developed flood plains and
particularly in communities that repeatedly have
experienced damaging floods. Since those communities
have already allowed significant flood plain development, however, the most effective mitigation measures,
such as land acquisition, are often no longer viable.
Many of the most effective responses to the flood
hazard are anticipatory in nature, but to be effective
they require political support, which is inherently
reactive in nature. A key question which must be
addressed, when considering policies to improve community flood plain management, is: what policies can
help generate the political support needed for an
effective management program?

Generating political support for flood plain
management is often viewed by local government
personnel as someone else's responsibility, but some
program components may help generate additional public
support. Programs which increase community awareness
of the flood hazard, for example, should have a
positive influence on public support for flood plain
management activities. Programs which include a significant amount of participation by flood plain land
owners and occupants can be expected to increase
political support. Linking flood management with other
community goals, such as protection of open space,
assurance of good water quality, and provision of
recreational facilities, is another means of garnering
support for flood plain land use management.
Mechanisms which channel state and federal technical
and financial support to local initiatives can also
capitalize on any political support that may develop in
a local community. For example, after a major flood
communities are often willing to consider programs to
mitigate the hazard; if technical assistance is
available from a regional or state agency, it can take
advantage of heightened local interest in the flood
problem to help the community formulate an effective
flood plain management program.

The three case studies discussed in Chapter 7
illustrate the variety of settings in which flood plain
land use management occurs. Given that variety, simple
regulations, such as those required by the National

Flood Insurance Program, cannot be expected to stem
flood plain development or to reduce flood losses significantly, in all cases. More diversity in the composition of local programs is a clear prerequisite to
more effective flood plain land use management. The
analysis in Chapter 6 indicates that programs must be
tailored to fit local situations. One basic aim of
flood plain management programs at all levels of
government should be to encourage communities to
formulate and adopt a set of land use management
measures that are likely to work best given the unique
circumstances of each community.

Program scope is strongly associated with program
effectiveness. That suggests that communities should
increase the number of methods they are using to deal
with the flood problem. New program components, particularly methods such as land acquisition and
relocation that attack the problem directly, will tend
to increase program effectiveness. Comprehensive
planning for flood plains helps communities to understand that flood plain management can include a number
of community goals in addition to flood loss reduction.
As suggested above, open space, water quality, and
recreational objectives that also serve flood hazard
mitigation aims can be used to stimulate interest in
flood plain management and may provide the justifica-
tion needed to use a broader array of program measures.
In addition, as programs increase in complexity,
planning becomes important to integrate the various
components.

Three types of communities require greater than
normal attention to flood plain management: (1) communities with heavily developed flood plains and few
alternative development sites; (2) communities with
large undeveloped flood plains; and (3) communities
which are subject to coastal flooding. Program
responses for each type of community are outlined
below.

In communities with heavily developed flood plains
and limited alternative development sites, flood plain
land use management should be linked with redevelopment
efforts and structural flood control measures. Our
research indicates that flood plain land use management
is not a very effective management response in that
type of community. Land use management can only keep
the problem from getting worse; structural flood control measures or redevelopment efforts are needed to
solve the existing problems. Redevelopment programs
are needed to address the blighted character of
developed flood plains in many urban areas. Redevelopment can include clearance of hazard area structures,

relocation of people and structures or floodproofing to
make existing structures safer. As the Littleton
experience demonstrated, redevelopment, when used in
conjunction with structural control of the hazard, can
increase the local tax base, while reducing the flood
hazard and removing blighted flood plain development.
Some communities with heavily developed hazard areas
may find emergency warning systems useful mechanisms
for saving lives and in some cases reducing potential
property losses.

In communities with heavily developed hazard
areas, it should be noted that the property at risk
includes large amounts of public investment as well as
significant private capital. Water and sewer systems,
roads, highways and bridges are all in place to support
existing flood plain development. Thus, the flood
problem affects the entire population of the community,
not only flood plain residents and land owners. These
communities should consider ways to protect or insure
their infrastructure investment. Protection might take
the form of floodproofing capital facilities or small
scale flood control measures. Self insurance, possibly
financed through special assesments or user fees, may
be used to cover the possible flood damages to such
facilities, if they cannot be adequately protected.
Our research suggests that communities where heavy
flood plain development presents a clear and present
danger should have the easiest time generating
political support for some type of response to the
hazard. The exact nature of that response will, of
course, depend on the details of the flood problem and
the availability of resources available to mount a
local flood hazard management program.

Management of undeveloped flood plains provides
the best opportunity to stem the increasing investment
at risk to the flood hazard. To date, relatively few
communities have realized the importance of limiting
the development of flood hazard areas so that a flood
problem is not created. That suggests a critical
deficiency in the way communities plan for new urban
development. In undeveloped flood plains the emphasis
should be on preservation of the natural values of the
flood plain and the prevention of uneconomic new flood
plain development. Regulation alone, however, is
seldom sufficient to prevent flood plain development
where the flood plain has locational advantages for
urban growth.

Our research suggests that land acquisition is a
key program component in that type of community. A
major problem exists because land acquisition usually
requires funding levels beyond the capability of local

government and is difficult for local officials to justify based solely on eliminating hypothetical future flood damages. Grants from state or federal agencies or cooperation with private land trusts can provide funding for acquisition. Long term acquisition with relatively modest, but continuous, annual funding or issuance of bonds for large-scale acquisition are two methods to spread the costs of acquisition over a longer time period. Dedication of flood plain land as a part of the subdivision permitting process provides one low cost means of acquisition if mechanisms for long term management and maintenance can be found.

Prevention of flood plain invasion seems to require special attention in a community's comprehensive planning process. While a majority of communities report that they are using comprehensive planning as a part of their flood plain programs, greater emphasis on planning is needed in communities attempting to preserve undeveloped flood plains. Comprehensive planning provides the means of coordinating the variety of goals and methods necessary to prevent unwise flood plain development. It also increases awareness of the flood hazard before development takes place.

Careful placement of community infrastructure is another powerful method which can be used to discourage development of flood plains. The effect of new water and sewer lines on the location of development with respect to the flood hazard should be considered in local capital facility planning. The locations of new roads and highways, while not always completely within local control, should also be evaluated as to their influence on flood plain development. Public facility location can play a significant role in preventing the invasion of undeveloped flood plains, but it has not been fully utilized in most flood-prone communities.

Communities subject to coastal flooding seem to be unique in several ways. First, the rate of hazard area development seems to be much higher than in communities subject to riverine flooding. The economic pressures which cause development of hazardous areas are much stronger in coastal communities due to the unique appeal of an oceanfront location for many activities. There are few comparable sites available which are not floodprone. Second, while most coastal communities have fairly heavily developed hazard areas, structural measures and redevelopment are generally not appropriate responses given the nature of the hazard and the type of development present. Third, the hurricane hazard which affects many coastal communities is more life-threatening than most riverine flood hazards.

Given their unique setting, coastal communities should focus on floodproofing and emergency warning systems to deal with their existing hazard problems. New structures should be elevated well above the height of the expected storm surge and reinforced to sustain wind and wave impacts. Placement of water, sewer, roads and bridges should be used to guide development away from the most hazardous locations. Sand dune protection ordinances should be used to preserve these natural barriers. Communities subject to coastal flooding should seek to limit their overall growth to a level that can be safely evacuated by existing roads and bridges.

In all types of flood-prone communities there is a clear need for more flood plain management training. Staff members, including administrators, planners, engineers, building inspectors and public works directors, need better training in flood hazard mitigation. Elected and appointed officials, such as city council persons and planning commissioners, also need better training. While an individual community cannot be expected to develop its own training program, it can encourage its staff and officials to improve their hazard management knowledge and skills through training courses offered by professional associations, local colleges and universities, and state and federal agencies. Such training should go a long way toward improving local flood plain management. Public education can also be undertaken at the local level. Hazard location, mitigation alternatives and emergency response information should all be included in such a program.

Clearly, there are a number of things a community can do to deal with the flood hazard. While regulation as required by the NFIP can play a role in all types of communities, other mechanisms tailored to the specific local situation are probably necessary to deal with the flood hazard effectively. To integrate these various types of activities and to provide for a level of citizen involvement likely to generate necessary political support, a flood plain planning program should be undertaken by any local community with significant amounts of flood-prone land, whether it is currently developed or not. The planning program would likely widen the scope of flood plain land use management goals adopted by local communities and would provide a framework within which a wider variety of management options could be considered. Such a planning program should include accurate and up-to-date mapping of the entire flood hazard area and estimates of damages likely to result from floods of various sizes. By including damage estimates associated with various sizes of floods and from different mitigation measures, the planning process would increase the awareness of public officials and citizens regarding the flood hazard. It also would allow public officials to compare the costs and benefits of alternative mitigation strategies.

It is clear that the funding and staff requirements for such a planning program provide key limitations in many communities. Given current spending levels, any detailed planning of urban flood plains is beyond the means of a number of communities. However, many communities do have some type of comprehensive planning process. Additional emphasis on the disposition and management of flood hazard areas could be handled as a part of this process for little or no additional cost. Pilot programs funded by other levels of government provide a way of beginning to implement a more detailed planning approach. Planning requirements in state comprehensive planning statutes or as a part of the National Flood Insurance Program could also be used to mandate this activity at the local level.

A ROLE FOR REGIONAL AGENCIES

Since flood problems often cross jurisdictional lines, regional agencies, either councils of governments (COG's) or flood control and water management districts, can play an important role in solving the flood problem. Regional agencies are frequently involved in providing communities with technical support in subjects, such as hydrology, where many communities currently lack sufficient expertise. While many regional agencies report they are providing technical assistance, this role could be significantly strengthened and expanded. Regional agencies can also be used to provide local governments with a better understanding of state and federal programs that can assist with flood plain management activities. Few local governments are familiar with all of the redevelopment, land acquisition and structural programs that can be brought to bear on their flood problems. By serving as a clearinghouse for that type of programatic information, regional agencies could provide local governments with a much better idea of what their flood plain management options are. Similarly, regional agencies could provide model ordinances and other materials to help communities develop an effective response to the flood hazard. Regional agencies could also sponsor training programs for local officials involved in flood plain management. Thus,

providing various forms of technical assistance is the
primary role for regional agencies in flood plain
management.

In some cases regional agencies may be appropriate
vehicles for implementing structural solutions,
acquiring flood prone land or even regulating flood
hazard areas. While Chapter Five shows these management activities to be fairly rare, they appear to be
strongly associated with effectiveness in preventing
increased flood losses. Regional agencies seem
especially appropriate for implementing structural
solutions or acquiring land in urban areas because such
projects often cross numerous community boundaries.
Councils-of-governments, which are voluntary associations of local jurisdictions, might be used for
regional land acquisition, but they would almost never
be appropriate for regulation. Special purpose
regional agencies, which are generally created by
states to deal with water management or urban drainage
and flood control problems, can and often do have
regulatory roles. Many of these agencies have been
given the authority to regulate flood plain development
in the absence of adequate local management. Such
special purpose agencies provide a model for effective
regional involvement in flood plain management.

Regional agencies also may have a role in the
review and approval of federally funded water, sewer
and highway projects. That review could be used to
help direct infrastructure (and the urban development
it supports) to non-hazardous areas. By coupling review and comment on federally funded public investments
with their planning activities, regional agencies may
be able to help direct growth away from hazardous
areas.

Regional agencies can also provide hazard information beyond that supplied by the NFIP. Some regional
agencies, for example, provide flood plain maps based
on the runoff associated with full development of urban
watersheds. Such flood plain maps will often differ
considerably from flood insurance maps that are based
on runoff under existing development conditions. This
type of hazard information can be made available to
local governments and to the public, as well. By
providing hazard information to the public, regional
agencies can increase the support for the flood plain
management activities of local governments.

STATE SUPPORT OF LOCAL ACTIVITIES

There are a number of important functions that

states can perform, especially given their ability to legally mandate certain local activities. States can directly regulate flood plain development through critical areas programs. They can also use direct regulation when local management of flood plains is not effective. States clearly have the authority and the responsibility to intervene if local actions provide a threat to public safety. The potential for such intervention provides a strong stimulus toward effective local management efforts.

States also provide the best level at which to monitor and evaluate local implementation of mandated regulatory and inspection activities. Monitoring of compliance under the NFIP has demonstrated that the federal government is too far removed from the local level to provide adequate oversight. The placement of monitoring responsibilities at the state level makes it more probable that those doing the monitoring will be familiar with local situations. Strong state monitoring of local flood plain management, combined with provisions for state regulation of the flood hazard area in the absence of adequate local management and the provision of state-supplied technical assistance, would greatly improve local effectiveness in the short run.

States already have the means to require more local attention to flood plains through state mandates of the elements to be included in comprehensive plans, which local governments are required to prepare in many of the states. State governments could go further and require that each community's comprehensive plan include a separate element for its flood plain. Alternatively, such a flood plain plan could be made a part of larger integrated hazards plan, which would include other hazards in addition to flooding. Any type of flood plain planning program should include accurate mapping of the flood hazard area and an analysis of flood risk. The risk analysis would include estimates of expected flood losses for current and future levels of urban development. Requirements for adequate citizen participation in such a planning process would also increase public awareness of the flood hazard.

States also have the ability to undertake single purpose programs targeted at a particular class of communities, such as those with large, undeveloped flood plains or those with significant redevelopment potential. In such cases grants-in-aid are more appropriate than regulatory approaches. State grants to support local efforts in land acquisition or flood plain redevelopment would begin to increase the diversity of local approaches. In those states with constrained revenue sources to support new programs, an attempt to direct a variety of federal grant programs toward solving flood problems could provide an initial source of funding.

IMPLEMENTING DIVERSE FEDERAL OBJECTIVES

Local communities are receiving a number of benefits from the federal interest in flood hazard management, including hazard insurance, disaster relief, flood control structures, and technical assistance. The major thrust of all of those programs is to protect urban development from flood damage, rather than to preserve the flood plain in its natural state. Those federal programs, to a large extent, make possible increased urbanization of the flood plain by reducing flood losses, both to society as a whole and to the individuals occupying the flood plain. But communities also experience a number of other effects from federal programs. Many of these flood plain impacts are generated by programs that are not ordinarily considered related to flood plain development. Federal programs that provide funding for highways and for water and sewer systems often have the unintended consequence of encouraging flood plain development. Coordinating the wide range of federal activities so that they support local flood plain management should be a major concern at the federal level.

The National Flood Insurance Program directly affects more flood-prone communities than any other federal activity. This program has clearly exerted, and continues to have, a strong effect in inducing communities to adopt policies and regulations to reduce property losses from flooding. As a result of the NFIP, billions of dollars in flood plain development are now covered by federally backed insurance. The amount of property at risk and the federal exposure to insurance losses has continued to rise during the life of the flood insurance program. Whether the availability of flood insurance has encouraged flood plain development or not is hotly debated. It seems clear that in at least some cases flood insurance has encouraged additional flood plain development, particularly in coastal areas.

Innovative means of reducing the amount of property at risk should be tried. Acquisition of substantially damaged property uner Section 1362 of the National Flood Insurance Act provides one mechanism for removing property from the hazard area, but that provision of the act has never been funded adequately.

The National Flood Insurance Program has also
provided valuable technical assistance to local
communities in the form of model ordinances and hazard
mapping. The NFIP has been responsible for a major
hazard mapping effort to delineate the 100- and 500-
year flood plains in thousands of communities. Flood
Insurance Rate Maps provide useful information for
flood plain land use management that generally was not
available prior to the NFIP. The costs of updating
those hazard maps is likely to be substantial as communities' boundaries change and as hydrology changes
due to continued upstream development in urban watersheds. The full costs of producing accurate maps and
updating them to account for the effects of new urbanization should be included within the flood insurance
rate structure. In addition to updated hazard maps,
communities need estimates of aggregate property at
risk to various levels of flood hazard. Perhaps the
Corps of Engineers could provide this service through
its technical assistance program, if the National Flood
Insurance Program cannot fill the need.

The model ordinances provided by the NFIP have
formed the basis for most communities' flood plain
management programs. However, communities need other
types of assistance in developing their programs. They
need examples of acquisition programs, model redevelopment programs, and information on funding sources for
other innovative management strategies.

Training is another form of technical assistance
provided by the National Flood Insurance Program.
While local staff members are currently the primary
targets of these training programs, more efforts must
be made to educate elected and appointed officials as
well. One mechanism to improve participation by these
officials would be to mount mobile training workshops
which would go to local communities instead of bringing
the officials to the training sessions. Another
mechanism which should be pursued is to get better
flood management training incorporated in the college
and university engineering, planning, law, architecture
and public administration programs. This could be
accomplished by training educators in these disciplines
and by producing course materials which could be incorporated into existing curricula.

In addition to the National Flood Insurance
Program, continuing federal involvement in providing
structural solutions for heavily developed flood plains
is certainly warranted. It is also clear that there
will never be enough funds available to "solve" the
flood problem by structural means. Strict application
of benefit-cost analysis is essential to assure that

limited construction resources are directed towards
areas of maximum benefit. Benefit-cost analyses should
include environmental and equity criteria as well as
economic efficiency concerns. Coordination of flood
control measures with other federal actions, particularly infrastructure funding and housing and economic
development programs, could be improved and would
likely produce more effective results all around. Currently, local governments must attempt to coordinate a
variety of federal programs at the local level.

While the majority of the federal effort is
directed toward protecting property in the flood plain,
a number of federal policy instruments, such as
Executive Order 11988, the Coastal Barriers Resources
Act, and the "Principles and Standards for Water
Resource Planning" promulgated by the U.S. Water
Resources Council indicate that preservation of the
flood plain and its natural environment is becoming an
equally important concern. That represents a significant widening of basic federal objectives. The future
evolution of federal policy should include funding to
implement programs which reflect a wider set of
objectives in addition to the current focus on protecting property.

A program aimed at preventing the development of
underdeveloped riverine flood plains could be modeled
on the Coastal Barriers Resources Act. A pilot program
which limits federal support for the extension of water
and sewer lines and roads into riverine flood plains
should be tried in several states or river basins.
Such a program should probably be coordinated with land
acquisition assistance for particularly suitable sites.

Several demonstration projects which focus
economic development programs on redevelopment of
urbanized flood hazard areas would also be useful.
These programs could bring together funds from existing
programs, such as HUD's Urban Development Action Grants
or Community Development Block Grants, to show how they
can be used in flood plain management.

Thus, the federal government can encourage
diversity at the local level by moving to implement its
own widening set of goals. Special purpose programs
aimed at communities with particular types of flood
hazard, as discussed earlier, and increased technical
assistance to each of the other levels of government
provide the best directions for new federal initiatives. Such fitting of flood plain land use management
programs to local circumstances is essential to improving community response to the flood hazard.

FUTURE RESEARCH

While the general outlines of community flood
plain management and related policies at other levels
of government are clear, further research is needed.
Subjects for future research include the role of tax
policy in hazard mitigation, the use of infrastructure
location to guide urban development to non-hazard
areas, risk analysis methods for local flood plain
management, and the use of hazard information in development decisions. Additional research on how
political support for flood plain management can best
be developed also seems to be warranted by our
findings.

Local tax policies and user fees provide an entirely new approach to hazard mitigation which could be
combined with the present regulatory and acquisition
approaches. Tax policy could conceivably be used to
direct new development away from hazardous areas or to
encourage redevelopment and floodproofing of existing
structures. Higher property taxes or user fees in the
flood hazard area could also be used to indemnify the
infrastructure needed to service flood plain development. By using such a tax policy a local government
could provide a form of self-insurance against flood
damage to flood plain water and sewer systems and
streets and bridges. Key research questions regarding
tax policy would be the legal feasibility of such an
approach in the various states, estimation of potential
damages and infrastructure replacement costs, and the
economic side effects of such policies.

The ability of local communities to control the
location of their infrastructure and the resulting
economic effects of locating infrastructure in nonflood plain locations also warrant additional research.
The flat topography of many communities' flood plains
make them relatively inexpensive and appealing sites
for sewer systems and roads. While the cost of locating such systems in less hazardous areas will vary from
one community to another, a comparison of those costs
with the benefits of reduced flood losses in several
types of communities would be very useful.

A method which local communities could use to
analyze the risk posed by the flood hazard also requires further research and development. Such a method
should be able to estimate expected damages for the
existing level of development and for future land use
scenarios. The method would use stage damage relationships for various types of structures to estimate
losses for floods of various sizes with known proba-
bilities. When combined with an existing or proposed

hazard area land use inventory the method would produce
an estimate of expected damage. This type of risk
analysis would allow local decision makers to weigh the
costs and benefits of various mitigation strategies.

Finally, the use of hazard information in development decision making is not well understood. Research
is needed on the way in which public officials use this
type of information in such activities as planning,
zoning and subdivision review. How professionals both
in and out of government use flood plain information is
also of key importance. How the architects, engineers,
and planners hired by the developer use hazards information in site planning and design is not well
understood. While the role of hazard information in
individual location decisions has received some attention, the way that this information affects developers
and the owners of undeveloped land requires more study.
Similarly, the role of hazard information in generating
political support for flood plain management has been
left largely untouched.

In several of these areas demonstration projects
would be the most appropriate format for future research. Demonstration projects, in which one or more
state or federal agencies fund innovative flood plain
programs at the local, state or regional level, could
provide the basis for stimulating additional research.
Such demonstration projects should be considered ex-
periements in which new policies are subjected to
rigorous evaluation. By testing and evaluating a
number of innovative approaches in this manner, important new insights into how to make flood plain
management more effective should be possible. Successful demonstrations wold then serve as models which
other communities could emulate.

Thus, there seems to be a number of important
areas related to flood plain management which require
further research. While the last ten years have seen
giant strides in what we know about how communities
manage their flood plains, clearly much is left to be
done.

References

Abeles, Schwartz, et al. 1979. Feasibility of
Flooded Property Purchase Under Section 1362 of
the National Flood Insurance Act. Draft Report
Prepared for the U.S. Department of Housing and
Urban Development. Washington: U.S. Department
of Housing and Urban Development.

Allee, D.J. and M.F. Walter. 1977. "Implementation
of Non-structural Flood Risk Management in the
Northeastern United States: A Review of
Information Needs," in Implementation of
Non-structural Alternatives in Flood Damage
Abatement, Waldon R. Kerns, ed. Blacksburg,
Va.: Virginia Polytechnic Institute and State
University, pp. 3-15.

American Institute of Planners Research Office.
1976. Survey of State Land Use Planning
Activity. Prepared for the Department of
Housing and Urban Development. Washington:
U.S. Department of Housing and Urban
Development. April.

American Society of Civil Engineers. 1973. An
Evaluation of Urban Floodplains. Springfield,
Va: National Technical Information Service.

American Society of Civil Engineers, Task Force on
Flood Plain Regulations. 1962. A Guide for
the Development of Flood Plain Regulations.
January.

Anderson, Dan R. 1974. "The National Flood
Insurance Program--Problems and Potential," The
Journal of Risk and Insurance, Vol. 41: 579.

Baker, Earl J. 1976. "Toward and Evaluation of
Policy Alternatives Governing Hazard Zone Land
Uses." Tallahassee, Fl: Florida State
University.

Baker, Earl J. 1977. "Public Attitudes Toward Hazard
Zone Controls," Journal of the American Institute
of Planners, Vol. 43 (October): 401-408.

Baker, Earl J. and Joe Gordon McPhee. 1975. Land
Use Management and Regulation in Hazardous
Areas: A Research Assessment. Boulder:

Institute of Behavioral Science, The University of Colorado.

Banfield, Edward C. and James Q. Wilson. 1963. City Politics. Cambridge: Harvard University Press.

Bardach, Eugene. 1977. The Implementation Game: What Happens After a Bill Becomes a Law. Cambridge, Mass.: The MIT Press.

Bialas, Wayne F. and Daniel P. Loucks. 1978. "Nonstructural Floodplain Planning," Water Resources Research, Vol. 14 (February): 67-74.

Bick, Thomas K. 1977. "Third Interim Review of EPA 201 Wastewater Treatment Facility Grant Program Documents for Land Use Impacts, NEPA Compliance, and Public Participation, October 1, 1977." Washington: National Wildlife Federation, April.

Bingham, Richard D. 1976. The Adoption of Innovation by Local Governments. Lexington, Mass.: Lexington Books, D.C. Heath and Co.

Boisvert, Richard N. and Michael J. Rettger. 1979. Public and Private Impacts of Alternative Flood Assistance, Insurance, and Recovery Efforts. Ithaca, N.Y.: Center for Environmental Research, Cornell University, May.

Bloomgren, Patricia A. 1980. Strengthening State Floodplain Management. Washington: U.S. Water Resources Council.

Bolt, B.A., W.L. Horn and R.F. Scott. 1979. "Hazard Mitigation and Control," in Geologic Hazards. Revised, 2nd Edition. New York: Springer Verlag.

Booker Associates. 1982. Flood Hazard Mitigation: A Guidebook for the Appalachian Region. Washington: Federal Emergency Management Agency.

Bosselman, Fred and David Callies. 1972. The Quiet Revolution in Land Use Control. Washington: U.S. Government Printing Office.

Bosselman, Fred, Duane Feurez, and Tobin M. Richter. 1977. Federal Land Use Regulation. New York: Practicing Law Institute.

Brown, Nancy Benziger and Jones E. Tysinger. 1978. "Implementing Floodplain Management." Paper presented at the American Institute of Planners, National Planning Conference, New Orleans.

Burby, Raymond J. 1968. Planning and Politics: Toward a Model of Planning-Related Policy Outputs in Local Government. Chapel Hill: Center for Urban and Regional Studies, University of North Carolina at Chapel Hill.

Burby, Raymond J. and Steven P. French. 1980. "The U.S. Experience in Managing Flood Plain Land Use," Disasters: The International Journal of Disaster Studies and Practice, Vol. 4 (December): 451-457.

Burby, Raymond J. and Steven P. French. 1981. "Coping with Floods: The Land Use Management Paradox," Journal of the American Planning Association. Vol. 47 (July): 289-300.

Burby, Raymond, Steven French and Edward Kaiser. 1979. A Conceptual Framework for Evaluating the Effectiveness of Flood Plain Land Use Management. Chapel Hill: Center for Urban and Regional Studies, University of North Carolina at Chapel Hill, April.

Burby, Raymond J. and Scott Verner. 1984. "Managing Flood Hazards in the Western States," Western Planner, Vol. 5 (May): 5-6.

Burton, Ian. 1961. "Invasion and Escape on the Little Calumet," in Papers on Flood Problems, Gilbert F. White, ed. Chicago: Department of Geography, University of Chicago, pp. 84-92.

Burton, Ian. 1972. "Cultural and Personality Variables in the Perception of Natural Hazards," in Environment and the Social Sciences: Perspectives and Applications. Joachim F. Wohwill and Daniel H. Carson, eds. Washington: American Psychological Association, pp. 184-195.

Burton, Ian, Robert W. Kates, and Rodman E. Snead. 1969. The Human Ecology of Coastal Flood Hazard in Megalopolis. Department of Geography Research Paper No. 115. Chicago: Department of Geography, University of Chicago.

Campbell, William and Milton Heath. 1979. Legal Aspects of Flood Plain Management. Raleigh: Water Resources Research Institute, University of North Carolina.

Chapin, F. Stuart, Jr. 1963. "Taking Stock of Techniques for Shaping Urban Growth," Journal of the American Institute of Planners, Vol. 24 (May): 76-87.

Cheatham, Leo R. 1977. An Analysis of the Effectiveness of Land Use Regulations Required for Flood Insurance Eligibility. Mississippi State, Miss.: Water Resources Research Institute, Mississippi State University.

Cheatham, Leo R. 1979. An Assessment of Some Economic Effects of FIA Land Use Requirements on Urban Coastal Zone Development. Mississippi State, Miss.: Water Resources Research Institute, Mississippi State University, November.

Cheny, Philip B. 1974. A Report to the New England River Basins Commission on Non-structural Measures for Floodplain Management and Flood Damage Management with Application to the Connecticut River Basin Supplemental Flood Management Study. Phase II: The Formulation and Evaluation of

232

Specific Alternatives. Springfield, Va.:
National Technical Information Service. November.

Cochran, Harold C. 1975. Natural Hazards and Their
Distributive Effects. Boulder: Institute of
Behavioral Science, University of Colorado.

Committee on Geology and Public Policy. 1978. Floods
and People: A Geological Perspective.
Washington: Geological Society of America,
October.

Comptroller General of the United States. 1975.
National Attempts to Reduce Losses from Floods by
Planning for and Controlling the Uses of
Flood-Prone Lands. Washington: U.S. General
Accounting Office.

Comptroller General of the United States. 1976.
Formidable Administrative Problems Challenge
Achieving National Flood Insurance Program
Objectives. Washington: U.S. General Accounting
Office.

Comptroller General of the United States. 1977. The
Johnstown Area Flood of 1977: A Case Study for
the Future. Washington: U.S. General Accounting
Office.

Comptroller General of the United States. 1981.
Requests for Federal Disaster Assistance Need
Better Evaluation. Washington: U.S. General
Accounting Office.

Comptroller General of the United States. 1982.
National Flood Insurance: Marginal Impact on
Flood Plain Development; Administrative
Improvement Needed. Washington: U.S. General
Accounting Office.

Conservation Foundation. 1977. Physical Management of
Coastal Floodplains: Guidelines for Hazards and
Ecosystems Management. Washington: The
Foundation.

Conservation Foundation. 1980. Coastal Environmental
Management: Guidelines for Conservation of
Resources and Protection Against Storm Hazards.
Washington: U.S. Government Printing Office.

Council of State Governments. 1974. Intergovernmental
Relations in State Land Use Planning. Land Use
Policy and Program Analysis, Number 1. Lexington,
Ky.: The Council, September.

Council of State Governments. 1979. The States and
Natural Hazards. Lexington, Ky: The Council.

Dacy, Douglas C. and Howard Kunreuther. 1969. The
Economics of Natural Disasters: Implications for
Federal Policy. New York: The Free Press.

Damianos, Demetrios. 1975. The Influence of Flood
Hazards Upon Residential Property Values.
Blacksburg, Va.: Virginia Polytechnic Institute
and State University.

233

Daminianos, Demetrios and Leonard A. Shabman. 1976.
Land Prices in Flood Hazard Areas: Applying
Methods of Land Value Analysis. Blacksburg, Va.:
Virginia Polytechnic Institute and State
University.
Daniel, Donnie L. and D.C. Williams, Jr. 1979. Costs
of Errors in Defining a Community's Flood Plain.
Mississippi State, Miss.: Water Resources
Research Institute, Mississippi State University.
David, Elizabeth and Judith Mayer. 1984. "Comparing
the Costs of Alternative Flood Hazard Mitigation
Plans: The Case of Soldiers Grove, Wisconsin,"
Journal of the American Planning Association, Vol.
50 (Winter): 22-35.
Davis, Daryl. 1976. Comprehensive Flood Plain Studies
Using Spatial Data Management Techniques.
Washington: U.S. Army Corps of Engineers, The
Hydrolic Engineering Center.
DeGrove, John M. 1976. Land Management: New
Direction for State Governments, Paper prepared
for the Urban Policy Roundtable.
DeGrove, John M. 1984. Land, Growth and Politics.
Chicago: APA Planners Press.
Delafons, John. 1962. Land Use Controls in the United
States. Cambridge, Mass.: Joint Center for Urban
Studies of the Massachusetts Institute of
Technology and Harvard University.
Dingman, S. Lawrence and Rutherford Platt. 1977.
"Floodplain Zoning: Implications of Hydrologic
and Legal Uncertainty," Water Resources Research,
Vol. 13 (June): 519-523.
Dunham, Allison. 1959. "Flood Control Via the Police
Power," in University of Pennsylvania Law Review,
Vol. 107.
Dunshire, Andrew. 1978. Implementation in a
Bureaucracy. New York: St. Martin's Press.
Dzurik, Andrew A. 1980. "Floodplain Management
Trends," Water Spectrum, Vol. 12 (Summer): 35-42.
Federal Emergency Management Agency. 1979.
Natural Disaster Recovery Planning for Local
Public Officials. Washington: Federal Emergency
Management Agency.
Federal Emergency Management Agency. 1981. Design
Guidelines for Flood Damage Reduction.
Washington: American Institute of Architects
Foundation.
Federal Emergency Management Agency. 1981. Flood
Hazard Mitigation: Handbook of Common Procedures.
Washington: Federal Emergency Management Agency.
Federal Insurance Administration. 1976. Statutory
Land Use Control Enabling Authority in the Fifty
States. Washington: U.S. Department of Housing
and Urban Development.

Flack, J. Ernest. 1977. "Assessment of Research Needs on Non-structural Alternatives in Flood Damage Abatement," in Implementation of Non-Structural Alternatives in Flood Damage Abatement, Waldon R. Kerns, ed. Blacksburg, Va.: Virginia Polytechnic Institute and State University, pp. 37-45.

Flack, J. Ernest. 1978. "Economic Analysis of Structural Flood Proofing," Journal of the Water Resources Planning and Management Division. (November).

Foster, Harold D. 1980. Disaster Planning: The Preservation of Life and Property. New York: Springer Verlag.

French, Steven. 1979. "The Urbanization of Hazardous Areas, Flood Plains and Barrier Islands in North Carolina," in Perspectives on Urban Affairs in North Carolina, Warren J. Wicker, ed. Chapel Hill: University of North Carolina.

French, Steven P. 1980. Flood Plain Land Use Management: Analysis of Context, Program and Impacts. Chapel Hill: Center for Urban and Regional Studies, University of North Carolina at Chapel Hill.

French, Steven P. and Raymond J. Burby. 1980a. "Current Practice in Managing Coastal Flood Hazards," in Coastal Zone '80, Billy L. Edge, ed. New York: American Society of Civil Engineers.

French, Steven P. and Raymond J. Burby. 1980b. Managing Flood Hazard Areas: The State of Practice. Chapel Hill: Center for Urban and Regional Studies, University of North Carolina at Chapel Hill.

French, Steven P., Todd L. Miller, Raymond J. Burby, and David H. Moreau. 1980. Managing Flood Hazard Areas: A Field Evaluation of Local Experience. Chapel Hill: Center for Urban and Regional Studies, University of North Carolina at Chapel Hill.

Friesema, H. Paul., James Caporaso, Gerald Goldstein, Robert Lineberry, Richard McCleary. 1979. Aftermath: Communities After Natural Disasters. Beverly Hills, Calif.: Sage Publications.

Goddard, James E. 1958. "Floods and How to Avoid Them," Industrial and Manufacturers Record, Vol. 127 (July): 6-8.

Gray, Aelrod J. 1961. "Communities and Floods," National Civic Review, Vol. 50 (March): 134-138.

Healy, Robert G. and John S. Rosenberg. 1979. Land Use and the States, Second Edition. Baltimore, Md.: Published for Resources for the Future, Inc. by the Johns Hopkins University Press.

Heberlein, Thomas A. 1974. "The Three Fixes: Technological, Cognitive, and Structural," in

Water and Community Development: Social and
Economic Perspectives, Donald R. Field, James C.
Barrom and Burl F. Long, eds. Ann Arbor, Mich.:
Ann Arbor Science Publishers, Inc., pp. 279-296.

Helfand, Gloria. 1978. "You Lose If the National
Flood Insurance Program Increases Flood Losses."
New York: Natural Resources Defense Council,
May.

Heritage Conservation and Recreation Service, et al.
1979. Alternative Policies for Protecting Barrier
Islands Along the Atlantic and Gulf Coasts of the
United States and Draft Environmental Impact
Statement. Washington: The Service, December.

Howells, David H. 1977. "Urban Flood Management:
Problems and Research Needs," Journal of the Water
Resources Planning and Management Division
(November).

Hoyt, William G. and Walter B. Langbein. 1955.
Floods. Princeton, N.J.: Princeton University
Press.

Hutton, Janice R. and Dennis S. Mileti with William B.
Lord, John H. Sorensen and Marvin Waterstone.
1979. Analysis of Adoption and Implementation of
Community Land Use Regulations for Floodplains.
San Francisco: Woodward-Clyde Consultants,
October.

Institute of Public Administration. 1974. Criteria
for Evaluation of Social Impacts of Flood
Management Alternatives. Prepared for New England
River Basins Commission. Springfield, Va.:
National Technical Information Service, March.

The Institute of Rational Design, Inc. 1977. National
Flood Insurance Program: Guidebook for
Communities. New York: The Institute, September.

Ives, Sallie and Owen J. Furuseth. No Date. Immediate
Response to Headwater Flooding in Neighborhoods in
Charlotte, North Carolina. Charlotte: University
of North Carolina at Charlotte.

J.H. Wiggins Company. 1978. Building Losses From
Natural Hazards: Yesterday, Today and Tomorrow.
Redondo Beach, Calif.: The Company.

James, Joel W., Joel B. Kreger, and H. Dru Barrineau.
1977. Factors Affecting Public Acceptance of
Flood Insurance in Larimer and Weld Counties,
Colorado. Fort Collins, Col.: Environmental
Resource Center, Colorado State University.

James, L. Douglas. 1968. Economic Analysis of
Alternative Flood Control Measures. Lexington,
Ky.: University of Kentucky Press.

James, L. Douglas. 1972. "Role of Economics in
Planning Flood Plain Land Use," Journal of the
Hydraulic Division, ASCE, Vol. 98 (June):
981-992.

James, L. Douglas. 1974. The Use of Questionnaires in Collecting Information for Urban Flood Control Planning. Prepared for Office of Water Resources Research. Springfield, Va.: National Technical Information Service.

James, L. Douglas. 1977. "Information Needs to Facilitate Implementation of Non-Structural Alternatives," in Implementation of Non-Structural Alternatives in Flood Damage Abatement, Waldron R. Kerns, ed. Blacksburg, Va.: Virginia Polytechnic Institute and State University, pp. 16-28.

James, L. Douglas, Arthur C. Benke and Harvey L. Ragsdale. 1978. "Integrating Ecological and Social Considerations into Urban Flood Control Programs," Water Resources Research, Vol. 14, (April).

James, L. Douglas, Guy J. Keinhofer, G. Roy Elmore and Eugene A. Laurent. 1971. The Peachtree Creek: A Case History in Urban Floodplain Development. Atlanta: Georgia Institute of Technology, October.

James, L. Douglas, Eugene A. Laurent and Duane W. Hill. 1971. The Flood Plain as a Residential Choice: Resident Attitudes and Perceptions and Their Implications to Flood Plain Management Policy. Atlanta: Environmental Resources Center, Georgia Institute of Technology.

James, L. Douglas, et al. 1975. Integration of Hydrolic, Economic, Ecologic, Social and Well-being Factors in Planning Flood Control Measures for Urban Streams. Springfield, Va.: National Technical Information Service.

Jimenez, Gloria M. 1979. "A Redirection of the National Flood Insurance Program," Washington: Federal Emergency Management Agency, May.

Johnson, Eugene O. 1969. "Coordination of Urban Planning and Flood Plain Development," in Flood Plain Management: Iowa's Experience, Merwin D. Dougal, ed. Ames, Ia.: The Iowa State University Press, pp. 103-111.

Johnson, Steven L. and Douglas M. Sayre. 1973. Effects of Urbanization on Floods in the Houston, Texas Metropolitan Area. Washington: U.S. Geological Survey, April.

Kaiser, Edward J., Karl Elfers, Sidney Cohn, Peggy Reichert, Maynard M. Hufschmidt, and Raymond Stanland, Jr. 1973. Promoting Environmental Quality Through Urban Planning and Controls. Washington: U.S. Environmental Protection Agency, June.

Kates, Robert W. 1962. Hazard and Choice Perception in Flood Plain Management. Department of Geography Research Paper No. 78. Chicago: Department of Geography, University of Chicago.

Kates, Robert W. 1971. "Natural Hazard in Human Ecological Perspective: Hypotheses and Models," Economic Geography, Vol. 47: 438-451.

Kates, Robert W. and Gilbert F. White. 1961. "Flood Hazard Evaluation," in Papers on Flood Problems, Gilbert F. White, ed. Chicago: Department of Geography, University of Chicago, pp. 135-147.

Kennedy, Edward J. 1976. "Hydrological Viewpoint of Flood-Plain Use," Transportation Research Circular. No. 178 (June).

Krimm, Richard. 1980. "Interagency Agreement for Nonstructural Damage Reduction Measures as Applied to Common Flood Disaster Planning and Post-flood Recovery Practices." Memorandum from Federal Emergency Management Agency. December 15.

Krutilla, John V. 1966. "An Economic Approach to Coping with Flood Damage," Water Resources Research, Vol. 2 (Second Quarter): 183-190.

Kunreuther, Howard with Ralph Ginsberg, Louis Miller, Philip Sagi, Paul Slovic, Bradley Borkan and Norman Katz. 1978. Disaster Insurance Protection: Public Policy Lessons. New York: John Wiley and Sons.

Kusler, Jon A. 1971. Water Resources Policy in Wisconsin: Flood Management. Madison: University of Wisconsin, Water Resource Center.

Kusler, Jon A. 1976. A Perspective on Flood Plain Regulations for Flood Plain Management. Washington: Department of the Army.

Kusler, Jon A. 1979a. Emerging Issues in Wetland/Floodplain Management, Draft. Report of a Seminar Series. Washington: U.S. Water Resources Council.

Kusler, Jon A. 1979b. Floodplain Acquisition: Issues and Options in Strengthening Federal Policy. Washington: U.S. Water Resources Council, October 1.

Kusler, Jon A. 1980. Regulating Sensitive Lands. Cambridge, Mass.: Ballenger Publishing Company.

Kusler, Jon A. 1982a. Innovation in Local Floodplain Management: A Summary of Community Experience. Boulder: Natural Hazards Research and Applications Information Center, Institute of Behavioral Science, University of Colorado.

Kusler, Jon A. 1982b. Regulation of Flood Hazard Areas to Reduce Flood Losses. Volume 3. Boulder: Natural Hazards Research and Applications Information Center, Institute of Behavioral Science, University of Colorado.

Kusler, Jon A. and Thomas Lee. 1972. Regulations for Flood Plains. Planning Advisory Service, Report No. 277. Chicago: American Society of Planning Officials.

Leik, Robert, T. Michael Carter, and John Clark. 1978.
Community Response to Natural Hazard Warnings.
Minneapolis: University of Minnesota.

Leman Powell Associates. 1979. "A Process for
Community Flood Plain Management." Washington:
Office of Water Research and Technology, U.S.
Department of the Interior.

Leopold, Luna B. 1968. Hydrology for Urban Land
Planning--A Guidebook on the Hydrologic Effects
of Urban Land Use. Geologic Survey Circular 554.
Washington: U.S. Geological Survey.

Levin, Melvin R., Jerome G. Rose, and Joseph S. Slavet.
New Approaches to State Land Use Policies.
Lexington, Mass.: Lexington Books, D.C. Heath and
Co.

Lind, C. Robert. 1967. "Flood Control Alternatives
and the Economics of Flood Protection," Water
Resources Research, Vol. 3 (Second Quarter):
345-357.

Luloff, A.E. and Kenneth P. Wilkinson. 1979.
"Participation in the National Flood Insurance
Program: A Study of Community Activeness," Rural
Sociology, Vol. 44 (Spring): 137-152.

Mazmanian, Daniel A. and Paul A. Sabatier. 1978.
"Policy Evaluation and Legislative Reformulation:
The California Coastal Commissions," Presented at
the Policy Implementation Workshop at Pomona
College, Claremont, California. November.

Mazmanian, Daniel and Paul Sabatier, eds. 1981.
Effective Policy Implementation. Lexington,
Mass.: Lexington Books, D.C. Heath and Co.

Mazmanian, Daniel A. and Paul A. Sabatier. 1983.
Implementation and Public Policy. Dallas, Tex.:
Scott, Foresman and Company.

Mileti, Dennis, Thomas Drabek, and J. Eugene Haas.
1975. Human Systems in Extreme Environments: A
Sociological Perspective. Boulder: Institute of
Behavioral Science, University of Colorado.

Miller, H. Crane. 1975. "Coastal Flood Plain
Management and the National Flood Insurance
Program: A Case Study of Three Rhode Island
Communities," Environmental Comment (November).

Miller, H. Crane. 1977a. Coastal Flood Hazards and
the National Flood Insurance Program, Washington:
U.S. Department of Housing and Urban Development,
Office of Federal Insurance Administration.

Miller, H. Crane. 1977b. "The National Flood
Insurance Program: A Quest for Effective Coastal
Floodplain Management," Environmental Comment
(June): 5-8.

Miller, H. Crane. 1980-1981. "Federal Policies in
Barrier Island Development," Oceanus, Vol. 23
(Winter), Woods Hole Oceanographic Institution.

Mitchell, James Kenneth. 1974. Community Response to
    Coastal Erosion: Individual and Collective
    Adjustments to Hazard on the Atlantic Shore.
    Chicago: University of Chicago Press.
Mogulof, Melvin B. 1974. "Intergovernmental Relations
    in Land Use Control: The Case of the California
    Coastal Zone." Draft Working Paper. Washington:
    The Urban Institute.
Moore, Dan E. and Randolph L. Cantrell. 1976.
    "Community Response to External Demands: An
    Analysis of Participation in the Federal Flood
    Insurance Program," Rural Sociology, Vol. 41
    (Winter): 484-508.
Morse, Henry F. 1962. Role of the States in Guiding
    Land Use in Floodplains. Atlanta Ga.: Georgia
    Institute of Technology. Special Report No. 38.
Murphy, Francis C. 1958. Regulating Flood Plain
    Development. Department of Geography Research
    Paper No. 56. Chicago: Department of Geography,
    University of Chicago.
National Institute for Advanced Studies. 1978.
    Capability and Experiences of Small Communities
    with Respect to the National Flood Insurance
    Program. Washington: National Institute for
    Advanced Studies.
National Science Foundation. 1980. A Report on Flood
    Hazard Mitigation. Washington: National Science
    Foundation.
New England River Basins Commission. 1976. The
    River's Reach: Flood Plain Management in the
    Connecticut River Basin. Boston: New England
    River Basins Commissions.
Office of Technology Assessment, Congress of the United
    States. 1978. Issues and Options in Flood
    Hazards Management. Washington: Office of
    Technology Assessment, Congress of the United
    States, June.
Orfeo, Marian A. 1978. "Non-Structural Flood Plain
    Management Measures: A Handbook for Local
    Governments," Departmental Paper Submitted to
    University of North Carolina in partial
    fulfillment of M.R.P. requirements, Chapel Hill.
Owen, H. James and Glen R. Wall. 1981. Floodplain
    Management Handbook. Washington: U.S. Government
    Printing Office.
Paulson, Steven K. and Wayne E. Lawrence. 1978.
    Survey and Evaluation of Social Science Research
    on Flood Abatement. Blacksburg, Va.: Virginia
    Water Resources Center.
Pelham, Thomas G. 1979. State Land-Use Planning and
    Regulation: Florida, the Model Code, and Beyond.
    Lexington, Mass.: D.C. Heath and Company,
    Lexington Books.

Petak, William J. and Arthur A. Atkinson. 1982. _Natural Hazard Risk Assessment and Public Policy: Anticipating the Unexpected._ New York: Springer-Verlag.

Pietras, Marianne Elizabeth. 1979. "Implementation Issues in the National Flood Insurance Program," Ph.D. Dissertation, Department of Sociology, University of Massachusetts.

Planning Advisory Service. 1953. _Flood Plain. Regulation._ Information Report No. 53. Chicago: American Society of Planning Officials.

Platt, Rutherford H. 1976. "The National Flood Insurance Program: Some Midstream Perspectives," _Journal of the American Institute of Planners,_ Vol. 42 (July): 303-313.

Platt, Rutherford H. 1978. "Coastal Hazard and National Policy: A Jury Rig Approach," _Journal of the American Institute of Planners,_ Vol. 44 (April): 170-179.

Platt, Rutherford H. 1979. _Options to Improve Federal Nonstructural Response to Floods._ Washington: U.S. Water Resources Council. December.

Platt, Rutherford H. 1980. "Retooling National Flood Policy: The Pearl River Flood at Jackson, Mississippi," Draft, Amherst, Mass.: Department of Geology/Geography, University of Massachusetts, April 15, 1980.

Platt, Rutherford H. 1982. "The Jackson Flood of 1979: A Public Policy Disaster," _Journal of the American Planning Asociation,_ Vol. 48 (Summer): 219-231.

Platt, Rutherford H. and Jon Kusler. 1978. "Intergovernmental Floodplain Management Project: Project Summary." Amherst, Mass.: Department of Geology/Geography, University of Massachusetts.

Platt, Rutherford H. and George M. McMullen. 1979. _Fragmentation of Public Authority Over Floodplains: The Charles River Response._ Publication No. 101, Amherst, Mass.: Water Resources Research Center, University of Massachusetts at Amherst, January.

Platt, Rutherford H. and George M. McMullen. 1980. _Post-Flood Recovery and Hazard Mitigation: Lessons From the Massachusetts Coast, February, 1978._ Amherst, Mass.: Water Resources Research Center, University of Massachusetts at Amherst.

Platt, Rutherford, et al. 1980. _Intergovernmental Management of Floodplains._ Boulder: Institute of Behavioral Science, University of Colorado.

Poertner, Herbert G. 1980. _Stormwater Management in the United States: A Study of Institutional Problems and Impacts._ Bolingbrook, Ill.: Stormwater Consultants.

Pressman, Jeffrey L. and Aaron Wildavsky. 1973.
    Implementation. Berkeley: University of
    California Press.
Preston, James C., Dan E. Moore and Tully Cornick.
    1975. Community Response to the Flood Disaster
    Protection Act of 1973. Ithaca, N.Y.: Water
    Resources Center anmd Department of Rural
    Sociology, Cornell University.
Ralph M. Field Associates. 1979. Feasibility of
    Flooded Property Purchase Under Section 1362 of
    the National Flood Insurance Act. Draft Report
    Prepared for the U.S. Department of Housing and
    Urban Development. Washington: U.S. Department
    of Housing and Urban Development.
Ralph M. Field Associates, Inc. 1981. State and Local
    Acquisition of Floodplains and Wetlands.
    Washington: U.S. Water Resources Council,
    September.
Reps, John. 1964. "Requiem for Zoning," in Planning
    1964. Chicago: American Society of Planning
    Officials.
Research Group, Inc. 1978a. Floodplain Development
    Pressures and Federal Programs. Prepared for the
    Office of Federal Activities, U.S. Environmental
    Protection Agency. Washington: U.S.
    Environmental Protection Agency, June.
Research Group, Inc. 1978b. Methods Used by Federal
    Programs to Reduce Floodplain Development
    Pressures. Atlanta, Ga.: The Research Group,
    Inc.
Rettger, Michael J. 1977. An Economic Analysis of
    Alternative Federal Flood Damage Assistance
    Programs. Ithaca, N.Y.: Center for Environmental
    Research, Cornell University, August.
Roder, Wolf. 1961. "Attitudes and Knowledge on the
    Topeka Flood Plain," in Papers on Flood Problems,
    Gilbert F. White, ed. Chicago: Department of
    Geography, University of Chicago, pp. 61-83.
Rogers, Harrell and Charles Bullock. 1976. Coercion
    to Compliance. Lexington, Mass.: Lexington
    Books, D.C. Heath and Co.
Rosenbaum, Nelson. 1978. "Statutory Stringency and
    Policy Implementation: The Case of Wetlands
    Regulation." Prepared for Delivery at the Policy
    Implementation Workshop, Pomona College, Claremont
    California, November 16-17.
Rossi, Peter H., James D. Wright, and Eleanor
    Weber-Burdin. 1982. Natural Hazards and Public
    Choice: The State and Local Politics of Hazard
    Mitigation. New York: Academic Press.
Rossi, Peter H., James D. Wright, Eleanor Weber-Burdin,
    and Joseph Pereira. 1983. Victims of the
    Environment: Loss From Natural Hazards in the

United States, 1970-1980. New York: Plenum Press.

Rubin, Claire. 1979. "Disaster Mitigation: Challenge to Managers," Public Administration Times, Vol. 2 (January).

Rubin, Claire B. 1981. Long Term Recovery from Natural Disasters: A Comparative Analysis of Six Local Experiences. Washington: Academy for Contemporary Problems.

Sabatier, Paul A. 1977. "Regulatory Policy-Making: Toward a Framework of Analysis," Natural Resources Journal, Vol. 17 (July): 415-460.

Sabatier, Paul A. and Daniel Mazmanian. 1978. "The Conditions of Effective Implementation: A Guide to Accomplishing Policy Objectives." Pomona, Calif.: Pomona College.

Sabatier, Paul A. and Daniel Mazmanian. 1979a. Can Regulation Work? The Implementation of Regulatory Policy. Davis, Calif.: Institute of Governmental Affairs, University of California at Davis.

Sabatier, Paul A. and Daniel Mazmanian. 1979b. The Implementation of Regulatory Policy: A Framework of Analysis. Davis, Calif.: Institute of Governmental Affairs, University of California at Davis.

Schneider, William J. and James E. Goddard. 1974. Extent and Development of Urban Flood Plains, Geological Survey Circular 601-J. Washington: U.S. Geological Survey.

Schneider, William J., David A. Rickert and Andrew M. Spieker. 1973. Role of Water in Urban Planning and Management. Geological Survey Circular 601-H. Washington: U.S. Geological Survey.

Shabman, Leonard A. 1979. Improved Formulation and Evaluation of Nonstructural Elements for Water Resources Plans in Flood Hazard Areas. Washington: U.S. Water Resources Council.

Sheaffer, John R. 1960. Flood Proofing: An Element in a Flood Damage Reduction Program. Department of Geography Paper No. 65. Chicago: Department of Geography, University of Chicago.

Sheaffer, John R., George W. Davis, Alan P. Richmond. 1970. Community Goals--Management Opportunities: An Approach to Flood Plain Management. Chicago: Center for Urban Studies, University of Chicago, May 1970.

Sheaffer, John R. and Louis Rozaklis. 1980. "Barrier Islands Purchase: A Cost-Effective Approach to Management," Presented to the House Committee on Interior and Insular Affairs, Subcommittee on National Parks and Insular Affairs, on HR 5981, March 27.

Sheaffer, John R., et al. 1967. Introduction to Flood Proofing: An Outline of Principles and Methods. Chicago: Center for Urban Studies, University of Chicago.

Sheaffer, John R., et al. 1976. Flood Hazard Mitigation Through Safe Land Use and Construction Practices. Chicago: Keifer and Associates, Inc., December.

Sheaffer and Roland, Inc. 1981a. Barrier Island Development Near Four National Seashores. Prepared for the Council on Environmental Quality, Federal Emergency Management Agency, Department of the Interior and Department of Commerce. Chicago: Sheaffer and Roland, Inc., April.

Sheaffer and Roland, Inc. 1981b. Evaluation of the Economic, Social and Environmental Effects of Floodplain Regulations. Washington: Federal Emergency Management Agency.

Shows, E.W. 1977. "National Flood Insurance and the Coastal Zone: A Case Study of Hurricane Eloise," Water Resources Bulletin, Vol. 13 (October): 973-982.

Singer, Daniel and Norman Walzer. 1975. Flood Hazard and Patterns of Urban Development in the Upper Midwest. Macomb, Ill.: Public Policy Research Institute, Western Illinois University, January.

U.S. Army Corps of Engineers. 1972a. A Computer Simulation Model for Flood Plain Development. Part 1: Land Use Planning and Benefit Evaluation. Springfield, Va: National Technical Information Services.

U.S. Army Corps of Engineers. 1972b. Flood Proofing Regulations. Washington: U.S. Army.

U.S. Army Corps of Engineers. 1979. "Evaluation of Nonstructural Measures (ER 1105-2-353): Proposed Evaluation Procedures," Federal Register, Vol. 44: 20350-20352.

U.S. Army Corps of Engineers. 1980. National Economic Development Benefits for Nonstructural Measures. Washington: U.S. Army Corps of Engineers.

U.S. Army Corps of Engineers, Baltimore District. 1977. Cost Report on Non-Structural Flood Damage Reduction Measures for Residential Buildings Within the Baltimore District. Baltimore: Institute for Water Resources.

U.S. Army Corps of Engineers, St. Paul District. 1979. The Development of Nonstructural Alternatives. St. Paul: The District.

U.S. Department of Housing and Urban Development. 1966. Insurance and Other Programs of Financial Assistance to Flood Victims. Washington: The Department, August 8.

244

U.S. Senate Committee on Banking and Currency, 89th
Congress. 1966. Insurance and Other Programs for
Financial Assistance to Flood Victims.
Washington: U.S. Government Printing Office.

U.S. Senate, Committee on Interior and Insular Affairs,
94th Congress, First Session. 1975. Land Use
Management and Regulation in Hazardous Areas.
Washington: U.S. Government Printing Office.

U.S. Water Resources Council. 1971. Regulation of
Flood Hazard Areas to Reduce Flood Losses, Volume
I. Washington: U.S. Government Printing Office.

U.S. Water Resources Council. 1972. Flood Hazard
Evaluation Guidelines for Federal Executive
Agencies. Springfield, Va.: National Technical
Information Service.

U.S. Water Resources Council. 1972. Regulation of
Flood Hazard Areas to Reduce Flood Losses, Volume
II. Washington: U.S. Government Printing Office.

U.S. Water Resources Council. 1973. "Principles and
Standards for Planning Water and Related Land
Resources," Federal Register, Vol. 44:
72978-72990.

U.S. Water Resources Council. 1976. A Unified
National Program for Flood Plain Management.
Washington: U.S. Water Resources Council, July.

U.S. Water Resources Council. 1978a. "Floodplain
Management Guidelines for Implementing E.O.
11988," Federal Register (February).

U.S. Water Resources Council. 1978b. The Nation's
Water Resources: 1975-2000, Volume 1: Summary.
Washington: U.S. Government Printing Office,
December.

U. S. Water Resources Council. 1979. A Unified
National Program for Floodplain Management.
Washington: U.S. Water Resources Council.

Urban Systems Research and Engineering, Inc. 1976.
The Growth Shapers--The Land Use Impacts of
Infrastructure Investments. Prepared for the
Council on Environmental Quality. Washington:
U.S. Government Printing Office.

Van Horn, Carl E. and Donald S. Van Meter. 1976. "The
Implementation of Intergovernmental Policy," in
Public Policy Making in a Federal System, Charles
O. Jones and Robert D. Thomas, eds. Beverly Hills,
Calif.: Sage Publications, pp. 39-62.

Van Meter, Donald and Carl E. Van Horn. 1975. "The
Policy Implementation Process: A Conceptual
Framework," Administration and Society, Volume 6
(February): 445-488.

Vitek, John D. and Donald G. Richards. 1978.
"Incorporating Inherent Map Error into
Flood-Hazard Analysis," Professional Geographer,
Volume 30 (May): 168-173.

White, Gilbert F. 1945. Human Adjustment to Flood. Chicago: University of Chicago Press.

White, Gilbert F. 1961. "Introduction: The Strategy of Using Flood Plains," in Papers on Flood Problems, Gilbert F. White, ed. Chicago: University of Chicago, Department of Geography, pp. 1-4.

White, Gilbert F. 1964. Choice of Adjustment to Floods. Department of Geography Research Paper No. 93. Chicago: Department of Geography, University of Chicago.

White, Gilbert F. 1969. Strategies of American Water Management. Ann Arbor: The University of Michigan Press.

White, Gilbert F. 1975. Flood Hazard in the United States: A Research Reassessment. Boulder: Institute of Behavioral Science, The University of Colorado.

White, Gilbert F. and J. Eugene Haas. 1975. Assessment of Research on Natural Hazards. Cambridge, Mass.: The MIT Press.

White, Gilbert F., et al. 1958. Changes in the Urban Occupancy of Flood Plains in the United States. Chicago: Department of Geography, University of Chicago.

White, Gilbert F., et al. 1976. Natural Hazard Management in Coastal Areas. Prepared under contract for the U.S. Department of Commerce. Boulder: Instiute for Behavioral Science, University of Colorado.

Whittow, John. 1979. The Anatomy of Environmental Hazards: Disasters. Athens, Ga.: The University of Georgia Press.

Williams, Walter. 1975. "Implementation Analysis and Assessment," Policy Analysis, Volume 1: 531-566.

Wilson, John D., Daniel L. Trescott, DeeEll, Fifield, and Vera MacIntyre Hayes. 1980. Hurricane Hazard Mitigation at the Local Government Level: The Roles of the Building Code and Other Development Strategies. Tallahassee, Fl.: Bureau of Disaster Preparedness, Department of Community Affairs.

Wiseman, Robert F. 1977. Dynamics of Urban Development on Flood Plains. Washington: Office of Water Research and Technology, U.S. Department of the Interior.

Wright, James D. and Peter H. Rossi. 1981. Social Science and Natural Hazards. Cambridge, Mass.: Abt Books.

Wright, James D., Peter H. Rossi, Sonia R. Wright, and Eleanor Weber-Burdin. 1979. After the Clean-Up: Long-Range Effects of Natural Disasters, Beverly Hills, Calif.: Sage Publications.

About the Authors

RAYMOND J. BURBY is assistant director for research of the Center for Urban and Regional Studies, University of North Carolina at Chapel Hill, and co-editor of the _Journal of the American Planning Association_. He received his A.B. in government from The George Washington University, and his M.R.P. and Ph.D. in planning from the University of North Carolina at Chapel Hill. Dr. Burby has had extensive experience in research focusing on environmental planning and management, serving as the principal or co-principal investigator on some 30 sponsored research projects. He is the author of eight books and numerous journal articles and conference papers, including recent works dealing with flood hazard management, watershed protection, and the relationship between land use and health. He currently serves on the executive council of the Southern Regional Science Association, the editorial board of the _Journal of Planning Literature_, on the board of directors of the North Carolina Land Use Congress, Inc., and is vice-president of the North Carolina Water Resources Association.

STEVEN P. FRENCH is associate professor of planning, California State Polytechnic University at San Luis Obispo. He received his A.B. from the University of Virginia, his M.U.P. from the University of Colorado at Denver, and his Ph.D. in planning from the University of North Carolina at Chapel Hill. Dr. French has extensive experience in local government, having served as a county planning director in Colorado. In recent years, his research has focused on the mitigation of natural hazards. He is the author of several articles dealing with both flood and earthquake hazard mitigation. His current research focuses on

247

248

methods of incorporating hazards risk analysis in land use planning.

BEVERLY A. CIGLER is associate professor of political science and public administration at North Carolina State University. She has conducted research and published widely on growth management, federal-state-local intergovernmental relations, local energy policy, and local government capacity building.. She teaches courses dealing with environmental policy, state policy and politics, and program management. Dr. Cigler serves as president of the Research Triangle chapter of the American Society for Public Administration.

EDWARD J. KAISER is professor of planning at the University of North Carolina at Chapel Hill, where he teaches planning methods and land use planning in the Department of City and Regional Planning. He received his undergraduate training in architecture at the Illinois Institute of Technology and his Ph.D. in planning from the University of North Carolina at Chapel Hill. Dr. Kaiser is coeditor of the Journal of the American Planning Association and coauthor of Urban Land Use Planning. He is a past officer of the Association of Collegiate Schools of Planning and currently serves as vice president for professional development of the North Carolina chapter of the American Planning Association.

DAVID H. MOREAU is director of the Water Resources Research Institute, University of North Carolina, and professor of planning at the University of North Carolina at Chapel Hill. He received his Ph.D. in Water Resources from Harvard University. In addition to various research activities in urban water planning and management, he has been a consultant to the U.S. Environmental Protection Agency and local governments on environmental planning. He serves as chairman of the Orange Water and Sewer Authority in North Carolina.

BRUCE STIFTEL is assistant professor of urban and regional planning at The Florida State University. His current teaching and research interests focus on planning theory, representation of interests in environmental planning processes, environmental planning processes, environmental mediation, and hazard mitigation planning. He received degrees in environmental studies and biology from the State University of New York at Stony Brook and in city and regional planning from the University of North Carolina at Chapel Hill, where he is now a candidate for the Ph.D.

Professor Stiftel served as community planner with the
U.S. Environmental Protection Agency and as research
associate with the University of North Carolina.